DETERMINING THE VALUE OF NON-MARKETED GOODS

Economic, Psychological, and Policy Relevant Aspects of Contingent Valuation Methods

Studies in Risk and Uncertainty

edited by W. Kip Viscusi
Harvard Law School
Cambridge, MA 02138

Previously published books in the series:

Luken, R.: ENVIRONMENTAL REGULATION: TECHNOLOGY, AMBIENT AND BENEFITS-BASED APPROACHES
Shubik, M.: RISK, ORGANIZATIONS AND SOCIETY
Edwards, W.: UTILITY THEORIES: MEASUREMENTS AND APPLICATIONS
Martin, W.: ENVIRONMENTAL ECONOMICS AND THE MINING INDUSTRY
Kunreuther, H. and Easterling, D.: THE DILEMMA OF A SITING OF HIGH-LEVEL NUCLEAR WASTE REPOSITORY
Kniesner, T. and Leeth, J.: SIMULATING WORKPLACE SAFETY POLICY
Christe, N.G.S. and Soguel, N.C. CONTINGENT VALUATION, TRANSPORT SAFETY
Battigalli, P., Montesano, A. and Panunzi, F.: DECISIONS, GAMES AND MARKETS
Freeman, P. and Kunreuther, H.: MANAGING ENVIRONMENTAL RISK THROUGH INSURANCE

DETERMINING THE VALUE OF NON-MARKETED GOODS

Economic, Psychological, and Policy Relevant Aspects of Contingent Valuation Methods

edited by

R. J. Kopp
Resources for the Future

W. W. Pommerehne†
University of Saarland

and

N. Schwarz
University of Michigan

SPRINGER SCIENCE+BUSINESS MEDIA, LLC

Library of Congress Cataloging-in-Publication Data
Determining the value of non-marketed goods : economics, psychological, and policy relevant aspects of contingent valuation methods / edited by R.J. Kopp, W.W. Pommerehne, and N. Schwarz.
p. cm. -- (Studies in risk and uncertainty ; 10)
Includes bibliographical references and index.
ISBN 978-0-7923-9980-3 ISBN 978-94-011-5364-5 (eBook)
DOI 10.1007/978-94-011-5364-5
1. Contingent valuation. I. Kopp, Raymond J. II. Pommerehne, Werner W. III. Schwarz, Norbert, Dr. phil. IV. Series.
HB846.55.D47 1997
363.7--dc21 97-25764
CIP

Printed on acid-free paper.

TABLE OF CONTENTS

Contributing Authors vii

Acknowledgements ix

1
Editors' Introduction
Norbert Schwarz & Raymond Kopp 1

BACKGROUND AND THEORY

2
Contingent Valuation: Economics, Law and Politics
Raymond J. Kopp & Katherine A. Pease 7

3
Measuring the Non-Use Values: Theory and Application
Richard Bishop, Patricia A. Champ, Thomas C. Brown,
& Daniel W. McCollum 59

4
Economic and Psychological Aspects of Valuing Risk Reduction
W. Kip Viscusi 83

METHODOLOGICAL ISSUES IN CONTINGENT VALUATION

5
Constructing Measures of Economic Value
Raymond J. Kopp and V. Kerry Smith 101

6
Contingent Valuation Surveys and Tests of Insensitivity to Scope
Richard T. Carson 127

7
Cognition, Communication, and Survey Measurement: Implications for Contingent Valuation Surveys
Norbert Schwarz 165

8
What do Psychologists Want? Contingent Valuation as a Special Case of Asking Questions
Baruch Fischhoff 189

9
The Effect of Giving Respondents "Time-to-Think" on Tests of Scope
Dale Whittington, KyeongAe Choe, and Donald Lauria 219

APPLYING CONTINGENT VALUATION

10
Practical Problems in Contingent Valuation
Bengt Kriström 235

11
Communication Devices in Contingent Valuation Surveys - Experiments with Video[1]
Ståle Navrud 273

12
Limits to the Applicability of the CV Approach? A Case Study
Werner W. Pommerehne† & Albert Hart 299

Subject Index 323

†deceased

CONTRIBUTING AUTHORS

Richard C. Bishop, Department of Agricultural Economics and Institute for Environmental Studies, University of Wisconsin, Madison, WI 53706-1513, USA

Thomas C. Brown, Rocky Mountain Forest and Range Experiment Station, Fort Collins, CO 80524, USA.

Richard Carson, Department of Economics, University of California at San Diego, La Jolla, CA 92093, USA

Patricia A. Champ, Rocky Mountain Forest and Range Experiment Station, Fort Collins, CO 80524, USA.

KyeongAe Choe, Center for International Development, Research Triangle Institute, Research Triangle Park, North Carolina, USA

Baruch Fischhoff, Department of Social and Decision Sciences and Department of Engineering and Public Policy, Carnegie Mellon University, Pittsburgh, PA 15213-3890, USA

Albert Hart, Department of Economics, University of the Saarland, D-6600 Saarbrücken, Germany

Raymond J. Kopp, Resources for the Future, Washington, DC 20036, USA

Bengt Kriström, Department of Forest Economics, Swedish University of Agricultural Sciences, S-90183 Umea, Sweden

Donald Lauria, Department of Environmental Sciences and Engineering, School of Public Health, University of North Carolina, Chapel Hill, NC 27599-7400, USA

Daniel W. McCollum, Rocky Mountain Forest and Range Experiment Station, Fort Collins, CO 80524, USA.

Ståle Navrud, Department of Economics and Social Sciences, Agricultural University of Norway, N-1432-5003 Aas, Norway.

Katherine A. Pease, National Oceanic and Atmospheric Administration, Long Beach, CA 90802.

Werner Pommerehne†, Department of Economics, University of the Saarland, D-6600 Saarbrücken, Germany

---

†deceased

Norbert Schwarz, Department of Psychology and Institute for Social Research, University of Michigan, Ann Arbor, MI 48106-1248, USA

V. Kerry Smith, Department of Economics, Duke University, Durham, NC 27708-90328, USA

W. Kip Viscusi, Harvard Law School, Harvard University, Cambridge, MA 02138, USA

Dale Whittington, Department of Environmental Sciences and Engineering, School of Public Health, University of North Carolina, Chapel Hill, NC 27599-7400, USA

ACKNOWLEDGEMENTS

We gratefully acknowledge the support of the Werner Reimers Foundation, Bad Homburg, Germany. The plan for this volume was developed at a conference held at the Werner Reimers Conference Center and the Foundation's financial support and hospitality during the conference greatly contributed to the successful completion of this project. We thank Jenny Covington for her skillfull preparation of the manuscript.

1

EDITORS' INTRODUCTION

On the night of March 24, 1989 the Exxon Valdez departed from the normal shipping lanes as it passed through the Valdez Narrows to avoid icebergs from the nearby Columbia Glacier. The tanker's crew failed to realize how far off the shipping lanes the tanker had strayed and suddenly ran into the submerged rocks of Bligh Reef releasing 11 million gallons of Prudo Bay crude oil into the waters of Prince William Sound. The Exxon Valdez oil spill led to a massive clean-up effort and years of bitter litigation. In addition is was responsible for the passage of legislation designed to reduce the likelihood of future spills and for an unprecedented level of public and academic interest in an economic technique known as contingent valuation (CV).

CV became a topic of intense interest for two reasons -- because it was and still is the only technique capable of measuring what is known as passive use value, or as it has often been previously termed, nonuse or existence value; and because the State of Alaska intended to sue the parties responsible for the oil spill for lost passive use value (expected to be a quite large dollar amount). Few participants in the debate argue with the concept of passive use value; rather both the public and academic discussion focuses on one question -- can CV produce reliable estimates of passive use value?

The contingent valuation method was first proposed in 1947 and its first reported application was by Davis (1963) in his Harvard Ph.D. dissertation on the economic value of recreation in the Maine woods.[1] Additional applications of the method to various public goods and studies of its methodological properties were conducted in the 1970's and 1980's both in the United States and, increasingly, in other countries. A review of the theoretical and empirical basis of contingent valuation at the end of this period is presented in Mitchell and Carson (1989). A recent contingent valuation bibliography (Carson *et al.*, 1995) contains over 1600 references to books, articles, and reports on the method.

Prior to the Valdez oil spill, the CV method had become increasingly accepted for measuring the benefits of environmental policy actions. In 1979, the U.S. Water Resources Council included CV as one of three recommended methods for determining the benefits of federal water and related land resource projects. Since that time, various US federal and state agencies have used the method for purposes of policy evaluation.

CV measures of economic value rely on the same logic that underlies all economic monetary valuation concepts, that is, choice. In CV studies, choices are posed to people in surveys; analysts then use the responses to these choice questions to construct monetary measures of value. The specific mechanism used to elicit respondents' choices can take a variety of forms, including asking survey respondents whether they would purchase, vote, or pay for a program or some other well-defined object of choice. It can also be a direct elicitation of the amount each respondent would be willing to pay (WTP) to obtain an object of choice or the amount each respondent would be willing to accept (WTA) in compensation to give it up.

When used in the context of an environmental policy, a CV survey presents each respondent with an opportunity to make a choice, where the object of choice is usually a plan or program to alter the status of environmental or natural resources, for example to improve drinking water quality, reduce air pollution, or protect some endangered specie. The context for choice can be any setting that is regarded as credible by survey respondents. Because the elements of the choice can be presented in some detail to each respondent, there is no need to rely on historical choices and impose the assumptions required to link those choices to the object to be valued.[2]

CV is of obvious interest to economists because it is a tool that permits economic values to be constructed for various public programs for which there are no observable market prices. However, CV is also of interest to psychologists and sociologists because the technique requires individuals to form complex judgments based on information provided to them and to make choices based on their construal of the described program. While some economists include psychologists and sociologists in their CV study teams, the practice is not routine and more often than not, economists are not aware of the relevant psychological and sociological concepts and literature that bear on the construction of CV surveys and the interpretation of results.

In the summer of 1994 a conference was organized by Werner Pommerehne† of the University of Saarland, Germany and Norbert Schwarz of the University of Michigan. With the support of the Werner Reimers Stiftung Foundation, the conference was held in the small German town of Bad Homburg. The express purpose of bringing together economists, psychologists and sociologists was to discuss issues and exchange ideas having to do with CV. In addition, the breadth of the available expertise was broadened by mixing European economists, psychologists and sociologists with their US colleagues. This volume contains revisions of the papers that were presented and discussed at that conference. The

†deceased

completion of the volume was delayed by the unexpected death of Werner Pommerehne shortly after the conference. We dedicate this volume to his memory.

This volume is composed of three sections. The papers comprising the first section provide background into the issues underlying the public and academic discussion regarding CV and the reliability of CV estimates of economic value. In addition, these papers review the theory underlying the measurement of economic value and discuss those aspects of the theory most relevant to CV. The papers in the second section focus on issues that have formed the core of the CV discussions these last several years. These issues include: sensitivity of WTP estimates to the size of the program offered, tests for theoretical consistency of CV results, and the sensitivity of results to context and numerous other features of the survey and its administration. The final section addresses the application of CV to actual economic valuation tasks. The papers discuss the types of practical problems the CV researcher will encounter and then provides two new applications of the CV technique to current policy evaluations. These applications consider hydroelectric development in Norway and the sighting of nuclear waste repositories in Switzerland.

As the reader moves through these chapters it may be advantageous to keep a few issues in mind.

Assumed Economic Rationality

The theoretic coherence of the economic values constructed from responses to CV surveys rests on the assumption that the behavior of the respondents when answering the CV questions corresponds to the notion of "economic rationality." At its base, economic rationality implies two things. First, individuals possess preferences over "states of the world," where these states can be defined so broadly that they can encompass the distribution of normal private goods and services, the provision of public goods like environmental quality, government programs of all types, political polices, and even intangibles like the codes of ethical conduct a individual chooses to abide by. Second, given these preferences which rank states of the world for the individual; when provided with the opportunity to make choices between alternative states of the world, the individual makes those choices on the basis of his or her preferences, choosing that state which is most preferred.

The conclusion one draws from the economic rationality assumption is that human behavior is quite purposeful and that if an outside observer knew the preferences of any given individual as the individual knows them, that knowledge could be used to explain a considerable amount of human behavior as it relates to choices. It should be noted that economic rationality does not imply "unbounded rationality." Surely there are cognitive limits to any person's ability to make complex choices in a manner fully consistent with their preferences. Rather, rationality implies the intent to make these choices in a manner consistent with preferences given cognitive ability and information endowments.

Few would argue that people don't make a vast majority of their decisions on the basis of their preferences (this is certainly so for private goods), but there are critics of economic rationality that argue that the underlying preferences are non-ridged and in fact quite malleable in the sense that preferences are manipulated or indeed formed by the context in which the choice decision takes place. Changing the decision context therefore changes the preferences and thus the outcome of the choice. If this interpretation of preferences is true, an observer who knows only preferences under one set of contextual circumstances cannot hope to explain choice behavior in another context.

Mean and Ends

Estimates of the economic value of public goods derived from CV surveys are bundled within a larger "commodity" that contains both the public good and the process by which the public good is provided. Examples of this bundling might include the increase in the provision of a public good like wildlife habitat via a government program that raises taxes and uses the proceeds to purchase 1000 acres of privately owned habitat lands to form a wildlife refuge. In this case, CV valuation includes both means, the program to tax and acquire lands and an ends, the provision of habitat.

In most simple economic models of individual behavior, only ends are assumed to be the states of the world over which individuals have preferences. A strict application of this view of preferences would imply that the value individuals place on a bundled commodity like that described above (taxing to raise revenue to purchases 1000 acres and form a refuge) should not depend on how the 1000 acres are obtained as long as the cost to the individual is the same. Thus a CV survey that elicits an economic value for the 1000 acres via the government approach above should be equal to the value that would be obtained if households were asked to make similar monetary contributions to a private charity that was intending to purchase the lands. Should two studies like this be conducted and the elicited value differ, proponents of the "ends only" view of preferences would blame the inconsistency in the values on the CV methodology. However, one may just as easily criticize the ends-only assumption.

Individual Heterogeneity

CV estimates of economic value reveal the great heterogeneity of preferences that exist across households. This heterogeneity is quite obvious when one examines the CV choices made by individuals when the objects of the choice are environmental goods. In this case the wide distribution of preferences regarding human action and environmental consequences is apparent in the distribution of elicited values for environmental goods. Individuals self-described as "strong environmentalists" are, all other things equal, willing to pay significantly more for a given level of environmental improvement than those who describe themselves otherwise.

Of course it is not a surprising result to find that individuals with strong environmental preferences would be willing to pay more for environmental goods, but it is a result that can be used to shed some light on the important issue of the reliability of CV measures of economic value. For example, if we had found that self-characterized "strong environmentalists" were willing to pay *less* than "anti-environmentalists," some doubt would be raised about the reliability of the CV estimate of economic value. Thus, to the extent we can form prior expectations regarding the relationship between CV measures of economic value and heterogeneous attributes of individuals distributed over the sample, we can conduct statistical tests to see if those prior expectations hold. The ability to conduct such tests and shed light on the reliability issue is a due to the fact that individual heterogeneity is preserved in the CV results, unlike more common "representative consumer" models which ignore heterogeneity.

ENDNOTES

1 See Portney (1994) for a brief history of contingent valuation.

2 See Chapter 5 for further discussion of the nature of the assumptions required when the analyst utilizes indirect or revealed preferences approaches to construct values for objects of choice.

REFERENCES

Carson, Richard T., Jennifer Wright, Anna Alberini, Nancy Carson and Nicholas Flores, 1995. *A Bibliography of Contingent Valuation Studies and Papers*, Natural Resource Damage Assessment, Inc., La Jolla, Ca.

Davis, R.K. 1963, "The Value of Outdoor Recreation: An Economic Study of the Maine Woods," Dissertation, Harvard University.

Mitchell, Robert C., and Richard T. Carson. *Using surveys to value public goods: The contingent valuation method.* Washington: Resources for the Future, 1989.

Portney, Paul, R., 1994, "The Contingent Valuation Debate: Why Economists Should Care," *Economic Perspectives*, Vol. 8, No. 4, 3-18.

2

CONTINGENT VALUATION: ECONOMICS, LAW AND POLITICS

Raymond J. Kopp and Katherine A. Pease

INTRODUCTION

There exists within the U.S. today, a debate that draws interest from three spheres of activity that only on occasion have interests in common. The debate concerns the technique of public good valuation known as contingent valuation (CV), and the participants in the debate are drawn from the distinct worlds of academic social science research, law, and politics. The last significant collision of economics, law and politics in the U.S. resulted in the court ordered breakup of the U.S. telecommunications monopoly (AT&T), the political trend toward deregulation of some major U.S. industries (transportation being the most notable) and the ushering in of a new and highly productive era for an old sub-discipline in economics known as industrial organization. It is likely, although not assured, that the debate surrounding CV could lead to similarly substantive results in the areas of law, public policy and social science research.

The purpose of this paper is to describe the debate to those who are not direct participants. But more importantly, we hope to identify the elements in the debate that have caused it to be a topic of conversation and heated controversy in the academic, legal and political communities. It is our view that one of the major elements in the debate, if not the major element, is not CV at all, but rather is the "thing" CV is used to measure -- passive use value (or nonuse value).[1] Were it not for the legal and policy implications of passive use, one could reasonably argue that discussions regarding CV would be largely confined to academia. Since we attribute a great deal of the fury surrounding CV to the concept of passive use, much of the discussion in the paper will focus on the economic, legal and political reactions to the role that quantified passive use does and potentially could play in the legal and public decision making arenas.

Comprehending the CV and passive use debate requires an understanding of the concept *economic value* and how economists measure economic value. This paper provides a brief discussion of the theoretical foundation for *total economic value* (a term that encompasses passive use) and describes how the structure of a CV study is used to measure total value. This paper next discusses the role that monetary estimates of passive use play in judicial proceedings and public decision making -- the adjudication of civil claims for public compensation due as a result of injuries to natural resources and the political use of such estimates in formal cost-benefit analysis of government policies undertaken by regulatory agencies.

Because much of the debate focuses on the validity of CV estimates of passive use, the paper next addresses the validity/reliability issue and touches upon the academic arguments and the legal requirements likely to be imposed on CV estimates of lost passive use if they are to be admitted as evidence in U.S. courts. The paper closes with some thoughts regarding the future path of the debate and speculates about the role CV estimates of passive use might play in public decision making.

THE CONCEPT OF ECONOMIC VALUE

The Role Played by Choice

To economists, the term "value" has a very specific meaning. The most important but often overlooked feature of economic value is that it is a theoretical construct and that monetary measures of economic value are inferred (constructed) by analysts from the choices that individuals make. Economic value cannot exist independent of a choice.

For microeconomists, the study of choice is the raison d'être and from the study of choice, economic values can be defined and empirically constructed.[2] A choice implies that an individual is confronted with a selection of alternatives and the consideration of the alternatives by the individual defines a tradeoff. Contemporary economic theory of individual behavior when confronted by choices suggests that what is chosen must be at least as desirable, from the perspective of the individual making the choice, as the alternatives that were not chosen. The theory implies that the alternative chosen is at least as good, or as valuable, as the alternatives that were not chosen and thereby defines value for the alternative chosen in terms of the alternatives foregone. For example, if an individual chooses to relinquish three apples for a peach, an observing analyst can state that under the circumstances of the choice (perhaps known in their entirety only to that individual), the economic value to that individual of the peach is at least three apples. If the choice were giving up $1 for the peach, and the individual chose the peach, then the analyst would conclude under the circumstances of the choice that the value of the peach to that person was at least $1.[3]

Objects of Choice

Economic values are constructed for *objects of choice* under *particular circumstances of choice*. From the analyst's perspective, the object of choice is the thing for which an economic value is desired. Objects of choice may be quite general and extend far beyond our normal conception of private goods sold in markets. Objects of choice can be public goods like local police protection, ambient air and water quality, or species and habitat protection. But the list does not stop here. Objects of choice can be any tangible or intangible object, process or activity that can be described in a way that allows a choice to be fashioned.

Each object of choice has a set of defining and perhaps unique attributes. These attributes are perceived by the individuals who confront a choice involving the object and the attributes may or may not be perceived similarly across all such individuals. Any peach may look attractive to one person but not to others. Should an observing analyst assume that all individuals share a common perception of the attributes of the object of choice, she may be mistaken. If one observes individuals choosing to live in areas of Los Angeles that are less subject to air pollution than others, the analyst could assume that they are choosing the less polluted locale (the object of choice) due to reduced risk of minor respiratory discomfort (an attribute of the object of choice). However, it may well be the case that improved visibility of the surrounding mountains is an important attribute that the analyst has overlooked.

An analyst's failure to capture all of the object's attributes is an important omission in some instances but unimportant in others. Return to the peach example and assume that all the analyst wishes to know is the economic value of the peach to the individual making the choice. The individual perceives the peach's attributes, but the analyst does not. However, the analyst would still use the dollar foregone as the economic value. In this case the information about attributes had no bearing on the construction of the economic value.

On the other hand, lack of information about attributes of an item can lead to errors in the valuation of an object. Consider again the example of the individual choosing to live in a less polluted section of Los Angeles and presumably paying a housing premium. Suppose first that the object to valued is a reduction in minor respiratory discomfort and second that the analyst believes that the attribute set fully describing the object of choice (this particular housing location) consists only of reductions to respiratory discomfort. If an individual moves to this locale and foregoes a sum of money equal to the housing premium, the analyst might assign an economic value to reduced respiratory discomfort equal to the housing premium. In fact, that housing premium is the value of a much more expansive object of choice (at least including improved visibility), and the analyst has overstated the value of reduced respiratory discomfort.

The failure to capture the total value of an object of choice is endemic to most economic valuation of objects that do not trade on markets and indeed, can plague market objects as well. Suppose a decision maker would like to know the economic value of a program designed to set aside wilderness areas as protected preserves and retains an analyst to construct the value. The analyst assumes (implicitly or explicitly) that the object of choice is characterized by an attribute set that contains outdoor recreational opportunities for individuals and nothing more. The analyst then examines historical choices where values for identical recreational activities have been constructed and uses these values in the analysis of the program to set aside wilderness areas. If the attribute set as perceived by individuals included other attributes, for example passive use, the value constructed by the analyst is not a total economic value, but rather a reflection of the assumptions made regarding the attributes of the object of choice.

How could the analyst have constructed a total value for the wilderness set aside program? Would the analyst have to know the attribute perceptions of all relevant individuals? From the previous peach example, we know that complete knowledge of the attribute set is not required. What is required in the absence of complete knowledge is the ability to provide a choice situation in which individuals can learn of the object of choice, confront a tradeoff and make a choice on the basis of their own perceptions regarding the attribute set. The economic value constructed from such a choice encompasses passive use and thereby captures total value.

Circumstances of Choice

Objects of choice, together with the circumstances of choice, completely describe the *elements of the choice* for the purpose of constructing an economic value. The circumstances of choice describe the context in which a choice is made. At a minimum these circumstances include: (a) the consequences of the choice (the nature of the tradeoff), *i.e.,* what is foregone by the choice and what is gained; (b) the specified rights of assignment, *i.e.,* with what specified individual or group of individuals do elements of control over the object of choice reside; and (c) the choice mechanism, *i.e.,* the manner in which the individual exercises the choice, for example, through private market transactions, political processes like voting, or other unspecified behaviors.

It was argued in the previous section that an analyst need not know the individual's perceptions regarding the attributes of an object of choice to construct an economic value from a choice that involves that object. What is required is that the object to be valued and the object of choice specified by the elements of choice are one and the same. Unfortunately, this acceptable level of analyst ignorance does not carry over to knowledge requirements regarding the circumstances of the choice. With regard to the circumstances, the analyst must know the choice alternatives (what could have been chosen), what was gained and what was foregone. In instances where the analyst has control over the full elements of choice (*i.e.,* specifies the object and circumstances of the choice) as in the case of CV, this information requirement is met. However, when the analyst employs observed historical choices, the information requirement becomes more burdensome and is usually met by making largely unverifiable assumptions.[4]

In addition to other features of the choice, the circumstances of choice specify the *rights of assignment* over elements of control of the object of choice. There are two choice situations: (1) giving something up to receive the object of choice, corresponding to the *willingness to pay* (WTP) concept, and (2) receiving something to give up the object of choice, corresponding to the *willingness to accept* (WTA) concept.

WTP and WTA are the fundamental monetary measures of value in economics. All economic valuation can be shown to correspond to one or the other. In WTP choice situations, the economic value of the object of choice is constrained by the *wealth* of the individual (*i.e.*, by the personal possessions an individual can give up). Thus, while an individual may be willing to give up all of his/her wealth to obtain some highly desired object of choice, the economic value is constrained by what he/she owns.

Constraining the economic value of an object of choice to available wealth does not arise in the WTA choice context. Here the item to be valued is something the individual already possesses and the item is part of his/her wealth. The decision tradeoff requires the specification of *something* the individual will freely accept in exchange for the object. Because in this choice situation the object is already part of the individual's wealth, the *something* an individual will freely accept in return for that object is not constrained by the individual's wealth.

Instead a person agrees to give up something in exchange for monetary wealth. The object of choice is what must be given up as part of this trade-off. While this choice may seem atypical, it is not -- selling anything places people in this situation. Thus, when people accept a job (*i.e.*, sell labor services), sell a house or a car, or agree to permit a solid waste facility to be located in their neighborhood in return for compensation payments, the choices involve a WTA trade-off and, hence, allow the construction of an economic value for the object of choice foregone. If the choice posed to the individual involves a monetary payment to the individual in exchange for the object of choice, then the compensation payment becomes the basis for the monetary value of the object.

Contingent Valuation -- Contingent Choices

All determinations of economic value are constructions from choices. The elements of a choice relevant for economic valuation are described by the object of choice and the circumstances of choice. Failure to match the attributes of an object to be valued with the attributes of the object of choice will imply a general failure to measure total economic value for the desired object. The circumstances of choice specify the assignment of rights of control over the object of choice and determine the relevant valuation perspective -- WTP or WTA. Under particular assumptions, monetary measures of value for the same object of choice constructed from two choice situations characterized by alternative circumstances of choice (*i.e.*, WTP versus WTA) can be equal. However, as a general rule they are not expected to be equal.

The technique of contingent valuation permits the analyst to specify and maintain control over the full elements of the choice. In this way CV differs dramatically from revealed preference approaches where historical records of past choices must be assembled and the objects and circumstances of those choices *made to fit* (by the use of suitable assumptions) the object to be valued. In contrast, the analyst employing the CV technique can define the object of choice to be one and the same with the object for which an economic estimate of total value is desired. CV permits the attributes of the object to be perceived by individuals making the choice in any manner they wish, ensuring that a total value can be constructed from the choice. Finally, the analyst can set the circumstances of the choice to conform to the same assignment of rights that exist for the object to be valued.

POLITICS AND LAW

It is fair to say that the current heat generated by the debate over CV and passive use is most intensely felt within the U.S. federal government as it wrestles with the two not entirely unrelated issues of (a) rules and procedures for the assessment of damages to natural resources due to releases of oil and hazardous substances, and (b) agency guidelines for cost-benefit studies conducted as part of major new regulation promulgation. These two activities are influenced by the political concerns of the Executive Branch and will undoubtedly be shaped by those concerns. However, there are other inputs and influences including researchers knowledgeable in the areas of CV and passive use, past legal opinions, and potential future legal action regarding the damage assessment regulations which can be challenged in court after final promulgation.

Since the most obvious debate is taking place over the damage assessment regulations, we first begin by tracing that history and commenting on the current status of the rulemakings. We then turn our attention to the much less visible, but perhaps no less important, debate concerning CV's future in mandated cost-benefit studies of regulatory programs.

The Damage Assessment Rulemaking Process

The Role of Regulations

In recent years, federal agencies have promulgated numerous regulations covering many aspects of American society. These regulations are based on underlying statutes passed by Congress whereby Congress has basically delegated aspects of its legislative function to the Executive Branch. Such delegation has been upheld as permissible by the U.S. Supreme Court and is not consider a violation of the separation-of-powers Constitutional principle.

Generally, the U.S. judicial system is reluctant to set aside agency regulations and will likely defer to the agency's judgment. Such deference plays an important role in the natural resource damage assessment arena. If agencies promulgate regulations establishing guidelines or standards for structuring damage assessment within the appropriate statutory framework, those standards are likely to be upheld if challenged judicially. In turn, if trustees follow those regulatory guidelines, such studies are likely to be admitted into evidence in a judicial setting. *See* discussion *infra* on reliability. Thus, the types of standards or guidelines promulgated can play a pivotal role in the ultimate outcome of a natural resource damage assessment and perhaps the general application of CV in other settings, including academic research.

Important to any discussion of the use of CV to estimate natural resource damages is the role of the two regulatory agencies designated to promulgate natural resource damage assessment regulations -- the Department of the Interior (Interior) and the National Oceanic and Atmospheric Administration (NOAA). While these regulations are not mandatory, their promulgation serves several purposes. The most obvious is the provision of a logical framework for natural resource trustees to follow as they develop a damage assessment. But the public rulemaking process also provides the opportunity for diverse positions to be raised, varying view points to be weighed and compromises to be reached. In such a process, it is not unusual for strong differences to emerge, particularly when certain groups have a vested interest in the outcome. Certainly this tension is evident as one examines Interior's and NOAA's rulemakings.

Interior Initiates Rulemaking

In 1980, Congress passed the Comprehensive Environmental Response, Compensation and Liability Act (CERCLA) establishing a liability and compensation scheme to address releases of hazardous substances. It provides, in part, that the Executive Branch promulgate regulations "for the assessment of damages for injury to, destruction of, or loss of natural resources" resulting from the release of oil or hazardous substances. Those regulations would identify the "best available procedures to determine such[5] damages ... and shall take into consideration factors, including, but not limited to, replacement value, use value, and the ability of the ecosystem or resource to recover." The President delegated this responsibility to Interior.[6]

As Interior embarked on its rulemaking, it quickly became evident that a key factor in this process was the definition of the appropriate measure of damages.[7] In the preamble to its 1985 proposed rule, Interior noted that it had received extensive comments on the proper definition of damages and on appropriate methods for determining such damages. Some of these initial comments foreshadowed the subsequent legal challenges to the 1986 final rule and the framework for the continuing debate on the role of passive use values and CV in the damage assessment context.

Interestingly, the disagreement over the appropriate measure of damages appears to have been waged within Interior also. Interior's administrative record supporting the rulemaking includes a document called the Concept Paper for Development of CERCLA 301(c) Natural Resource Damage Assessment Regulations. That concept paper indicated that the Interior regulatory team proposed that "the damage value procedures included [sic] both restoration/replacement values and use values including option and existence values ...." Further, the Interior economist working on the regulations noted, according to the administrative record, that "the value of natural resources should include both option and existence values."[8,9]

However, the approach recommended in Interior's Concept Paper was substantially modified. In its 1985 proposed rulemaking, Interior fashioned a measure of damages composed of two important components -- the "lesser of" rule and a hierarchy of economic methodologies.[10] The "lesser of" rule provided that trustees may recover either the cost of restoration or replacement or diminution of use values, whichever was less, except where special resources were involved.[11]

Interior then restricted the measurement of the diminution of direct use values by establishing a hierarchy of methodologies. Under this hierarchy, the trustee must first use diminution in market price as the measure of lost value even though Interior recognized that such a measure did not necessarily equate to loss in social value. If the resource was not traded in a market, the proposed rule directed the trustees to use the appraisal method. If the trustees could do neither, they could use nonmarket methodologies such as travel costs, hedonic pricing, unit value, factor income, and CV.[12] Interior recognized CV as a method to survey direct use values but restricted its application in other areas by stating that CV can only be used "to estimate option and existence values ... if the authorized official determines that no other valuation technique will be feasible."[13]

The 1985 proposed rulemaking generated many comments, and again, a substantial number addressed the measure of damages issue. A number challenged the "lesser of" rule. Many others focused on the hierarchy of economic methodologies in general and CV in particular. In response to the various forces at play, Interior, in its 1986 final rule, retained the "lesser of" rule and further restricted the use of CV by stating that existence and option values could only be estimated when use values could not be determined.[14] While acknowledging that "[o]rdinarily, option and existence values would be added to use values," Interior justified its position by stating that CERCLA section 301(c) only mentions use values (ignoring the language "including, but not limited to") and that more is known about measuring use values as opposed to existence and option values.[15]

Ohio Litigation

The combination of the "lesser of rule," the hierarchy of measurement methodologies and the restrictions on estimating passive use values guarantee undervaluation of injuries to natural resources and calls into question whether meaningful restoration could be achieved. The restrictions on measurement of diminution in value imposed by Interior made it probable that restoration costs would rarely be "the lesser." Undoubtedly, this approach was appealing to those likely to be held liable for the costs, but was certain to raise concerns among some trustees and other interested groups.

With the considerable attention that Interior's rulemaking had generated, it is not surprising that litigation ensued and that several of the areas challenged concerned measure of damages and use of CV. *See Ohio, et al. v. Department of the Interior.*[16] Industry groups, environmental groups and states challenged different parts of the final rule. Among the many areas contested by State/Environmental Petitioners and Industry Petitioners, only those arguments related to the measure of damages will be discussed.

The *Ohio* Court viewed State/Environmental Petitioners' challenge to the "lesser of" rule as the most significant issue in the case. In this challenge, State/Environmental Petitioners asserted that the "lesser of" rule was inconsistent with CERCLA, its legislative history and the underlying objective of Congress which was to restore those resources injured by polluters. Addressing the hierarchy of allowable economic methodologies with its emphasis on a market based approach, State/Environmental Petitioners argued that this approach significantly undervalued natural resources because such an approach "prohibits trustees from taking into account the value of injured natural resources to anyone other than the persons who may trade the natural resources on the market." Moreover, when nonmarket methodologies were permitted, the hierarchy allowed only *direct* use values. The appropriate measure of damages, according to State/Environmental Petitioners, was lost intrinsic value, costs of restoration or replacement and use value.[17]

Industry Petitioners focused primarily on the use of CV for calculating direct use values, although they did touch briefly on passive use values.[18] They pointed out that they were "not argu[ing] that CV can never be used to assess natural resource injuries ... [r]ather ... that damage assessments performed according to CV should not be accorded the 'significant benefit' of a rebuttal presumption" because CV is 1) inconsistent with common law and 2) not one of the "best available procedures to determine such damages" as required by CERCLA section 301(c). According to Industry Petitioners, CV was "unreliable, imprecise, subject to bias and lacking in proper guidance."[19] Further, Industry Petitioners challenged Interior's 1986 rule on the ground that it provided very little guidance to avoid the problems associated with CV. Dismissing the guidance in Interior's technical support document[20] as inadequate, they asserted that the "[r]ule fails to provide any significant procedural checks on the conduct of a CV survey."[21]

Considering the challenge, the *Ohio* Court found that Interior's regulation establishing the "lesser of" rule was "directly contrary to the clearly expressed intent of Congress and is therefore invalid." It also held that the hierarchy of economic methodologies was not a reasonable interpretation of the CERCLA.[22] Finally, the *Ohio* Court rejected Industry Petitioners' challenge to the inclusion of CV.

The *Ohio* Court's discussion of resource valuation and the use of CV is important as it highlights issues that are being raised in Interior's and NOAA's on-going rulemakings as well as at numerous professional conferences and in legal and economic publications. It is this court's interpretation of CERCLA and its legislative history that Congress recognized that "natural resources have value that is not readily measured by traditional means." Because Congress intended the damage assessment process "to capture fully all aspects of loss," market prices "are not acceptable as primary measures of the use values of natural resources." The court also questioned why Interior had deviated from the views expressed by its regulatory team which had recognized that many natural resources have no market. The court noted that it was the "incompleteness of market processes that give rise to the need for contingent valuation techniques."[23]

Turning to passive use values, the court stated that Interior's limitation on the calculation of such values was based on an erroneous interpretation of CERCLA. It expounded that while "[o]ption and existence values may represent 'passive' use ... they nonetheless reflect utility received by humans from a resource, and thus, *prima facie,* ought to be included in a damage assessment."[24] The court again mentioned that Interior had ignored the position stated by its regulatory team on inclusion of such values. Concluding its discussion, the court declared that while Interior could rank methodologies according to its perception of their reliability, it could not base its exclusion of option and existence values on an "incorrect reading of the statute."[25]

The final issue of concern addressed by the *Ohio* Court was whether CV was a "best available procedure" under CERCLA. The court upheld Interior's inclusion of the method and observed that inclusion of CV was "reasonable and consistent with congressional intent" and entitled to deference from the court. In addressing some of the concerns raised by the Industry Petitioners, the court said that some of the arguments raised "strike at CERCLA, not CV's implementation ...."[26]

Next Round -- Interior's Revisions to the Rules

Faced with the remand of part of its 1986 final rule, Interior published a notice of proposed rulemaking in 1991 to respond to the issues raised in the *Ohio* decision. In this notice, Interior stated that the damage claim would consist of both restoration costs and "all reliably calculated values, including option and existence values ...."[27] To do so, Interior proposed the concept of "compensable value." Interior explained that "[c]ompensable value encompasses all of the public economic values associated with an injured resource, including use values and nonuse values such as option, existence and bequest values ...." The advantage of the compensable value concept is that it "allows for many different reasons why the public may value natural resources -- including reasons not represented by market prices."[28]

Interior did caution, however, that "[a]lthough nonuse values can theoretically exist for any natural resource, they are most significant for irreversible or long-lasting changes to well-known, unique natural resources." It noted that it would be unlikely that significant passive use values would exist for resources that recovery quickly or for resources with many substitutes. It concluded that the "[t]rustees might best substantiate their claims for lost nonuse values ... by demonstrating irreversible, or very long-lasting, adverse impacts to unique, widely-recognized natural resources."[29]

Also in response to the *Ohio* decision, Interior eliminated its hierarchy of economic methodologies. Again, it cautioned that removal of the hierarchy did not imply that all methods were "equally reliable or applicable." The trustee must consider the facts of the case and the data available.[30]

Since the *Ohio* decision, Interior had received many comments on the validity and use of CV in damage assessments. In reply, it stated that CV was a valid method that may be used by trustees in damage assessments, and the after the *Ohio* decision, use of CV is "no longer at issue ...." Comparing the use of CV to other methods for calculating direct use values, Interior said that "for nonmarketed use values ... CVM, when properly applied, has produced values comparable to values based on 'revealed preference' methods."[31] It then acknowledged that it was more difficult to reach consensus on reliability of CV for calculating passive use values as there was not the same "body of research comparing nonuse values to values based on revealed preference approaches." Thus, Interior considered CV the least reliable method when used to estimate passive use values, though still a reliable method. Interior concluded that CV for measuring passive use values may become more reliable as the "state of the art advances."[32]

NOAA Joins In -- OPA Rulemaking Process

While Interior continued its efforts to revise its 1986 final rule, NOAA began to address its new statutory responsibility of developing damage assessment regulations to address injuries caused by oil spills. The 1989 *Exxon Valdez* oil spill in Prince William Sound, Alaska, became the catalyst for Congressional revision of the Clean Water Act. Characterized as "the worst marine environmental disaster this nation has ever experienced,"[33] the *Exxon Valdez* oil spill was instrumental in the passage of the Oil Pollution Act (OPA)[34] in August 1990. OPA, among other things, established a new liability and compensation scheme designed to address more adequately the effects of oil pollution incidents. It also directed NOAA to promulgate natural resource damage assessment regulations for such incidents.

In some ways, the conceptual task faced by NOAA in drafting the portion of the regulations dealing with the measure of damages was simplified as NOAA could draw upon Interior's experiences, the *Ohio* decision and a more clearly articulated measure of damages in OPA.[35] Like Interior, NOAA sought comments and public input prior to the publication of its proposed rule. In its 1992 advance notice of proposed rulemaking,[36] NOAA summarized comments received on issues of concern. Not surprisingly, many comments dealt with economic issues such as valuing lost services, role of passive use values, and use of CV. While the role of passive use values evoked comments similar to those received by Interior, most comments dealing with valuation issues had some mention of CV.[37] NOAA recognized that CV was an established economic methodology, but acknowledged that its use for measuring passive values was controversial. Punting for the moment, NOAA sought further comments on use of CV.

NOAA CV Panel

Although it is unclear which events caused the increasing attention and controversy concerning the use of CV, one can point to likely candidates. Those include 1) the increasing interest of natural resource trustee agencies to pursue damage assessment cases; 2) possibility of a rebuttal presumption attaching to the valuation; 3) CV's use in a handful of damage assessment cases; 4) perceived favorable regulatory climate for business during the 1980's, 5) *Exxon Valdez* oil spill with its potential for large values; 6) *Ohio* decision; and 7) Cambridge Economics, Inc. Conference on CV funded by Exxon. Regardless of the causes, NOAA's and Interior's rulemakings faced increased scrutiny over the issue of CV.

In partial response to this heightened interest and the conflicting view points surrounding the issue, NOAA attempted to provide a forum for addressing the use of CV in a comprehensive, neutral fashion. On April 8, 1992, NOAA announced the formation of an expert Ppnel (hereafter, Panel) chaired by two Nobel laureates to evaluate the reliability of CV. Besides reviewing numerous written submissions, the Panel convened a public meeting to receive oral comments on the following issues: 1) whether constructed market methodologies could be implemented reliably to calculate passive use values and if so, under what circumstances and under what guidance; 2) if constructed market methodologies could not be implemented, what additional research or studies should be conducted to refine such methodologies so that they can reliably estimate passive use values; 3) what alternatives, if any, exist to measure passive use values.[38]

On January 15, 1993, NOAA released the Panel's report. That report concluded that if CV studies follow the guidelines suggested by the Panel that such studies "can produce estimates reliable enough to be the starting point of a judicial process of damage assessment, including lost passive-use values."[39] The Panel's guidance consisted of two categories -- that which should be met to ensure reliability and that which must be met. Most of the recommendations dealt with survey design, development and administration and basically embodied the standards being followed in any high quality survey. The Panel briefly considered whether "performance standards" could be used to determine whether reliable measures of passive use values had been obtained. It suggested that only one test in this area need be used -- responsiveness to the scope of the environmental insult.[40] The Panel's report is part of NOAA's administrative record in support of its OPA rulemaking.

At the same time the Panel prepared to issue its report, an unusual event occurred indicating again the role of politics in the rulemaking process. In the last days of the Republican Bush Administration, the Assistant Secretary for Policy, Management and Budget, a political appointee in the Interior Department, sent a set of final regulations concerning the use of CV to the Federal Register for publication, bypassing the normal clearance process. These regulations contained many restrictions on the use of CV to measure passive use values.[41] While it is unclear who actually drafted the regulations,[42] Interior acknowledged that the regulations "improperly referred to and relied upon information received outside the comment period...." Alerted to this development, the incoming Democratic administration prevented the publication of these "midnight" regulations.[43]

NOAA & Interior -- Continuing Rulemakings

The Panel's report gave pause to Interior's rulemaking on the issue of CV. Both NOAA and Interior recognized the need for consistency to the maximum extent possible between the two sets of regulations governing damage assessment activities. As a result, Interior delayed that portion of its regulations concerning the use of CV and sought additional comments in light of the Panel's report.

Based on the new set of comments received, Interior issued another proposed rule.[44] The beginning of the proposed rule reiterated positions taken in Interior's 1991 notice -- that the measure of damages was restoration costs and diminution in resource values and that CV was a legitimate valuation methodology. However, later in the discussion, Interior, in responding to comments, appeared to take a more critical approach to use of CV.

Once again, Interior had received numerous comments on calculation and recovery of passive use values. And once again, the comments fell into two widely divergent camps -- those supporting recovery of passive use values at the discretion of the trustees through the use of CV which was viewed as a reliable method and those taking the opposite view.[45] Turning to these comments, Interior first addressed inclusion of passive use values. It observed that the *Ohio* Court did not mandate inclusion of such values in a damage assessment claim. Rather, the court only required that any limitation on the recovery of passive use values be "based on considerations of reliability ...." Further, Interior stated that the court did not mandate unlimited use of CV and "did not address the difference between use of CVM to calculate use values and use of CVM to calculate nonuse values."[46]

Interior then expressed its concerns about reliability of CV to estimate passive use values. It stated that "there are potential reliability problems associated with any of the valuation methodologies listed in the proposed rule ... however these other techniques do not have the same potential to change the aggregate estimate of lost compensable value to the same degree that CVM does particularly when used to quantify nonuse values."[47] Despite this concern, Interior recognized that passive use values could be significant in some cases and should be recovered in such instances.[48]

The next major event in the development of the damage assessment regulations was the publication of NOAA's proposed regulations.[49] The measure of damages remained unchanged from that articulated in OPA -- the cost of restoration, diminution in value and reasonable assessment costs. NOAA determined that passive use values are part of diminution of value. Further, NOAA stated that it believed that "reliable estimates of lost passive use value due to discharges of oil can be estimated using CV so long as the CV study follows the standards provided in the proposed regulations."[50]

NOAA spent considerable time crafting CV standards and relied heavily upon the recommendations of the Panel. NOAA's standards cover three areas -- survey instrument design and development; survey administration; and nature of the results. Acknowledging that reliability of a CV estimate starts with the design and development of the survey instrument, NOAA proposed a number of standards and guidance in this area.[51] Noting that even carefully designed surveys could produce unreliable estimates without equally careful survey administration, NOAA proposed standards for survey administration.[52] Lastly, NOAA outlined a standard for evaluating the results of CV studies. Drawing upon the Panel's concern that respondents should be responsive to variations in the environmental insult, NOAA proposed a "scope" test to determine whether respondents are sensitive to the scope of the environmental insult.[53]

The NOAA proposed rule does contain an oddity -- the requirement that trustees calibrate or discount the estimated WTP. Unless trustees justify a different calibration factor, they are required to cut the estimated WTP in half. The rationale for this requirement appears to be based on two factors. The first is the lack of external validation, while the second is a few studies indicating that actual WTP is less than stated WTP.[54] Because NOAA's other proposed standards and guidance are designed to eliminate or greatly reduce any potential bias and to result in a conservative estimate of WTP, the requirement to halve the estimated WTP seems counter intuitive. Perhaps recognizing this, NOAA does ask commenters to propose other reasonable calibration tests. It states that the commenters "should consider adopting a stringent discount factor, while at the same time suggesting relaxing some of the other standards contained in the proposed rule."[55]

It is unclear what the tradeoff of standards for a "stringent" discount factor is really intended to address. If NOAA truly believes that its proposed standards are necessary to produce a reliable estimate of WTP in natural resource damage cases as stated in the preamble to the rule,[56] one would think that NOAA would not want to encourage "less reliable" results, particularly when such results may be used in litigation.

There is a belief by some that the calibration requirement may have been included by NOAA in response to pressure from other executive branch agencies. One comment included in NOAA's administrative record supporting this supposition states, in part, that "[w]e are writing to you to let you know our strong objection to the changes that were made, apparently in part at OMB's request, to NOAA's recently proposed natural resource damage assessment rules... .One of the most objectionable provisions that NOAA was required to include is a requirement that the results of a contingent valuation survey be cut in half. This is termed a 'calibration' of the results."[57]

Besides calibration, NOAA requested comments on the issues of an alternative "indirect" scope test;[58] response rate; additional tests for determining reliability to be included in a detailed guidance document; prior knowledge;[59] and threshold factor for using CV surveys.[60]

Shortly after NOAA published its 1994 proposed rule, another indication of Executive Branch controversy occurred. Although the details are unclear from the public record, it appears that Interior's next revision to its proposed damage assessment regulations did not encompass the same standards and guidelines on CV as did NOAA's proposed regulations. Further, it appeared that OMB would not officially "accept" Interior's proposed rule without conforming changes. These inferences are drawn from a document in the administrative record supporting NOAA's OPA rulemaking. That document states, in part, that:

> [w]e understand that the DOI proposed regulations do not contain some of the unreasonable and arbitrary limits on the use of contingent valuation, limits that NOAA was recently forced by OMB and others to accept in its proposed regulations under the Oil Pollution Act.
>
> ...
>
> Apparently, OMB is currently refusing even to lodge the DOI natural resource damage regulations. Until proposed regulations are lodged, OMB's 90 day review period under the Executive Order does not start to run. OMB must be urged to lodge the regulations ....[61]

Complicating Interior's rulemaking was the judicially supervised schedule for promulgation of regulations addressing the *Ohio* decision. No doubt realizing that internal Executive Branch disagreements could jeopardize Interior's ability to implement the court order, Interior bifurcated its rulemaking. On March 1994, Interior issued a final rule that established procedures for calculating a natural resource damage claim based on restoration costs and for estimating direct use value.[62] The preamble to the rule stated, however, that Interior would publish another proposed rule covering assessment of passive use values.[63]

Interior's final rule retained the measure of damages described in the proposed rule -- the cost of restoration as well as compensable value. Although receiving numerous comments on the use of CV, Interior postponed consideration of comments concerning the use of CV to calculate passive use values. It did address briefly the use of CV to estimate direct use value. In its 1991 proposed rulemaking, Interior had asserted that CV was as reliable as any other nonmarket methodology when used to estimate direct use value. Receiving no comments disputing this assertion, Interior, in its final rule, allows use of CV to assess direct use value subject only to the same restrictions applicable to any other methodology. The final rule also eliminates the ranking of valuation methods according to reliability that had been in the proposed rule.[64] Interior's approach in its final rule and the lack of comments concerning the use of CV for the calculation of direct use value seem to be a good indication that any former controversy surrounding the use of CV to calculate direct use value had ceased.[65] As for standards for the use of CV to estimate passive use values, Interior said that it would "soon be issuing a proposed set of standards to improve the reliably of CV ...."[66]

Following on the heels of the final rule, Interior published a notice of proposed rulemaking addressing use of CV to calculate passive use values and seeking comments on NOAA's 1994 proposed rulemaking concerning the same issue.[67] For the most part, Interior's 1994 proposed rule reiterated the guidance and standards found in NOAA's 1994 rule. In addition, Interior's proposed rule responded to comments submitted in response to its 1993 proposed rule and posed additional questions concerning portions of NOAA's proposed guidance and standards.

Once again, the comments received on the use of CV to calculate passive use values divided into two camps. The first supported the use of the methodology at the trustee's discretion while the second purported that CV produces unreliable results. Those opposing the inclusion of CV repeated many of the previously articulated concerns. However, another set of commenters focused on the legitimacy of recovering passive use values.[68]

In response to the comments questioning the inclusion of passive use values as part of the damage claim, Interior cited language from the *Ohio* decision that opined that reliably calculated lost values, including passive use values, should be included. Thus, Interior emphasized that "the focus of this notice is not whether lost nonuse values per se are an appropriate component of a natural resource damage assessment. This notice addressed whether lost nonuse values can be reliably calculated and, if so, under what conditions."[69] Turning to the reliability of CV methodology for passive use valuation, Interior stated that "based on the evidence received to date," CV is not a "fundamentally flawed methodology." A properly designed and administered survey can produce reliable results. Interior also observed that any CV carried out that followed the regulations "should satisfy judicial standards for admissibility of evidence."[70]

As mentioned at the beginning of the discussion on Interior's 1994 proposed rule, Interior imported into its notice most of the discussion, guidelines and standards published in NOAA's 1994 proposed rule on use of CV to calculate passive use values. Interior, however, did add to the discussion of the test designed to demonstrate that individuals are responsive to the scope of the environmental insult (scope test) and posed a number of probing question concerning the scope test, calibration, prior knowledge and screening/threshold factor.[71] Both Interior and NOAA extended the public comment period on the proposed rules to October 7, 1994.[72]

An analysis of the comments received concerning passive use and the use of CV to estimate passive use revealed little change in the types of comments received. Because the comments reiterate previous diverse positions, Interior and NOAA were once again in the position of attempting to satisfy conflicting viewpoints.

NOAA also appeared to be following in the footsteps of Interior's litigious history concerning the promulgation of the regulations. Like Interior in 1984, NOAA has been sued[73] for failure to promulgate its regulations within the two year time period established by Congress in OPA.

Rather than issuing a final rule based on the comments received on the 1994 proposed rule, NOAA published another notice of proposed rulemaking in August, 1995.[74] In the 1995 proposed rule, NOAA departed significantly from its previous approach. The proposed rule focused on restoration, and the determination of compensable values was relegated to a more secondary role. Methodologies for estimating human values can be used to determine the appropriate scale of compensatory restoration,[75] but only if a "service-to-service" based scaling[76] is not feasible. Gone are the guidelines for CV development, administration and interpretation. Instead, the proposed rule merely notes that contingent valuation is a methodology that may be used when a service-to-service approach is not appropriate. Because of the fundamental change in approach, NOAA sought comments on whether standards for the use of valuation methods should be included in the final rule.[77]

While most commenters supported the new approach proposed by NOAA, several requested that NOAA provide specific guidance for the use of CV. Eight commenters stated that passive use values should not be used in the scaling exercise, and nine noted that CV should not be used. Two commenters urged the use of both passive use values and CV when scaling compensatory restoration. An analysis of the comments disclosed no new criticisms of CV methodology.[78]

The NOAA final rule, very similar to that proposed in August, 1995, was published on January 5, 1996.[79] At this time it is unclear whether any party will challenge the final rule. Perhaps NOAA has broken the litigious cycle that has been an integral part of the promulgation of natural resource damage assessment regulations.

The Role of Passive Use in Regulatory Decision Making

Cost-Benefit Analysis and the Regulatory Process

On February 19, 1981, President Reagan signed Executive Order 12291 (E.O. 12291). This executive order required agencies proposing new major regulations to provide the Office of Management and Budget (OMB), part of the Executive Branch, a regulatory impact analysis (RIA) for such regulations. A major component of the RIA is a formal cost-benefit analysis of the proposed regulation.[80] This was the first time that formal cost-benefit analysis of new regulations was required. In the first year of the Clinton Administration, E.O. 12866 superseded E.O. 12291. However, E.O. 12866 retained the central role that cost-benefit analysis played in E.O. 12291.

For many years the U.S. Environmental Protection Agency (EPA) complied with the cost-benefit provisions of E.O. 12291. Many of the RIAs calculated the benefits for regulations promulgated under the Clean Air and Water Acts by considering only what might be termed use values.[81] However, as EPA moved to regulate substances under newer environmental statutes such as the Resource Conservation and Recovery Act (RCRA),[82] it began to calculate benefits using a total value concept thereby explicitly acknowledging passive use.[83]

It is reasonable to assume that EPA will continue to base its benefit calculations used in RIAs on a total value concept. Since it is generally recognized that total value estimates can only be obtained using CV, EPA has a vested interest in seeing that CV remains a technique available for such use. And it is here where the damage assessment rulemakings and the internal decisions of the Executive Branch regarding the procedures agencies use in conducting RIAs meet.

It is fair to say that EPA and perhaps other agencies currently using a total value context for benefit calculation in RIAs or considering such an approach are concerned about the results of the damage assessment rulemakings regarding use of CV. The concern is that procedures developed in the damage assessment rulemakings, designed to ensure that CV estimates of passive use are reliable enough to be admitted as evidence in legal proceedings, will be utilized by OMB as guidance in OMB's evaluation of the RIAs submitted by agencies. These same agencies believe that CV used in regulatory decision making should not be forced to abide by the litigation driven requirements that are not only overly restrictive and costly to implement, but could impede acceptance of new approaches that may be developed in the future.

Currently, an interagency working group has been formed to consider appropriate guidelines for CV estimation of passive use and the role these estimates should play in cost-benefit studies included as part of RIA packages to OMB. The working group is composed of EPA, the Department of Energy (Energy) and several other agencies including the President's Council of Economic Advisors (CEA). The group is headed by OMB. It is likely that the damage assessment guidance concerning use of CV is playing a central role in the working group's assessment.

Agency Motivations

While it is difficult for outsiders to know the true position of the agencies comprising the working group, one can develop reasonably informed opinions on the basis of agency responsibilities and public comments made by agency personnel. For example, it comes as no surprise that EPA wishes to develop RIA guidelines that provide for very flexible use of CV. By flexible, we mean guidelines that are far less specific and rigid than those expressed by the NOAA Panel or the guidelines contained in the proposed NOAA and Interior damage assessment rules. In contrast to the EPA position, the posture of the Department of Energy is one that seems to reject the total value basis for cost-benefit studies, preferring to rely solely on direct use values to compute benefits. Because limiting use of CV curtails the ability of agencies to pursue a total value approach, Energy's stance motivates its desire for very restrictive guidelines for use of CV.[84] OMB is clearly in the same court as Energy. OMB appears to favor restricting the use of CV and thereby limiting the ability of agencies to pursue a total value approach to benefits estimation.[85]

What lies at the heart of these opposing agency views regarding the total value basis for cost-benefit analysis and the application of CV? Let us first examine EPA. There are at least two views explaining the agency's stance -- one laudable and one cynical. On the laudable side, it is likely true that if one polled economists on the issue of the appropriateness of a total value basis of cost-benefit analysis, the majority would support such a paradigm. One can then say that EPA is simply following contemporary thinking regarding the appropriate basis of cost-benefit analysis. Since the total value basis requires the use of CV, EPA would logically be in favor of RIA guidelines that permitted the agency to use freely CV.

The cynical view of EPA's motivations would argue as follows. EPA has extensive regulatory responsibility resulting in an enormous amount of activity as required by the enabling legislation. For EPA to fulfill its statutory obligations, regulations must be promulgated. On the other hand, OMB views unfavorably proposed EPA regulations that fail to pass a cost-benefit test. Thus, one might argue that EPA has an interest in ensuring that its proposed regulations pass such tests. It might be argued that EPA believes adopting a total value framework for cost-benefit analysis rather than the more restrictive direct use basis enhances its chances of overcoming the cost-benefit hurdle.

While it is easy to speculate about EPA's position, it is more difficult to do so for Energy's and OMB's. To begin an examination of possible motivations, consider the critical comment by one Energy economist arguing against the total value basis for cost-benefit analysis -- "[i]f the concept of existence value is accepted for general use by economists and policy analysts, and a whole host of new existence values is identified, virtually any kind of project or proposal may become justifiable."[86]

Simply stated, the above quote implies that if total value is used as the basis for cost-benefit analysis, then "too many" regulatory programs will pass the cost-benefit test. For "too many" to have any honest appeal, one must make the prior assertion that on theoretical grounds total value is not the appropriate basis for cost-benefit analysis. Without such a prior assertion, stating that too many regulations pass a cost-benefit test is a baseless argument one might ascribe to heavily regulated industries that simply desire to have regulatory burdens reduced.

Why might Energy reside in the camp that believes adopting a total value framework would lead to too many regulations? While it may indeed believe in the commitment motivated choice argument[87] or some variant, its position has not been well articulated. On the other hand, one might construe the agency's position as supporting the views of private industries (in particular, heavily regulated energy companies) that believe additional regulation would reduce their international competitiveness. This view might lead Energy to endorse guidelines for RIAs that bar a total value approach to cost-benefit analysis in the hopes that fewer regulations would pass such a test.

While Energy may be pursuing its stance on the basis of firmly held intellectual beliefs, recent action by Energy suggests otherwise. It seems from recent remarks that Energy is currently funding a group of economists to investigate the feasibility of quantifying the passive use losses that might result from employment dislocations that environmental regulations could cause (*i.e.*, the loss of jobs in the Northwest forestry industry due to spotted owl habit protection regulations).[88] Energy has been arguing that employment losses due to regulation can give rise to passive use losses and that these should properly be counted on the cost side of the cost-benefit ledger. Suggestions to include passive use in the cost of regulations are not new, but this does suggest that Energy has no intellectual attachment to its anti-total value stance.

The motivations of OMB are perhaps the most difficult to grasp fully. OMB is not subject to the sort of pressures that may shape the actions of EPA and Energy, and thus likely does not share these agencies' political motivations. On the total value issue, OMB, or more properly the economists working in Office of Information and Regulatory Affairs, may genuinely believe the commitment motivated choice criticism of the total value basis for cost-benefit analysis. For example, a recent paper by two OMB economists clearly evidences this belief.[89] This paper suggests that the authors view motivations for choices that may based on societal concerns or upon actions ("the process by which decisions are made") as inappropriate choices upon which to construct values for the purposes of cost-benefit analysis. This suggests that OMB does indeed reject the total value basis for cost-benefit analysis.

We can examine and rationalize the stance OMB takes with regard to CV by first acknowledging the anti-total value view we have attributed to OMB. Like Energy, OMB may maintain intellectually compelling reasons for its stance. However, OMB is just as critical of CV estimates of passive use when used for natural resource damage assessment as it seems to be with the use of such estimates in cost-benefit analysis. OMB has not stated how the "commitment motivated choice" or other anti-total value arguments pertain to passive use losses estimated for the purpose of damage assessment. One might then conjecture that OMB has other motivations for its actions.

One alternative explanation for OMB's attitude may relate to the vast amount of regulations OMB must monitor and evaluate. OMB's staff is small relative to the staffs of some of the agencies proposing regulations. CV based cost-benefit analyses can be complex, and the proper evaluation of such studies requires expertise that extends beyond economics and likely beyond the expertise of OMB's staff. Barring CV from use in RIAs by placing restrictive requirements on its use may be a simple means to manipulate the OMB regulatory workload.

A second explanation is that OMB has no faith in cost-benefit analysis and believes that the economy is already over regulated. Therefore, new regulations are unnecessary regardless of the results of the cost-benefit analysis. A variation on this theme would be to conjecture that OMB has little or no faith that regulatory agencies will carry out objective, high quality cost-benefit analyses using CV. OMB might argue that since evaluating the quality and objectivity of a CV study is problematic, it is best that CV not be used.

There remain two other possible motivations for OMB's attitude that should be noted. The first is the reliability/validity of CV estimates of passive use, while the second is perhaps an argument for the position that too many projects pass a cost-benefit test. OMB has raised a number of concerns regarding the reliability of CV estimates -- most of which are not new, but deserve discussion. Section 4 discusses the legal and economic reliability of CV estimates. The argument that too many projects pass the cost-benefit hurdle can be given intellectual underpinnings, as we discuss below.

The Proper Role of Passive Use in Regulatory Decision Making

Suppose one is willing to concede that estimates of passive use are valid and reliable when constructed from the choices contained in well designed and executed CV surveys. Is there a case to be made for the position that using such estimates in cost-benefit analyses of government regulations will lead to "too many" programs passing the cost-benefit test? While such an argument can be made, there is a straightforward (at least conceptually) way to ensure that this does not happen. We note at the outset that too many programs passing a cost-benefit test is not reflective of some underlying inadequacy of CV as applied in the cost-benefit context, but rather indicates a failure on the part of the federal government to coordinate and conduct proper cost-benefit studies.

The "too many programs pass" phenomenon can be examined with a simple example. Consider the following hypothetical scenario. EPA is considering two major regulations -- one on air toxic emissions and one on ground water protection. It is thought by EPA that both regulatory programs would have significant passive use benefits and so a CV study is proposed to be used in each RIA. EPA designs two independent CV surveys that meet the relevant requirements for valid and reliable estimates of total value. One survey focuses exclusively on the air toxic regulation and the other on the water regulation. Both surveys use the same payment vehicle, a tax surcharge for the next five years.

EPA fields each survey to independent samples of U.S. households, constructs an aggregate estimate of WTP for each individual program, and then uses these WTP estimates as the basis for benefit estimates in each proposed regulation's RIA. If EPA intends these regulations to be put in place at approximately the same time , under particular circumstances one can argue that the benefits of either program may be overstated. The overstatement could come from at least two causes. First, there is the pure substitution effect. If some CV respondents viewed these programs as substitutes, then the WTP for one program, given that the other already exits, will be less than the WTP if the other program does not exist. Second, to the extent the required tax payments are sufficiently large to be binding on the income of some CV respondents, the WTP for either program will be less when the other program (and its associated tax) is in place.

Given the example above, one can imagine the problems OMB might face if numerous proposed regulations from various federal agencies use CV based estimates of benefits in their respective RIAs, but where independent respondents were asked about each proposed program in the absence of knowledge regarding the other programs. Each CV benefit estimate is valid and reliable given the circumstances of the choice as presented to the respondent, that is, no other public goods are offered. However, taken as a package of programs providing multiple public goods, respondents would view each component (proposed program) differently, where the WTP for the package would be less than or equal to the sum of the WTP for the individual components.[90]

If one believes that CV techniques will come to dominate cost-benefit analysis undertaken for RIAs, and one is convinced by the above argument that overstating the aggregate benefits of packaged regulations is a real possibility, what might be done? There is an easy answer to this question, but it would require the Executive Branch to coordinate the rulemakings of its various regulatory agencies.

Currently, each executive agency must publish semi-annually in the Federal Register an agenda of regulations under development or review.[91] However, there is no requirement for a comprehensive cost-benefit analysis of the regulatory package, but there could be a requirement that certain regulatory proposals expected to be promulgated over some defined future time period be grouped together to assess the costs and benefits of the package. The responsibility for this function could be delegated to an interagency task force under the supervision of the OMB, the President's Council of Economic Advisors or both.[92]

Such a coordinated approach to the regulatory review process has several desirable features. First, it would eliminate any chance that program benefits would be overstated due to the current piecemeal approach. Second, agency resources could be used more effectively by developing and administering a single, high quality CV survey. By merging the currently independent efforts, budget based excuses for poor quality studies would become less forceful. Third, forcing a coordinated regulatory review would bring certain proposed regulations together for a unified analysis.[93]

Another advantage of a coordinated review is that it also would reduce the potential for over or understatement of program *costs*. Like the analysis of program benefits, the current piecemeal approach to regulatory review examines the cost associated with each proposed regulation in isolation and does not consider the cost implications of joint implementation of the regulations. If the costs of regulations are supra or sub-additive,[94] a coordinated review on the cost side is just as important as it is on the benefits side.

Before leaving this section we wish to make an important point. There exists substantive differences in the appropriate framework to be used for the estimation of total value when one is considering the provision of new public goods or when one is estimating the compensation required due to natural resource injuries. These distinctions have been discussed by Kopp and Smith in this volume, but we note here that the greatest difference lies in fact that when estimating required compensation for the purposes of damage assessment, one would not seek to include the economic valuation of the natural resource injuries in a larger context that involves the simultaneous valuation of other public goods (as one might do when conducting a cost-benefit analysis for polices serving to increase the provision of public goods). When one seeks to measure compensation for natural resource injuries, WTA compensation is the appropriate frame of reference for economic valuation. Therefore it would be meaningless to mix a WTA compensation valuation with a set of WTP valuations for other public goods.[95]

THE VALIDITY (RELIABILITY) OF CV ESTIMATES OF LOST PASSIVE USE

This section focuses on the most debated issue in the economic, legal and political controversy surrounding CV and passive use -- the validity of CV estimates of passive use. We begin the section by describing the legal view regarding the validity (reliability) of admissible evidence and then turn to the academic perspective of CV reliability.

Recovery for Passive Use Values -- Legal Perspective

As in the economic profession, there is no serious debate in the legal profession about the existence, at least under certain circumstances, of passive use values. Rather, the discussion centers on whether such values are recoverable under the current statutory and regulatory frameworks, and if so, under what conditions.

Other than the *Ohio* Court, *see* previous discussion, few courts have considered recovery of passive use values pursuant to the federal statutory framework. This paucity of precedence is not surprising. Natural resource damage assessment is a relatively new area, and most cases are settled out of court. Based on the limited rulings to date, no court has held that passive use damages, in theory, cannot be recovered. For example, in a discussion on divisibility of natural resource damages, the court in the New Bedford Harbor/PCB case noted "the possibility of what have been termed 'existence' and 'intrinsic' values attributable to natural resources. Those values also may be injured."[96] The court in *Idaho v. Southern Refrigerated Transport, Inc.* also recognized that existence value would be an appropriate item of damage if proven at trial.[97] In the final case, *Utah v. Kennecott Corp.*, the court rejected a proposed settlement of the state's natural resource claims for failure to consider "non-consumptive use values of the aquifer, i.e., option and existence values." The court added that "people who live in a desert most likely would assign substantial value in just knowing that an aquifer exists."[98]

Reliability -- The Legal Perspective[99]

In the debate over the appropriate uses of CV, the word "reliability" is frequently heard. It is not apparent, however, that this word has the same meaning to all the participants in the debate. A recent U.S. Supreme Court decision concerning the admissibility of scientific evidence noted that while scientists "typically distinguish between 'validity' (does the principle support what it purports to show?) and 'reliability' (does application of the principle produce consistent results?)," the Court emphasized its "reference here is to evidentiary reliability -- that is, trustworthiness."[100] Thus, this discussion of reliability from a legal perspective adopts that definition.

When one considers the evolution of the common law, it is not surprising that modern courts continue to be concerned with the trustworthiness of evidence being proffered. The trier-of-fact, whether a judge or a jury, must be able to evaluate the credibility or trustworthiness of the evidence. Over the centuries rules have developed to guide the courts in determining what kinds of evidence should be considered. For example, a type of "secondhand" evidence called "hearsay"[101] is disfavored with some exceptions. Obviously, these rules play a critical role in determining the use of CV in a litigation context which can develop out of the natural resource damage assessment process.

One often heard criticism concerning the use of CV in the damage assessment context is that the method is not "reliable" enough to be used in litigation and would, therefore, be inadmissible in a court of law. This assertion, however, is likely to be unfounded for a well constructed and administered CV survey. In the legal area, consideration of evidence is a two step process. First, it must be admitted, and then the judge or jury must determine what weight, if any, to accord it.

Most courts will admit a properly administered survey as an exception to the hearsay rule, as nonhearsay or pursuant to the Federal Rules of Evidence. The Judicial Conference Study Group Handbook of Recommended Procedures for the Trial of Protracted Litigation, 25 F.R.D. 351 (1960), outlines the generally accepted survey principles that, if followed, are likely to result in the admission of the survey. Those standards are 1) the proper universe is examined; 2) a representative sample is chosen; 3) the mode of questioning respondents is correct; 4) persons conducting the survey are experts trained in survey techniques; 5) data are properly gathered and accurately reported; 6) the sample design, questionnaire, and interview techniques meet objective criteria; and 7) the survey is conducted independently of attorneys in the case -- interviewers and respondents are unaware of the purposes of the survey. These Judicial Conference standards are cited in many court opinions dealing with admissibility of surveys, though a court may considered other factors as well.[102]

The Federal Rules of Evidence also would support the admissibility of CV surveys used to estimate interim lost use value in the damage assessment context. For example, Rule 703 states:

> [t]he facts or data in the particular case upon which an expert bases an opinion or inference may be those perceived by or made known to him at or before the hearing. If of a type reasonably relied upon by experts in the particular field in forming opinions or inferences upon the subject, the facts or data need not be admissible in evidence.

The Notes of the Senate Advisory Committee on Rule 703 provide guidance on the scope of this rule. In part, the Notes explain:

> [t]he third source contemplated by the rule consists of presentation of data to the expert outside of court and other than by his own perception. In this respect the rule is designed to broaden the basis for expert opinions beyond that current in many jurisdictions and to bring the judicial practice into line with the practice of the experts themselves when not in court.

Further, the Notes state "[t]he rule also offers a more satisfactory basis for ruling upon the admissibility of public opinion poll evidence. Attention is directed to the validity of the techniques employed rather than to relatively fruitless inquiries whether hearsay is involved."

In considering the admissibility of a CV survey, a second rule of evidence, Rule 702, is also likely to be considered. Rule 702 provides that "[i]f scientific, technical, or other specialized knowledge will assist the trier of fact to understand the evidence or to determine a fact in issue, a witness qualified as an expert by knowledge, skill, experience, training, or education, may testify thereto in the form of an opinion or otherwise."

The Notes of the Senate Advisory Committee on Rule 702 indicate that the term "expert" should be broadly construed to include:

> [any] person qualified by "knowledge, skill, experience, training or education." Thus within the scope of the rule are not only experts in the strictest sense of the word, e.g., physicians, physicists, and architects, but also the large group sometimes called "skilled" witnesses, such as bankers or landowners testifying to land values.

The U.S. Supreme Court recently considered Rule 702 in the case *Daubert v. Merrell Dow Pharmaceuticals,* 113 S.Ct. 2786 (1993). There, the Court stated that under the Federal Rules of Evidence, the trial judge must ensure that all evidence admitted is both relevant and reliable. Evidence is relevant if it assists the judge or jury to understand evidence or to help to determine an issue in the case. Reliability, as noted previously, refers to "trustworthiness." When determining reliability, the trial judge should consider several questions. Those include 1) has the theory or technique been subject to peer review and publication;[103] 2) whether standards exist for the technique; and 3) has the method or technique achieved a "particular degree of acceptance" within the relevant community? Further, the Court observed that the "inquiry envisioned by Rule 702 is ... a flexible one .... [and] [t]he focus, of course, must be solely on principles and methodology, not on the conclusions that they generate."[104]

Federal courts are now beginning to apply *Daubert* when considering the admissibility of certain types of evidence such as DNA test results. Through such decisions, one can begin to glean the interpretation of the *Daubert* standards such as "particular degree of acceptance" within the relevant community. For example, in the case *United States v. Chischilly,* the court considered Chischilly's argument that the DNA profiling tests are controversial and have "divided the scientific community into opposing camps." Ruling that such evidence is admissible, the court stated that "evidence of opposing academic camps arrayed in virtual scholarly equipoise amidst the scientific journals is scarcely an indication of the 'minimal support within a community' that would give a trial court cause to view a known technique with skepticism under Daubert ...."[105]

Further, the *Chischilly* Court pointed out that the Supreme Court in *Daubert* "cautions lower courts not to confuse the role of judge and jury by forgetting that 'vigorous cross-examination, presentation of contrary evidence, and careful instruction on the burden of proof' rather than exclusion, 'are the traditional and appropriate means of attacking shaky but admissible evidence.'"[106]

More recently, the Ninth Circuit reconsidered *Daubert* in light of the Supreme Court's guidance. Stating that the "test under *Daubert* is not the correctness of the expert's conclusions but the soundness of his methodology, the court turned to publication as an indicia of this test. The court observed that research "accepted for publication in a reputable scientific journal after being subjected to the usual rigors of peer review is a significant indication that it is taken seriously by other scientists, i.e., that is meets at least the minimal criteria of good science." However, if the method has not been subject to peer review, such evidence may still be admitted if the experts "explain precisely how they went about reaching their conclusions and point to some objective source -- a learned treatise, the policy statement of a professional association, a published article in a reputable scientific journal or the like -- to show that they have followed the scientific method, as it is practiced by (at least) a recognized minority of scientists in their field."[107]

Concluding Remarks -- Legal Perspective

While the cases concerning admissibility of surveys referred to above do not deal with surveys designed to estimate lost value due to injuries to natural resources, there is no reason to believe that such surveys would be treated any differently if they met the *Daubert* standards and other rules of federal evidence. CV is a well established methodology having first been proposed in 1947 and first applied in 1963.[108] It has been the subject of many articles appearing in peer reviewed literature as well as in other publications and proceedings of professional meetings.[109] The judicial system of the United States has articulated admissibility standards for surveys in general, and survey research organizations have well established guidelines for administration of surveys.[110] Further, NOAA's panel recommended guidance to ensure reliability when using CV surveys to estimate passive use values.

Under *Daubert*, what is meant by acceptance of the methodology in the relevant community is not precisely defined. One thing is certain, however -- the Court clearly rejects general acceptance as the exclusive requirement for admissibility. Does the fact that there is controversy about the method mean that the method fails the *Daubert* test? As this article has discussed, there are two vocal camps vigorously espousing different positions on the reliability of CV surveys to estimate passive use values. That, alone, is not sufficient to cause a court to rule such a study inadmissible. See *Chischilly* discussion, *supra*. Rather, relevance may be the determining factor as discussed in *Daubert II*. If a well executed study would assist the trier of fact in considering a factual issue, it would likely be admitted into evidence. Certainly, an important issue under the existing statutory and regulatory framework governing natural resource damage assessment is the value of the lost or injured natural resources. CV methodology provides a means for estimating that value and remains the only method to estimate passive use values. Thus, one would expect a court to admit a properly designed and administered CV survey used in natural resource damage assessment.

CV Reliability -- the Academic Perspective

Nowhere have the issues surrounding the validity and reliability of CV estimates of passive use values been more hotly debated than in the pages of scholarly journals and at professional workshops, symposiums and conferences.[111] While examining the debate in its entirety is a task well beyond the scope of this paper, the NOAA Panel report provides an overview of the critical issues. In addition, readers are directed to the recent symposia on contingent valuation contained in the Fall 1994 issue of *Economic Perspectives.*[112]

The NOAA Panel and CV Reliability

The task of the NOAA Panel on CV can best be summed up by quoting directly from the Panel's report.

> The CV technique is the subject of great controversy. Its detractors argue that respondents give answers that are inconsistent with the tenets of rational choice, that these respondents do not understand what it is they are being asked to value (and thus, that stated values reflect more than that which they are being asked to value), that respondents fail to take CV questions seriously because the results of the surveys are not binding, and raise other objections as well. Proponents of the CV technique acknowledge that its early (and even some current) applications suffered from many of the problems critics have noted, but believe that more recent and comprehensive studies have already or soon will be able to deal with these objections.
>
> This (sometimes acrimonious) debate has put the National Oceanic and Atmospheric Administration (NOAA) in a very difficult spot. NOAA must decide in promulgating the regulations under the Oil Pollution Act whether the CV technique is capable of providing reliable information about lost existence or other passive-use values. Toward this end, NOAA appointed the Contingent Valuation Panel to consider this question and make recommendations to it.[113]

It seems clear that the Panel believed its charge was to assess the reliability of CV for the estimation of passive use in legal proceedings involving the assessment of damages to natural resources due to releases of oil.

The Panel acknowledges early in its report the difficulty encountered when one attempts to determine whether any given set of CV results is reliable. The Panel notes,

> [t]he contingent valuation method has been criticized for many reasons and the Panel believes that a number of these criticisms are particularly compelling. Before identifying and discussing these problems, however, it is worth pointing out that they all take on added importance in light of the impossibility of validating externally the results of CV studies.[114]

Here the Panel is expressing pessimism over the likelihood that the results of a CV study could ever be compared with the results from some other valuation technique as a means to verify independently the CV results. Given the "impossibility of validating externally the results of CV studies" the Panel turns from an *ex post* analysis of results to an *ex ante* concern with the quality of the study itself, and focuses its discussion on how to improve the quality of studies and thereby improve the reliability of the results.

The Panel's assessment resulted in a set of recommended survey design and administration guidelines and procedures that if followed, would in the opinion of the Panel, lead to reliable results. The Panel stated,

> The Panel concludes that under those conditions (and others specified above), CV studies convey useful information. We think it is fair to describe such information as reliable by the standards that seem to be implicit in similar contexts, like market analysis for new and innovative products and the assessment of other damages normally allowed in court proceedings. As in all such cases, the more closely the guidelines are followed, the more reliable the result will be. It is not necessary, however, that every single injunction be completely obeyed; inferences accepted in other contexts are not perfect either.[115]

The Panel's recommendations include guidelines for survey design and administration. On the administration front the Panel recommends: probability sampling, in-person interviews, minimizing nonresponse, careful pretesting, and an examination of interviewer effects. As far as survey design is concerned, the Panel recommends: a conservative design,[116] a WTP valuation format, a referendum style choice, an accurate description of the policy or program to be valued, checks on understanding and acceptance, voting choices followed by open-ended questions asking about reasons for voting one way or the other, deflection of transaction values, reminding respondents of alternative expenditure possibilities, reminding respondents of undamaged substitute commodities, and providing the opportunity to respondents not to vote.

The Panel guidelines for survey administration are nothing more than standard practice for any high quality survey effort. And while following these guidelines is expensive and time consuming, there is not a great deal of controversy that such practices would improve the reliability of the CV survey.[117] The Panel's recommendations on survey design are for the most part also standard practice. However, some are novel and controversial. These include: the use of a referendum format rather than a open ended question eliciting maximum WTP, the requirement for temporal averaging, and the explicit offer to the respondent of an opportunity not to vote. The requirements for temporal averaging and the explicit offer to the respondent of an opportunity not to vote are novel; however, recent evidence suggests they do nothing to improve CV reliability.[118]

While the Panel believes that independent verification of CV results is impossible, it suggests that the economic theory of rational choice might be drawn upon to create a test of CV reliability that can be used in addition to the survey design and administration guidelines to gauge the reliability of CV results. The Panel observed:

> Rationality in its weakest form requires certain kinds of consistency among choices made by individuals. . . . Usually, though not always, it is reasonable to suppose that more of something regarded as good is better so long as an individual is not satiated. This is, in general, translated into a willingness to pay somewhat more for more of a good, as judged by the individual. Also, if marginal or incremental willingness to pay for additional amounts does decline with the amount already available, it is usually not reasonable to assume that it declines very abruptly.[119]

The Panel then stated:

> Until such time as there is a set of reliable reference surveys, the burden of proof of reliability must rest on the survey designers. They must show through pretesting or other experiments that their survey does not suffer from the problems that these guidelines are intended to avoid. Specifically, if a CV survey suffered from any of the following maladies, we would judge its findings "unreliable."

One of the specified maladies described by the Panel was "[i]nadequate responsiveness to the scope of the environmental insult." This requirement has since been described as a *scope* test. The *scope* test requires that WTP estimates derived from CV surveys should be related to the "size"[120] of the object of choice. An alternative test has been proposed by Diamond, Hausman, Leonard and Denning (1993) and has been referred to as an *adding-up* test. This test is based on the assumption that an object of choice can be decomposed into pieces, and then it is argued that the sum of the WTP's for each part should equal the WTP for the whole.

Earlier in this volume Kopp and Smith noted that the scope test proposed by the NOAA Panel rests on a single, fairly weak assumption, that more of a good is preferred to less. While this may not be universally true for all goods, it has enough intuitive appeal to serve as a reasonable assumption upon which to construct a test. In contrast, the test by Diamond, Hausman, Leonard and Denning (1993) rests on a much stronger assumption regarding individual's preferences. In particular, the adding up test assumes that component pieces to be "added-up" are perfect substitutes for one another. This perfect substitution assumption is neither intuitive nor verifiable. Thus, tests of internal consistency of choices such as that proposed by Diamond, Hausman, Leonard and Denning, require auxiliary assumptions in addition to the simple axioms underlying economic theory to formulate empirical hypotheses. As a consequence, the adding up test of choice consistency considers composite hypotheses (the internal consistency condition and the relevant auxiliary assumptions). Therefore, it is equally plausible that behavior judged by an adding up test as inconsistent could be due to a violation in one or more of the required additional assumptions for the test and have nothing at all to do with consistency of choice. The weakness of the adding up test leaves only the NOAA Panel scope test as an appropriate test of the internal consistency of choices.

Kopp and Smith also present the results of two scope tests conducted by Smith and Colleagues. Both of these tests lend support to the position that WTP derived from CV

surveys is consistent with the NOAA Panel's weak assumption that more of a good should be preferred to less.

Testing for Construct Validity

In the opinion of the NOAA Panel, information provided by CV surveys that abide by the Panel's recommended survey design and administration guidelines can be judged "as reliable by the standards that seem to be implicit in similar contexts, like market analysis for new and innovative products and the assessment of other damages normally allowed in court proceedings."[121] Moreover, added credibility can be given to the results if the data show a sensitivity of WTP to the scope of the environmental insult, *i.e.*, pass a scope test.

While not mentioned by the Panel, there is a third aspect of CV studies that may be examined to shed light on reliability. Construct validity refers to the degree to which one measure relates to other measures predicted by theory.[122] In examining construct validity in the context of a CV study, one can seek to determine whether variation in the respondents' choices is systematically related to factors suggested by economic theory such as preferences for the object of choice, the cost of program offered to the respondent, and the ability to pay for it. In the context of natural resource damages, other factors relevant for construct validity might include measures of respondents' perceptions of the injuries and the characteristics of the program designed to remediate those injuries. The estimation of a multivariate choice function is a statistical method used to demonstrate construct validity. The choice function relates respondents' choices to their evaluations of the programs offered to them in CV surveys as well as to their demographic characteristics and attitudes.[123]

The first demonstration of construct validity for a CV study that meets most of the NOAA Panel guidelines is found in Carson *et al.* 1992. That study sought to measure the loss in passive use value due to the *Exxon Valdez* oil spill using a referendum style, in-person CV survey. Respondents were asked to vote on a plan that would cause taxes to be raised to fund a program using escort ships to protect Prince William Sound, Alaska from another oil spill causing natural resource injures comparable in magnitude to those of the Exxon Valdez. Several follow-up questions were asked regarding respondent demographics, attitudes, perceptions about the plan and injuries, and economic information about the respondent's household. Much of this information was used to test for construct validity.

Table 1 presents the results from the estimation of a construct validity equation. Since the data derived from respondent choices to the voting question are either a yes or no vote to a particular amount of tax the respondent would have to pay for the program, Carson *et al.* were not able to specify the respondents' maximum WTP for the Prince William Sound protection program. Rather they were able to place the maximum WTP with bounds (*i.e.,* between zero and $25 dollars if the respondent voted no for the plan if the tax amount was $25, and between $25 and infinity if the respondent voted yes). Given this "interval censored data" Carson *et al.* employed a parametric survival model based on a Weibull error structure in the estimation of the construct validity equation.[124]

TABLE 1: CONSTRUCT VALIDITY FUNCTION

Parameter	Estimate	Standard Error	Asymptotic t-Value
GMORE	0.867	0.284	3.06
LESS	-0.273	0.146	-1.88
NODAM	-0.794	0.432	-1.84
NWORK	-0.862	0.131	-6.57
NWORK	-1.754	0.200	-8.79
NAME	0.203	0.134	1.51
COASTA L	0.414	0.143	2.89
WILD	0.261	0.119	2.19
STENV	0.473	0.229	2.06

TABLE 1: CONSTRUCT VALIDITY FUNCTION			
LIKVIS	0.240	0.138	1.74
LINC	0.284	0.100	2.85
WHITE	0.423	0.151	2.80
PROTEST	-1.226	0.145	-8.45

The first four variables in Table 1, GMORE, MORE, LESS, and NODAM, are dummy variables indicating which respondents believed that the damage likely to occur in the absence of the escort ship plan would be different from that of the Exxon Valdez spill. Following the theoretical basis for the scope test (*i.e.*, more is preferred to less), one would predict that the greater the perception of damage in the absence of the escort ship plan, the greater will be the willingness to pay for the plan. The coefficients on all four of these variables are significant and follow the expected rank ordering. Those respondents who think that there would be a great deal more damage, GMORE, are willing to pay quite a bit more money than the average respondent. Those who think that there will be somewhat less, but still more damage, MORE, are willing to pay less than the GMORE respondents, but still quite a bit more than the average respondent. Those who think that there would be less damage, LESS, are willing to pay less than the average respondent; and those who think that there would likely be little or no damage, NODAM, are willing to pay less, but still something. While no explicit scope test was performed by Carson *et al.*, these four variables taken together provide suggestive evidence of respondent sensitivity to scope.The next two variables, MWORK and NWORK, indicate respondents who think that the plan will prevent less than a great deal of the injury, MWORK indicating those who think that the plan will prevent some of the injury and NWORK indicating those who think that the plan will not reduce the injury at all. In this case, theory would suggest that WTP should fall as the perception of the plan's effectiveness falls. Again, both variables are significant and of the expected negative sign. The NWORK coefficient is about twice the size of the MWORK coefficient in absolute value. The MWORK and NWORK variables provide further evidence undercutting the insensitivity to scope criticism, as they suggest that respondents' valuations and expressed WTP *are* responsive to the characteristics of the good being offered, in this case, the ability of the program to actually prevent the described injuries. NAME is a dummy variable for those respondents who spontaneously named the Exxon Valdez spill as one of the major environmental accidents caused by humans. As expected, this variable, which measures salience, has a positive influence on a respondent's willingness to pay. COASTAL, which is a dummy variable indicating which respondents said that protecting coastal areas from oil spills was "extremely important" or "very important," has a large and highly significant positive influence on a respondent's willingness to pay. Likewise, WILD, which is a dummy variable for those who felt that the government should set aside a "very large amount" or "large amount" of new land as wilderness, has a positive effect on a respondent's willingness to pay. STENV, identification of oneself as a strong environmentalist, and LIKVIS, a dummy variable for indicating that the household was "very likely" or "somewhat likely" to visit Alaska in the future, also suggest a higher willingness to pay. The results discussed above accord well with reasonable prior expectation one might have regarding the association between WTP and factors that one might think should be associated with WTP. Thus, in the Carson *et al.* (1992) study, tests for construct validity add to the confidence one can assign to the validity of the WTP estimates.

CONCLUSION

Four categories of issues appear to be shaping the current and future debate over the inclusion of passive use values in the context of damage assessment and in the execution of cost-benefit analyses of federal regulatory programs. Those categories are business concerns, political concerns, economic issues and legal issues. Two of these issues, economic and legal, have already been discussed in the body of this paper. In this remaining section we address the business and political concerns that appear to be the driving forces serving to shape the future public policy use of CV.

Business Concerns

Potentially responsible parties have raised several issues consistently. The first is that CV will be used extensively by trustees to estimate passive use values for all types of cases regardless of the degree of potential injury which will, in turn, generate large estimates of damage. This being the case, insurance companies may view such future claims as "unbounded" and thus be reluctant to insure certain activities that may give rise to natural resource damage claims. While business, obviously, would incorporate such potential liability as a cost of doing business, such added expenditures would render these American businesses less competitive in the world market.[125]

When one examines the record, it is quickly apparent thatCVs to measure passive use values have been used infrequently by trustees. This infrequent use is probably due to several factors. First is the nature and extent of the injury involved. In any number of circumstances, the trustees may decide not to calculate passive use values

-- for example, small spills not affecting a sensitive habitat or moderate size oil spills in an industrialized area. The second factor is the time and expense of conducting a CV survey that meets the recommended guidelines of NOAA's Panel and hence the admissibility standards of *Daubert*. If a trustee is attempting to conduct such a high quality CV study, it is unlikely that the method will be used unless the trustee anticipates substantial injury to natural resources. Further, when one examines cases where CV has been employed to estimated passive use values, the eventual recovery of damages is modest in comparison to the specter raised by industry. In the *Idarado* mining case in Colorado, the estimate of natural resource damages, based partially on CV, exceeded $100 million. However, that claim was settled for $1.1 million. In the *Nestucca* oil spill which killed over 50,000 seabirds, the preliminary estimate of natural resource damages was $110 million. The State of Washington settled its natural resource claim for $3.5 million while the Province of British Columbia settled for $3.4 million. If these cases are any indication, industry's concerns about unbounded liability appear vastly overstated.

When it comes to the use of total value measures in cost-benefit analyses, the complaint from the business community also seems to hinge on competitiveness arguments. That is, even if the concept of total economic value is appropriate for cost-benefit analysis and can be reliably measured, many in the business community would argue that regulations clearing a cost-benefit hurdle because of the inclusion of total value are too costly for U.S. firms and will destroy our international competitive position vis-a-vis countries that do not regulate as stringently as we do.

This argument has credibility if the cost-benefit studies conducted by the regulatory agencies routinely fail to analyze properly the competitive impacts of regulatory decisions. The proper criticism is not the inclusion of total value, but rather the possible exclusion of competitive impacts. Given the difficulty of even a simple cross country comparison of regulations,[126] not to mention the unresolved theoretical and empirical issues that arise when one attempts to quantify in any meaningful economic sense competitiveness, it is probably true that regulatory induced declines in competitive positions are poorly captured, if at all, in cost-benefit studies.

Political Concerns

There are undoubtedly many views regarding the political importance and implications of CV's widespread use. More than a few of these views would focus on CV's use in damage assessment. The November 1994 mid-term election resulted in a change of party control of the U.S. Congress. The new Republican controlled Congress is likely to be more receptive to industry's concerns about the inclusion of passive use value for damage assessment purposes. Industry for the past year and a half has been floating proposals to revise the measure of damages to exclude passive use values.

While the issue of passive use and CV is of obvious importance to the damage assessment debate, it is our view that the politically more important concern is the role of passive use and CV in the analysis of regulatory policy. In particular, it is the adoption of a total value framework for cost-benefit analyses (and therefore the necessity of using CV) that gives rise to the greatest political concern (see sections 3.2.1 and 3.2.2) and is the cause for most of the attention being paid to CV.

The future use of CV in cost-benefit analysis is influenced by the damage assessment debate and as a consequence, political concerns manifest themselves in attempts to influence the damage assessment regulations. Political influence is brought to bear on the formulation of the DOI and NOAA damage assessment regulations due to the legitimacy that these regulations can bestow on CV. Should these regulations endorse the use of CV for the assessment of natural resource damages, the agencies are providing CV with a rebuttable presumption in damage assessment legal proceedings. From such an action one could reasonably conclude that if CV is "good enough" as a basis for awarding damages in courts of law, it is surely good enough for use in government studies of proposed regulations. In the face of such an endorsement, it grows more difficult to argue that CV and total economic value are inappropriate for use in cost-benefit studies.

ENDNOTES

1 Passive use is now used interchangeably with nonuse value. There is a growing trend toward combining passive use (nonuse) and direct use (use) into a single measure of economic value termed total value. This trend is based on the belief that any dichotomy of total value involves arbitrary assumptions, and there is no theoretical need to maintain such a dichotomy.

2 One may be inclined to say that the analyst estimates the economic value rather than constructs the value. In fact, the economic literature routinely refers to "value estimates." However, we use the verb *constructs* to underscore the notion that economic value does not exist in a free standing fashion amenable to empirical measurement. Rather, economic value can only be measured with reference to a choice, and the characteristics of that choice largely determine the measured value.

3 This simple example points out three important properties of economic value. First, economic value is constructed by the analyst from a choice and the value depends on that choice. Second, economic value does not have to be expressed in monetary units, and third, economists do not assume that individuals maintain in memory monetary economic values for the many possible choices they confront.

4 One approach, termed *revealed preference*, uses observed past choices and attempts to gather all relevant information pertinent to the past choice (*i.e.*, object and circumstances of the choice). Generally, records of the choice are incomplete, and the analyst is left with partial information at best, and at worst, partial and erroneous information. Moreover, because all of the pertinent aspects of past choices can *never* match exactly the new choice involving the object one wishes to value (*i.e.*, at the very least, we know that time has passed since the past decisions were made), the analysis usually rests on important assumptions that are introduced in an effort to make past choices relevant for the current valuation.

5 CERCLA section 301(c), 42 U.S.C. § 9651(c).

6 Executive Order 12316, Aug. 14, 1981.

7 "Resolution of the definition of damage to be used in this proposed rule is of such importance that it has already been discussed at length ...." Department of the Interior, Proposed Rulemaking, "Natural Resource Damage Assessments," 50 Fed. Reg. 52126, 52147 (Dec. 20, 1985)(1985 Interior Proposed Rule).

8 Joint Opening Brief of Petitioning States of New York, Ohio, Colorado, Massachusetts, California, Maine, New Jersey, Connecticut, Rhode Island and Vermont, and National Wildlife Federation, Public Citizen Litigation Group, and Environmental Defense Fund, 4/25/88; *Ohio, et al. v. Department of the Interior, et al.*, No. 86-1529 and Consolidated Cases (D.C. Cir. 1988) at 62 (States/Environmental Petitioners' Joint Opening Brief).

9 However, Interior was not the only Federal agency with apparent disagreement on the appropriate measure of damages. In its first comment, EPA recommended exclusion of option and existence values because CV estimates of such values were unreliable. *See*, Letter from Allan Hirsch, Director, Office of Federal Activities, EPA, to Keith Eastin, Associate Solicitor, Interior, dated March 20, 1986. Just over a month later, EPA submitted a second comment that concurred with the inclusion of existence and option values. *See*, Letter from Allan Hirsch, Director, Office of Federal Activities, EPA, to Keith Eastin, Associate Solicitor, Interior, dated April 25, 1986. Perhaps someone at EPA

realized that its use of CV in cost benefit analyses might be compromised by its first comment.

10 1985 Interior Proposed Rule at 52132-33.

11 A special resource was one "set aside [legislatively] and committed to a specific use by law .... primarily for the preservation of wildlife habitat or other sensitive environments ... [but it] is not necessarily a unique or important resource ..." and did not include threatened or endangered species and their critical habitat. *Id.* at 52141.

12 *Id.* at 52143; 43 C.F.R. § 11.83.

13 43 C.F.R. § 11.83(d)(5).

14 43 C.F.R. § 11.83(b)(2) & (d)(5)(ii).

15 To clarify the proposed language, Interior stated that CV "is just as valid a method to estimate [direct] use values as other methods listed." Department of the Interior, Final Rule, "Natural Resource Damage Assessments," 51 Fed. Reg. 27674, 27719-20 (Aug. 1, 1986)(1986 Interior Final Rule).

16 880 F.2d 432 (D.C. Cir. 1989).

17 States/Environmental Petitioners' Joint Opening Brief at 11-12, 55, 57, n39, 64.

18 "[A]ny provision for the measurement of nonuse values is inconsistent with CERCLA on its face." Joint Reply Brief of Petitioners Chemical Manufacturers Ass'n, Public Service Electric and Gas Co., & the Dana Corp., 10/31/88; *Ohio, et al. v. Department of the Interior, et al.*, No. 86-1529 and Consolidated Cases (D.C. Cir. 1988) at 29 (Industry Petitioners' Joint Reply Brief).

19 In addition, the transaction was completely hypothetical, and, therefore, respondents were likely to overstate their willingness to pay if they believed that they would not have to pay. *Id.* at 2, 11.

20 "Techniques to Measure Damages to Natural Resources," June 1987.

21 Industry Petitioners' Joint Reply Brief at 14-15.

22 *Ohio v. Department of the Interior,* 880 F.2d at 438.

23 *Id.* at 457, 462-464.

24 Later in its opinion, the court states that "[o]ption and existence values are non-consumptive values compensable under the terms of CERCLA." *Id.* at 476, n77.

25 *Id.* at 464.

26 *See* discussion at 477.

27 Department of the Interior, Notice of Proposed Rulemaking, "Natural Resource Damage Assessments," 56 Fed. Reg. 19752, 19759 (Apr. 29, 1991)(1991 Interior Proposed Rule).

28 *Id.* at 19760.

29 *Id.*

30 *Id.* at 19759.

31 For calculating direct use values, Interior viewed CV to be as reliable as any other nonmarket valuation methodology. *Id.*

32 *Id.* at 19754, 19762, 19765, 19766.

33 Statement by President George Bush on Signing the Oil Pollution Act of 1990, 26 WEEKLY COMP. PRES. DOC. 1265 (Aug. 27, 1990).

34 33 U.S.C. §§ 2701, *et seq.*

35 OPA provides that the measure of damages includes the costs of restoration, replacement, rehabilitation, or acquisition of the equivalent resources (restoration), the diminution in value of those resources pending restoration, and reasonable costs of assessment. 33 U.S.C. § 2706(d)(1)

36 National Oceanic & Atmospheric Administration, Advance Notice of Proposed Rulemaking, "Natural Resource Damage Assessments," 57 Fed. Reg. 8964, *et seq*. (Mar. 13, 1992).

37 For a range of comments, *see id.* at 8976-77.

38 National Oceanic & Atmospheric Administration, Extension of Comment Period and Announcement of Public Meeting, "Natural Resource Damage Assessments Under the Oil Pollution Act of 1990," 57 Fed. Reg. 23067, *et seq.* (June 1, 1992).

39 National Oceanic & Atmospheric Administration, Advance Notice of Proposed Rulemaking, Extension of Comment Period and Release of Contingent Valuation Methodology Report, "Natural Resource Damage Assessments Under the Oil Pollution Act of 1990," 58 Fed. Reg. 4601, 4610 (Jan. 15, 1993)(NOAA CV Panel Report).

40 *Id.* at 4609.

41 These "regulations" established minimum standards of reliability for CV studies estimating passive use values. For example, to be considered reliable, the survey results must demonstrate that WTP and WTA for a given resource should not diverge significantly and that the value ascribed to a resource is not affected to a statistically significant degree by its aggregation with other resources.

42 Some members of private industry also had a copy of the regulations before they were sent to the Federal Register.

43 Department of the Interior, Final Rule, "Natural Resource Damage Assessments," 59 Fed. Reg. 14262, 14266 (Mar. 25, 1994) (DOI 1994 Final Rule).

44 Department of the Interior, Proposed Rule; Reopening of Comment Period, "Natural Resource Damage Assessments," 58 Fed. Reg. 39328, *et seq.* (July 22, 1993).

45 *See generally*, discussion at 39350-51.

46 *Id.* at 39351

47 Interior said that the potential "per-person bias" in measuring direct use value by CV will be multiplied by a relatively small number (actual users of the resource) and thus keeps in check the absolute amount of bias in the aggregate estimate of damages. This would not be the case for measurement of passive use values as the multiplier is potentially much greater. *Id.*

48 *Id.*

49 National Oceanic and Atmospheric Administration, Notice of Proposed Rulemaking, "Natural Resource Damage Assessments," 59 Fed. Reg. 1062, *et seq.* (Jan. 7, 1994) (1994 NOAA Proposed Rule).

50 *Id.* at 1143.

51 Those include willingness-to-pay elicitation; credible description of the commodity; natural resource context of the injured resources; reminder of respondents' budget constraints and alternative expenditure possibilities; credible choice mechanism that is incentive compatible; credible payment vehicle; and adequate field testing.

52 There, NOAA addressed determination of the relevant population to be sampled; probability sampling; adequate sample size to draw the necessary statistical inferences; high response rate; and use of an experienced survey research organization.

53 For this test the trustee must show statistically that "the aggregate WTP across all respondents for the prevention or restoration program increases (decreases) as the scope of the environmental insult is expanded (contracted). The scope of the environmental insult is characterized by the severity of the natural resource injuries and the level of effectiveness and timing of the restoration or prevention programs." Split samples must be used for this demonstration. *Id.* at § 990.78(b)(5)(iii).

54 NOAA does note that these studies used "lower quality survey design" than that being proposed in the rule. *Id.* at 1146.

55 *Id.*

56 The preamble states that "NOAA believes that the proposed standards are necessary when CV surveys are used for natural resource damage assessment, because such studies will be given a rebuttable presumption in litigation ...." *Id.* at 1143.

57 Letter from Natural Resource Defense Council, *et al.* to Leon Panetta, Director, Office of Management and Budget, March 10, 1994. *See also* Letter from Natural Resource Defense Council to Bruce Babbitt, Secretary of the Interior, February 10, 1994.

58 The indirect test "examines the sensitivity to scope indirectly through the use of a WTP valuation function, relying entirely on the base survey instrument ...

a WTP valuation function may relate the probability of a yes vote to a list of variables assumed to underlie the voting decision, (e.g., ... household demographics)" 1994 NOAA Proposed Rule at 1146.

59 NOAA requested comments on whether "it is appropriate to use information regarding pre-existing knowledge of respondents to reassign to zero any positive values expressed by individuals who were unaware of the injuries prior to the survey." *Id.*

60 To avoid the concern expressed by some commenters that a CV might be undertaken in cases where expected damages would be too small to justify the expense of the survey, NOAA asked whether a minimum or threshold level of expected damages should be established in determining whether to proceed with the study. NOAA also questioned whether this threshold should apply to total damages or just passive use losses. *Id.* at 1147-48.

61 Letter from Natural Resources Defense Council to the Honorable Bruce Babbitt, U.S. Secretary of the Interior, February 10, 1994.

62 Those regulations have since been challenged by several industry groups and states on a number of grounds. *See Chamber of Commerce, et al. v. United States Department of the Interior*, No. 94-1462 and Consolidated cases (D.C. Cir. 1994).

63 DOI 1994 Final Rule.

64 *Id.* at 14264-66. Those restrictions include the requirement that the selected methodology is "reliable for the particular incident and type of damage being measured." *Id.* at 14264.

65 *See* discussion on *Ohio* litigation *supra*. Nevertheless, Interior did note in its preamble to the final rule that it would "reconsider whether additional standards for the use of CV to estimates lost [direct] use value are appropriate" during its upcoming biannual review. *Id.* at 14265.

66 DOI 1994 Final Rule at 14265.

67 Department of the Interior, Notice of Proposed Rulemaking, Natural Resource Damage Assessment," 59 Fed. Reg. 23098, *et seq.* (May 4, 1994).

68 *I.e.*, some commenters asserted that lost passive use damages are punitive rather than compensatory as they are "charged PRPs (potentially responsible

parties) for hurting the public's feelings;" or that passive use values are not "actually economic values." *Id.* at 23107.

69 *Id.* at 23108.

70 *Id.* at 23108, 23110.

71 *See* discussion at *id.* at 23104-6.

72 Department of the Interior, Proposed Rule; Extension of Comment Period, "Natural Resource Damage Assessment," 59 Fed. Reg. 32175, *et seq.* (June 22, 1994); National Oceanic and Atmospheric Administration, Proposed Rule; Extension of Comment Period, "Natural Resource Damage Assessments," 59 Fed. Reg. 32148, *et seq.* (June 22, 1994). Besides extending the comment period, NOAA sought comments on a number of areas such as calibration, scope tests, response rates, prior knowledge, extent of market, and mode of administration. *Id.* at 32154-55.

73 *New Jersey, et al. v. Ruckelshaus, et al.*, No. 84-1668 (D.N.J. 1984); *Natural Resources Defense Council, et al. v. United States Coast Guard, et al.*, CV-94 4892 (E.D.N.Y. 1994).

74 National Oceanic and Atmospheric Administration, Notice of Proposed Rulemaking, "Natural Resource Damage Assessments," 60 Fed. Reg. 39804, *et seq.* (Aug. 3, 1995) (1995 NOAA Proposed Rule).

75 "Compensatory restoration" addresses the interim losses from the time the injury occurs until the resource recovers either naturally or through human intervention.

76 The preamble described the service-to-service approach as one where the "appropriate quantity of replacement services is determined by obtaining equivalency between lost and replacement services after discounting appropriately." One must consider whether the same type and quality of services are being provided. 1995 NOAA Proposed Rule at 39816.

77 *Id.*

78 Because NOAA mentioned conjoint analysis (another survey technique) as a possible methodology, several commenters suggested a host of standards, not unlike those previously advocated for CV. Because conjoint analysis might also capture passive use values, the criticism leveled at conjoint analysis

supports our proposition that CV opponents are really opposed to the inclusion of passive use values, regardless of the methodology used to estimate such values.

79 National Oceanic and Atmospheric Administration, Final Rule, "Natural Resource Damage Assessments," 61 Fed. Reg. 440, *et seq*. (January 5, 1996).

80 The executive order stated that "[r]egulatory action should not be undertaken unless the potential benefits to society for the regulation outweigh the potential costs to society" and "[r]egulatory objective shall be chosen to maximize the net benefits to society." 46 Fed. Reg. 13193 *et seq.* (Feb. 19, 1981).

81 For example, benefit studies conducted to support National Ambient Air Quality Standards for ground level ozone were based on economic values constructed for reduction of respiratory disease and damage that ozone can cause to agricultural crops.

82 RCRA governs the manufacture, transport and disposal of hazardous substances.

83 *See* RCRA Corrective Action Rule where EPA based the benefits of the rule (protection of ground water) on a total value calculation with passive use value comprising a large portion of the value estimate.

84 *See* Rosenthal and Nelson (1992) for an articulation of this position.

85 While OMB's posture on CV is not entirety clear, it appears that OMB intends to impose very rigid guidelines on CV through its guidance on the implementation of RIAs. *See* Belzer and Theroux (1993) at 15. Based on their current proposed regulations, NOAA's and Interior's positions are similar and lie somewhere between EPA and Energy/OMB.

86 *See* Rosenthal and Nelson 1992.

87 Commitment motivated choice sets out a class of choices individuals make that are not motivated by pure self-interest, but rather by some *commitment* to ethical norms. Brookshire, Eubanks and Sorg (1987) state:

If individuals can be motivated by a personally-held environmental ethic to pay for preservation of wildlife, there is an important implication for benefit-cost analysis. Specifically, a willingness to pay does not always represent an "economic value" as defined within the context of benefit-cost analysis. The inclusion of ethically motivated values in benefit-cost analysis is inappropriate for the relevant normative framework.

The implication of this argument is that there exists some theoretical reason to exclude passive use values from cost-benefit analyses.

88 Oral remarks of Donald Rosenthal (Office of Policy Analysis, Energy), Conference on "The New Rules for Natural Resource Damage Assessments and Claims Under CERCLA and OPA," American Bar Association, June 2-3, 1994, Washington, DC.

89 *See* Belzer and Theroux (1993) at 8-9.

90 There is an important caveat to this statement. And that is, for the statement to be valid the individual program CV surveys must not underestimate the WTP for the objects of choice offered respondents. This is not always guaranteed since there are several features of the survey design that could lead to an understatement of WTP. For example, respondents may not believe that governments can provide the environmental public goods as described in the survey, or they may feel the tax surcharge would not end after five years, or they may believe it is the polluter's financial responsibility to undertake the regulatory action. If the individual surveys do understate WTP, then even if they are conducted independent of one another, actual benefits of the package of programs may not the overstated.

91 This obligation is imposed by E.O. 12866 and the Regulatory Flexibility Act, P.L. 96-354.

92 We are quick to note that the idea of a coordinated regulatory review is simply an idea for discussion and not a well-thought out proposal for action. If one were to develop a proposal for such a review there are many issues that would need to be addressed including the type of proposals that one would group together due to substitution effects. For example, all environmental and natural resource regulation may be analyzed as a group and all financial regulation as another group.

93 We are not advocating a process such as that recently proposed by Breyer (1993), where a centralized administrative group would be formed to "rationalize" regulations across independent agencies. However, we do believe that a coordinated regulatory review, using the same framework for analysis already embodied in E.O. 12866, would naturally lead to a critical comparison of regulatory approaches.

94 Supra-additive means that the costs of each regulatory program in a package of programs calculated in isolation would sum to an amount less than the costs calculated for the package as a whole. On the other hand, sub-additivity would imply that the costs of the independent programs would sum to a number greater then the cost of the package of programs.

95 Such an approach is meaningless for at least two reasons. First, bundling valuations together for the purposes of cost-benefit analysis makes sense because we are interested in the economic values for each program considered. In the case of damage assessment, however, we are interested only in the compensation for the injuries. Second, the value of the required compensation would be dependent upon the nature of all the other programs that were valued in the bundle. This dependency is due to the fact that the respondent would believe that all the public goods presented can be changed simultaneously, when in fact, the appropriate basis for compensation would rest on the *status quo* with respect to all other public goods.

96 *In Re Acushnet River and New Bedford Harbor: Proceedings Re Alleged PCB Pollution*, 716 F. Supp. 676, 686, n15 (D. Mass. 1989).

97 Memorandum Opinion and Order, Case No. 88-1279 at 43 (D. Idaho Jan. 24, 1991). In declining to award damages for this category of injury, the court stated that this "does not mean to suggest that the steelhead has no existence value." Rather, the court questioned the applicability of the study proffered by the state.

98 Memorandum Decision and Order, Case No. 86-0902G at 42 (D. Utah Sept. 3, 1992). Because restoration appeared infeasible, the state based its claim on diminution of the market value of the water.

99 Some of this discussion is drawn from legal research by Cheryl Scannell, attorney, NOAA General Counsel.

100 The Court also noted that "the difference between accuracy, validity, and reliability may be such that each is distinct from the other by no more than a hen's kick." [citation omitted] *Daubert v. Merrell Dow Pharmaceuticals*, 113 S.Ct. 2786, 2795, n9 (1993).

101 "Hearsay" is an oral or written statement, made by a person who is not called as a witness at trial. With certain exceptions, hearsay is generally not admitted in a court proceeding as it is "secondhand" rather than original evidence. That is, the witness is repeating what she heard someone else say.

102 *I.e.*, in the seminal case, *Zippo Manufacturing Co. v. Rogers Imports, Inc.*, 216 F. Supp. 670 (S.D.N.Y. 1963), the factors which supported the court's decision to admit the survey included 1) survey designers and interviewers were qualified experts in the field of consumer surveys; 2) survey principles and procedures were described to the court and included the manner of arriving at the applicable universe and sample populations; the method of delimitation of particular respondents; procedures to avoid sampling errors; interviewer instructions; and procedures for processing questionnaires; 3) testimony of several interviewers concerning their experience in conducting interviews and the manner in which they conducted the interviews in question; 4) fact that interviewers did not know the purpose of the survey; 5) original responses to questions were available to the court; and 6) testimony of an independent survey expert that the project was designed objectively and scientifically.

103 The Court believed that subjecting the theory or technique to peer review and publication was an important factor because, in part, "it increases the likelihood that substantive flaws in methodology will be detected." The Court then states, however, that publication will be "a relevant, though not dispositive, consideration in assessing the scientific validity of a particular technique or methodology on which an opinion is premised." *Daubert v. Merrell Dow Pharmaceuticals*, 113 S.Ct. at 2797.

104 *Id.* In addition, the Court noted that the trial judge must be mindful of the other applicable rules of evidence such as Rule 703. *Id.* at 2797-98.

105 Daily App. Rept. 10316, 10321 (9th Cir. July 25, 1994).

106 *Id.* at 10320.

107 *Daubert v. Merrell Dow Pharmaceuticals, Inc.,* 95 C.D.O.S. 131, 133 (9th Cir. Jan. 4, 1995)(*Daubert II*). Although plaintiffs' experts had not published their work in a scientific journal nor solicited formal review by their colleagues and only the defendant's experts "deemed these studies worthy of verification, refutation or even comment," the court's decision on admissibility ultimately turned on the issue of relevance -- would the evidence "assist the trier of fact to ... determine a fact in issue." *Id.* at 134.

108 See Cirancy-Wantrup, S.V. (1947), "Capital Returns from Soil-Conservation Practice," *Journal of Farm Economics*, 29, 1181-1196; Davis, R.K. (1963), "The Value of Outdoor Recreation: An Economic Study of the Maine Woods," Dissertation, Harvard University.

109 See Carson, R.T., J.L. Wright, N.J. Carson, A. Alberini, and N.E. Flores (1995), *A Bibliography of Contingent Valuation Studies and Papers*, La Jolla, Calif., Natural Resource Damage Assessment, Inc., listing over 2,000 studies and papers.

110 See Council of American Survey Research Organizations' Code of Standards for Survey Research and the American Association for Public Opinion Research's Code of Professional Ethics and Practices.

111 Some confusion exists over the term *reliability* as applied to the results of a CV survey. As used by the *Ohio* Court and in the NOAA Panel report, the reliability of a measure is the degree to which it measures the theoretical construct under investigation. However, in the empirical social sciences, this preceding definition pertains to *validity*, whereas reliability is defined as the extent to which the variance of the measure is not due to random sources and systematic sources of error. While we believe that it is important to keep the distinction between validity and reliability clear, to avoid confusing readers who are unfamiliar with the social sciences, we follow the usage of the *Ohio* Court and the NOAA Panel and use the term *reliability* to refer to the degree to which CV surveys measure the theoretical construct under investigation.

112 In particular, Portney (1994), Diamond and Hausman (1994) and Hanemann (1994).

113 NOAA CV Panel at 4603.

114 *Id.*

115 *Id.* at 4610.

116 The Panel states: "Generally, when aspects of the survey design and the analysis of the responses are ambiguous, the option that tends to underestimate willingness to pay is preferred."

117 This is not to say there is no controversy. Those CV practitioners that hold mail surveys in high regard, bristle at the notion of conducting in-person interviews.

118 *See* Carson *et al.,* 1994a.

119 NOAA CV Panel at 4604.

120 Of course, scope tests rest on the premise that the respondents recognize one object of choice to be larger than another. Ensuring such recognition may pose problems for CV designers due to the fact that objects of choice may not have defined metrics by which their size may be determined.

121 NOAA CV Panel at 4610.

122 Mitchell and Carson (1989) at 191 discuss two forms of construct validity: convergent validity and theoretical validity. The former refers to whether the measure of interest is correlated with other measures of the same theoretical construct. For example, one way of estimating the total number of people employed in the US is to use self reports about employment status; an alternative measure of the same construct would be the number of people reported to be employed in businesses by Census business surveys. Theoretical validity asks whether the measure is related to other measures of other constructs in a manner predicted by theory. For example, economic theory predicts that a measure of the quantity of a good be inversely correlated with its prices. The concept of construct validity used here rests on the notion of theoretical validity and not convergent validity.

123 When we move from this general description of an evaluation of construct validity, it is important to acknowledge that most predictions are general and simply indicate whether the direction of the association between a variable and a respondent's choices should be positive or negative. Equally important, from the perspective statistical analysis, the efficacy of construct validity tests relies on observing a large enough number of individuals with the characteristics or attitudes hypothesized to be related to a choice to be able to estimate the parameters of the correlation with reasonable precision.

124 *See* Hanemann, Loomis, and Kanninen (1991) for details of interval censored models.

125 ALCOA recently presented a similar concern when testifying before the U.S. Senate's Committee on Environment and Public Works during hearings on reauthorization of CERCLA. Criticizing the current natural resource damage assessment process, the ALCOA representative stated "the current approach promotes virtually unbounded, totally arbitrary liability assessment which threaten the competitiveness of American industry and precipitate highly adversarial proceedings where natural resource trustees tend to assert enormous damage claims and take 'bet your company' negotiating positions in attempts to extract large settlements from industry." Testimony of Kevin L. McKnight, April 12, 1994. In response to a query from Senator Lautenberg asking how

many damage assessments are using CV, Mr. McKnight responded that it was his belief that all of them were.

126 *See, i.e.,* Kopp, Portney and DeWitt (1990).

REFERENCES

Arrow, K., R. Solow, P. R. Portney, E. E. Leamer, R. Radner and H. Schuman (1993): "Report of the NOAA Panel on Contingent Valuation," 58 *Fed. Reg.* 4601 *et seq*. (Jan. 15, 1993).

Belzer, R. B. and R. P. Theroux, "Criteria for Evaluating Results Obtained from Contingent Valuation Methods," Paper presented at the *Valuing Food Safety and Nutrition Workshop,* Alexandria, Va., June 2-4, 1993.

Breyer, Stephen, 1993, *Breaking the Vicious Circle*, Cambridge, MA: Harvard University Press.

Brookshire, D. S. Eubanks, L. S. and C. F. Sorg, 1987, "Existence Values and Normative Economics," in Peterson and Sorg (eds.), *Toward the Measurement of Total Value,* Rocky Mountain Forest and Range Experiment Station, U.S. Department of Agriculture, Fort Collins, Colorado.

Carson, Richard T., Robert C. Mitchell, W. Michael Hanemann, Raymond J. Kopp, Stanley Presser, Paul A. Ruud 1992 "A Contingent Valuation Study of Lost Passive Use Values Resulting From the Exxon Valdez Oil Spill," A Report to the Attorney General of the State of Alaska.

Carson, Richard T., Jennifer Wright, Anna Alberini, Nancy Carson and Nicholas Flores, 1995. *A Bibliography of Contingent Valuation Studies and Papers,* Natural Resource Damage Assessment, Inc., La Jolla, Ca.

Cirancy-Wantrup, S.V. 1947, "Capital Returns from Soil-Conservation Practice," *Journal of Farm Economics*, 29, 1181-1196.

Davis, R.K. 1963, "The Value of Outdoor Recreation: An Economic Study of the Maine Woods," Dissertation, Harvard University.

Desvousges, William H., F. Reed Johnson, Richard W. Dunford, Kevin J. Boyle, Sara P. Hudson, and K. Nicole Wilson, "Measuring Natural Resource Damages with Contingent Valuation: Tests of Validity and Reliability;" Paper presented at the Cambridge Economics, Inc., Symposium, Contingent Valuation: A Critical Assessment; Washington, D.C., April 1992.

Diamond, P.A., and J.A. Hausman, "On Contingent Valuation Measurement of Nonuse Values;" Paper presented at the Cambridge Economics, Inc. Symposium, Contingent Valuation: A Critical Assessment; Washington, D.C., April 1992.

Diamond, Peter A., Jerry A. Hausman, Gregory K. Leonard and Mike A. Denning, 1993. "Does Contingent Valuation Measure Preferences? Experimental Evidence" in J.A. Hausman editor *Contingent Valuation: A Critical Assessment* (Amsterdam: North Holland).

Diamond, Peter, and Jerry A. Hausman. "Contingent Valuation: Is Some Number Better Than No Number." *Journal of Economic Perspectives*, Fall 1994, 8(4), pp. 45-64.

Duffield, John W., and David A. Patterson, "Field Testing Existence Values: An Instream Flow Trust Fund for Montana Rivers," Paper presented at the annual meeting of the American Economic Association; New Orleans, January 1991.

Goulder, Lawrence H., 1994, "Environmental Taxation and the 'Double Dividend:' A Reader's Guide," Working Paper, Department of Economics, Stanford University.

Hanemann, W. Michael. "Valuing the Environment Through Contingent Valuation." *Journal of Economic Perspectives*, Fall 1994, 8(4), pp. 19-43.

Hanemann, W. Michael, John Loomis, and Barbara Kanninen. "Statistical Efficiency of Double-Bounded Dichotomous Choice Contingent Valuation." *American Journal of Agricultural Economics*, November 1991, 73(4), pp. 1255-1263.

Kahneman, Daniel and Jack Knetch, 1992, "Valuing Public Goods: The Purchase of Moral Satisfaction;" *Journal of Environmental Economics and Management*, Vol. 22, pp. 57-70.

Kopp, R. J., P. R. Portney and D. Dewitt, 1990, "International Comparisons of Environmental Regulations," in *Environmental Policy and the Cost of Capital*, American Council for Capital Formation, Washington, D.C., 1990.

Portney, Paul R. "The Contingent Valuation Debate: Why Economists Should Care." *Journal of Economic Perspectives*, Fall 1994, 8(4), pp. 3-17.

Rosenthal, D. H. and R. H. Nelson, 1992, "Why Existence Value Should Not Be Used in Cost-Benefit Analysis," *Journal of Policy Analysis and Management*, Vol. 11, No. 1, pp. 116-22.

Seip, Kalle, and Jon Strand, 1992, "Willingness to Pay for Environmental Goods in Norway: A Contingent Valuation Study with Real Payment," Paper prepared for the SAF Center for Applied Research, Department of Economics, University of Oslo.

Sen, A. K., 1977, "Rational Fools: A Critique of the Behavioral Foundations of Economic Theory," *Philosophy and Public Affairs*, Vol. 6, pp. 317-344.

Smith, V. K., 1992 "Arbitrary Values, Good Causes, and Premature Verdicts," *Journal of Environmental Economics and Management*, Vol. 22, No. 1 pp. 71-89.

3

MEASURING NON-USE VALUES: THEORY AND EMPIRICAL APPLICATIONS

Richard C. Bishop, Patricia A. Champ, Thomas C. Brown and Daniel W. McCollum

INTRODUCTION

In keeping with our assignment, this paper will focus on measurement. We will devote far less time to the microeconomic theory of non-use values than many readers might expect. Non-use values are now well entrenched in the theory of the consumer (Krutilla 1967; Randall and Stoll 1983; Madariaga and McConnell 1987; Boyle and Bishop 1987; Smith 1987; Bishop and Welsh 1992; Freeman 1993). We shall want to briefly review the theory as a foundation for what will follow, but need not dwell on it at length. The central focus will instead be on measurement.

To date, contingent valuation (CV) is the only tool for estimating non-use values that has a substantial following among researchers. As most readers are no doubt aware, CV is currently the subject of debate in the U.S. Respected researchers currently disagree about whether CV can produce sufficiently accurate values to support damage assessments and policy analyses. This debate may have already begun in other countries and will almost certainly intensify there as applications of CV expand. The premise of this paper is that progress in this debate is impeded by the lack, within economics, of a well-articulated *theory of measurement* that is consistently applied across valuation studies. Mitchell and Carson (1989), drawing on the psychological theory of testing (Bohrnstedt 1983), have laid a foundation for such a theory. This paper will attempt to elaborate on their work with specific reference to non-use values.

In psychology, such abstract concepts as intelligence have long been the subject of research. Tests, such as IQ tests, are a major tool in psychometrics. We economists today face problems that are in many ways comparable to the problems that pioneers in psychology must have faced. We have the abstract concepts of willingness to pay (WTP) and willingness to accept (WTA) that we seek to measure. WTP and WTA, like intelligence, are fundamentally abstract, theoretical concepts that are not directly and fully observable in the real world. Both economists and psychologists must try to infer something about the magnitudes of their constructs from data that are thought to be indicative of those magnitudes. In this endeavor, both must rely--implicitly or explicitly--on a theory of measurement to guide research design and the interpretation of results. In fact, one might reinterpret CV questions as "WTP tests" analogous to IQ and other psychological tests. Thus, an economic theory of measurement has much to learn from the psychometric theory of measurement.

We begin by defining theoretical WTP, a concept that will play a role here comparable to that of a "true value" in psychometrics. That is, the validity of observed WTP can only be evaluated with reference to inherently unobservable theoretical WTP. Once theoretical WTP has been defined, we will consider alternative forms of evidence for estimating it. Values estimating using market data have long been considered credible, but this does not alter the fact that they too are estimates of unobservable theoretical WTP and thus share with CV the problems associated with validity assessment. To address the thorny relationships between observable and unobservable values, we will consider the dual criteria of reliability and validity and adapt these concepts to reflect the goals of CV studies. We then turn to a triad of concepts that might be termed the "Three C's": content validity, construct validity, and criterion validity. These concepts represent mutually reinforcing strategies for assessing validity. Much of the paper focuses on how these strategies can be applied to assess the validity of individual CV studies. We will also emphasize that validity at the level of the individual study is a prerequisite for trying to draw empirical conclusions about the validity of the CV method as a whole.

THEORETICAL WTP

Let us work with WTP, always bearing in mind that WTA is an alternative definition of economic value with equal theoretical standing. To define theoretical WTP, let us consider the effects of an "intervention" in the economy on the welfare of a theoretical consumer. Such interventions may take the form of proposed governmental policies, projects, or regulations that will in some way affect the natural environment.[1] Or, interventions might be releases of oil or a toxic substance with adverse environmental repercussions. In addition to environmental services, interventions may change other economic parameters such as the prices paid or the income received by consumers. Some environmental parameters may be relevant because the consumer "uses" the environment services in question. For example, the intervention may affect fish populations where the consumer goes fishing. Other parameters may be relevant to the consumer for reasons other than personal use. For example, the consumer may gain utility from being altruistic toward others who are users or toward animals or toward future generations. It is through effects on environmental and other economic parameters that interventions generate environmental "values," both use values and non-use values.

Suppose that the consumer maximizes a "well-behaved" utility function subject to a budget constraint of the standard form. To keep it simple, assume away time, uncertainty, and other complicating factors. Let us represent the consumer's indirect utility function by

$$v(P, d, Y)$$

where P symbolizes a vector of market prices, d symbolizes the status of an environmental resource that would be affected by the intervention, and Y symbolizes income. Let P_o, d_o, and Y_o represent the levels of these parameters in the absence of the intervention and P_w, d_w, and Y_w represent the levels of the parameters if the intervention is completed. Let WTP_t represent the theoretical WTP associated with the intervention. If the intervention has a positive effect on the consumer, that is,

$$v(P_w, d_w, Y_w) > v(P_o, d_o, Y_o),$$

then theoretical willingness to pay is defined implicitly by

$$v(P_w, d_w, Y_w - WTP_t) = v(P_o, d_o, Y_o).$$

On the other hand, if the intervention will make the consumer worse off, that is,

$$v(P_w, d_w, Y_w) < v(P_o, d_o, Y_o),$$

then the implicit definition becomes

$$v(P_w, d_w, Y_w) = v(P_o, d_o, Y_o - WTP_t).$$

Where the intervention leads to an improvement in welfare, WTP_t is most naturally interpreted as Hicksian compensating surplus, while it should be interpreted as Hicksian equivalent surplus if welfare will decline.

WTP_t as just defined must be viewed as a theoretical construct, a useful scientific fiction describing what would be measured under idealized circumstances. We economists use the WTP_t construct with such ease and confidence that it takes on a reality of its own in our minds, though it does not exist in reality. The utility maximization framework is a highly stylized version of how real human beings think and behave.

Consider, for example, how we conceptualize the process by which utility is maximized. Do we really believe that human beings decide at one point in time what they intend to consume during the next period of time? What unit of time are we thinking of, a month, a year, a lifetime? Is the "utility counter" set at zero on January 1 of each year? Human choice must, in reality, be a much more dynamic, complex process than the simple theory allows.

The very concept of "consumer" involves an abstraction from reality. Do we mean that consumption decisions are made by individual human beings acting in isolation from those around them? This does not seem square with reality. Groups of individuals (couples, families, unrelated individuals who share dwellings) make joint decisions, often subject to constraints that involve multiple incomes. Thus, it is not unusual to find discussions that refer to the consuming unit as a "household." However, more rigorous treatments of the subject refer only to individuals as the basic consuming unit because, if group decision processes were permitted, basic assumptions about preferences such as completeness, transitivity, and continuity would be much more difficult to justify. These assumptions underlie the utility functions needed to define WTP_t (and theoretical WTA) in the usual manner and to develop hypotheses about the relationships between values and other economic parameters. To the extent that the theoretical concept of "the consumer" has no full counterpart in the real world, neither does WTP_t. WTP_t is in principle unobservable because it does not exist in reality.

Why deal in such abstractions at all? People appear to be willing to pay some amounts, but not other amounts, for conventional goods and services. It is not much of a leap to infer that real people might also be willing to pay something to obtain environmental amenities and avoid environmental "bads." Why not stop there, defining theoretical WTP as the maximum willingness to pay of real people? The answer is that such an approach would not be very rich theoretically speaking. It would not readily yield testable hypotheses about how willingness to pay, thus defined, might be related to the other economic parameters confronted by these same real world people. Whether one wishes to consider relatively simple relationships (e.g., the relationship between WTP and income) or more complex ones (e.g., the relationships between WTP for two or more commodities or WTP for public goods) abstract "modeling" of economic behavior is necessary. Abstraction makes it possible to explore seemingly fundamental relationships without having to deal with all the complexities and ambiguities inherent in the behavior of real world people. Consumer theory and welfare economics are useful in designing empirical studies and interpreting results. Gains of this kind are only realized, however, by assuming away potentially important parts of reality.

Thus, WTP_t gives rich conceptual meaning to the otherwise rather loosely defined concept of economic value. To implement the concept requires real world evidence. Having defined the theoretical construct that is to be the objective of measurement, the next step is to consider possible sources of data that could be used to estimate WTP_t.

Alternative sources of evidence regarding WTP

Market data have been central to efforts to quantify economic values. This is the so-called revealed preference approach to value estimation. People spend money on goods and services, and such spending has great credibility among economists as evidence of values. Without quarreling at all with the credence that economists place on market data, it is worth emphasizing that market values are not direct observations on WTP_t. This is the case for both conceptual and empirical reasons.

From a conceptual perspective, to admit that economic theory is abstract is to admit that it may not and probably will not fully represent decision processes of real world consumers in the marketplace. People making market choices will hopefully engage in processes and apply criteria like those depicted in theory. Nevertheless, to say that theory is abstract is to say that what we shall term "other factors," factors not considered in the theory, may also impinge on consumer choices. Other factors could include, for example, the influences of group decision making within the household and strategies devised by real human beings to cope with uncertainty. To the extent that other factors enter into market choices, market values may diverge from WTP_t.[2]

In addition to theoretical concerns about interpreting market values as WTP_t, it must also be remembered that empirical estimation of demand and supply relationships inevitably involves simplifying assumptions. Errors in variables, model specification errors, missing data, extrapolations beyond the range of the data, and other potential sources of error may prove unavoidable. Benefit-cost analysis almost invariably involves extrapolations into the future of values inferred from past behavior, a process that is far from perfect. Thus, even if real world consumers did behave exactly like the consumer as depicted in economic theory, econometric errors would make estimated market values imperfect measures of WTP_t. Despite these concerns, market data may well provide useful, though imperfect, evidence about economic values where such data exist.

However, for many goods and services, including many services from the natural environment, there are no markets. For various reasons, interventions involve more direct provision of such goods and services by governmental units. Nevertheless, market behavior may reveal something about the values of non-market goods and services. Expenditures to avoid environmental "bads" or repair the damages done by them reveal something about how much people would value being free of such bads. People may reveal their preferences for local environmental amenities when they buy and sell real property or accept lower incomes to live nearby. Travel and related costs may serve as proxies for market prices in estimating the demand for publicly provided recreational services.

One perhaps underutilized possible source of evidence about the values of non-market goods and services is voting behavior, especially voting in referenda. Votes for or against referenda involving commitments to pay taxes or other fees might provide credible evidence for estimating WTP_t, although questions do arise about such an interpretation. It is conceivable, for example, that people who themselves would favor a proposition (indicating that their WTP values exceeding the monetary commitments) might still vote against it if, for example, they felt that it was unfair to impose a tax on others. To call referenda "political markets" is perhaps stretching the concept of markets a bit. Nevertheless, the fact that voting for such referenda involves real commitments to pay gives voting clout as evidence about economic values. At least one study has explored this possibility (Deacon and Shapiro 1975).

Whereas traditionally only actual commitments of money in markets and perhaps in referenda have been acceptable as evidence of WTP_t, beginning 20 years ago, economic researchers began to introduce responses to CV survey questions as potentially valid evidence. When any new idea is introduced into a traditional discipline like economics, it will be subjected to considerable scrutiny. In the case of CV, the theory of public goods points to incentives that may lead people to intentionally state misleading values where environmental quality is to be valued, especially if real commitments of money are not required. This has led to the supposition that responses might bias contingent values away from WTP_t. From a psychological perspective (e.g., Kahneman and Knetsch (1992)), speculation has focused on whether people will have trouble constructing accurate estimates of WTP_t in response to survey questions.

Questioning of new methods of measurement is healthy in science, but progress comes from empirical work and not simply speculating about possible problems. The accuracy of any valuation method must be assessed in terms of how close it comes to measuring the ideal. If WTP_t were observable, then there would be no problem. One would simply observe it. Given that WTP_t is not observable, more complex criteria and "rules of evidence" are needed to assess accuracy. Continuing to borrow from psychology, accuracy in measurement depends on the reliability and validity of the data and analyses that are used in measurement.

RELIABILITY AND VALIDITY

These concepts are clearly laid out by Mitchell and Carson (1989, pp.120-125). A measurement technique is unreliable if random errors in measurement reach unacceptable levels. Stated differently, measures are more reliable the less "noisy" are the data. Validity involves systematic errors in measurement. As Mitchell and Carson (1989, 190) have pointed out, "The validity of a measure is the degree to which it measures the theoretical construct under investigation." In the current context, the "theoretical construct under investigation" is WTP_t. A CV measure (or a measure derived using market evaluation or any other method) is "biased," and hence invalid, if it tends to depart in a systematic way from WTP_t.

The economist is interested in reliability and validity on a different level from the psychologist. When psychologists use these terms they are primarily interested in accuracy at the level of the individual human being. Think about IQ testing, for example. While psychologists interested in intelligence may have some interest in the average IQ of aggregates of people, they are primarily concerned about measuring intelligence of individuals. On the other hand, economists seeking to evaluate changes in economic welfare are interested in the accuracy of average values for populations and aggregate over those populations. A considerable amount of unreliability in observed WTP is tolerable, provided bias is non-existent or at least within tolerable bounds. Accurate estimates of mean WTP_t can be made in the face of unreliability by simply increasing sample size. Reliability issues are not totally dissipated by this change in emphasis. For example, the reliability of mean estimated WTP over time may still be an issue. Unreliability in observed values at the individual level can lead to biased estimates of higher moments. Nevertheless, research on CV and other valuation methods focuses primarily on the validity of estimated average WTP over appropriately defined aggregates of individuals.

Current practice in CV requires that we raise one other issue relating to the concept of validity. Application of CV, like any empirical undertaking, involves numerous issues that must be resolved based on the judgement of the researcher. In damage assessments, and to a substantial degree in benefit-cost applications as well, researchers today will often resolve these issues by choosing the "conservative" course. That is, in exercising judgement, they make choices that will, if anything, lead to lower estimates for mean WTP_t. If, as some fear, CV studies tend to overestimate mean WTP_t, then conservatism, at least within limits, may pull estimated values toward the theoretical value. However, if, as others believe, CV tends to provided accurate measures of mean WTP_t, conservatism must be viewed as an expedient departure from normal scientific practice. To arrive at estimates of average WTP_t that are more easily defended in court or the policy arena, researchers make conservative choices in study design and execution, thus intentionally introducing possible sources of downward bias. The target is no longer WTP_t, but an underestimate of it. Whatever the practical merits of conservatism, the ultimate scientific goal of CV studies is still to estimate aggregate WTP_t for the population in question. Conservatism in measurement must be viewed as an attempt to arrive at lower bounds for the desired values. In the long-run, refinements will hopefully lead to estimates that approach mean and aggregate WTP_t from below.

Because mean WTP_t is in principle unobservable, inferences about validity must be based on indirect evidence rather than direct comparisons of estimated WTP to WTP_t. Such indirect evidence may relate to the content validity, the construct validity, or the criterion validity of a measure.

Content validity

Content validity has to do with whether the design and execution of a study are conducive to the revelation of WTP_t. In other words, assessing content validity involves examining the "content" of the study procedures. For CV studies, assessing content validity involves four steps. First, the study design must be compared to the economic theory underlying WTP_t. Second, the extent to which the study communicates effectively to the relevant population must be evaluated. These first two steps might be summarized by saying that a valid CV study must deal with both

Homo economicus and *Homo sapiens* in ways that support WTP_t estimation. Third, whether various facets of study execution were adequate must be assessed. Here, such matters as sampling and response rates are considered. Fourth, the econometrics used to estimate mean and aggregate WTP_t and other statistics are examined. We now consider each of these aspects of content validity in more detail.

In dealing with *Homo economicus*, the scenario of a valid study provides the context and information that would lead a theoretical consumer to reveal his or her WTP_t. Fischoff and Furby (1988) provide a useful framework for developing a CV scenario with content validity. (Also see Bishop, Champ and Mullarkey 1995). The premise of Fischoff and Furby's framework is that a CV exercise should fulfill the requirements of a satisfactory transaction. They define a satisfactory transaction as one "involving individuals who are fully informed, uncoerced, and able to identify their own best interests" (Fischoff and Furby 1988, 148). Three aspects of the transaction must be adequately defined and understood by participants: the good, the payment, and the marketplace. All three can affect the value an individual places on a good.

The good

"Goods may be thought of as bundles of *attributes*, representing outcomes of accepting the transaction that might be valued either positively or negatively" (Fischoff and Furby 1988, 153). The researcher must determine which attributes affect the value an individual places on a good, a particularly challenging task if the individual is not familiar with the good prior to receiving the survey. Fischoff and Furby also mention the importance of specifying the reference and target levels of the good. Borrowing from benefit-cost terminology, survey respondents need to know the level of provision of the environmental attributes "without" and "with" the intervention.

The payment

In most CV studies, the hypothetical payment is made in dollars. However, as use of CV expands to other contexts, alternative forms of payment such as labor hours are also being used (Swallow and Wondyalew 1994). Respondents need to be clear on the numeraire, whatever it is. The direction of payment must also be made clear. Will the individual pay for the good or will the individual be compensated? Another important aspect is the mechanism through which the payment will be made. Commonly used "payment vehicles" include income taxes, property taxes, sales taxes, entrance fees, changes in market prices of goods and services, and donations to special funds.

The marketplace or context for valuation

The third aspect of the CV scenario that must be specified is what Fischoff and Furby term the "marketplace." Since a market per se, as that term is normally understood, need not be involved, we prefer to think in terms of the "context" in which the transaction is to take place. The scenario may need to explain the extent of the market (who the other potential participants are), how and when the environmental amenity might be provided, and the decision rule for the provision (e.g. majority vote, individual payment, etc.). Most researchers would agree that it is desirable to use an incentive compatible context in CV questions to avoid incentives for strategic responses.

Whether one takes the theoretical perspective of *Homo economicus* or the practical perspective of *Homo sapiens*, information on the good, the payment, and the context are central. *Homo sapiens* have certain additional needs that must be attended to. It is not difficult to imagine a study that covers all the theoretical aspects well but fails to effectively communicate the terms of the proposed "transaction" to the individuals whose values are to be estimated. Thus, Mitchell and Carson (1989, 192) recommended asking the following questions when assessing the content validity of a CV scenario:

> Does the description of the good and how it is to be paid for appear to be unambiguous? Is it likely to be meaningful to the respondents? Is there anything in the scenario that might suggest to some respondents that the good would not be paid for? Are the property right and the market for the good defined in such a way that the respondents will accept the WTP format as plausible? Does the scenario appear to force reluctant respondents to come up with WTP amounts?

CV researchers are increasingly recognizing that dealing with *Homo sapiens* is not a trivial problem. The result is increasing emphasis on "qualitative research" to support CV survey design. Focus groups, verbal protocols, observed one-on-one interviews, pretests, and pilot studies can be used to determine how information and questions can be most understandably presented.

While including qualitative research procedures in CV studies is commendable, their limitations in establishing the content validity of CV studies must be recognized. Focus groups, verbal protocols, observed one-on-one interviews, and other such procedures involve small samples which may not be representative. Furthermore, standard methods for conducting such procedures and for reporting results do not exist, at least at present. Typically, the outsider who is attempting to assess the content validity of a completed study is left with little more than a statement to the effect that a certain number of focus groups were conducted. There is always the danger that such exercises were conducted in such a way that points of confusion and misunderstanding did not surface. Research to standardize procedures may be helpful. Pretests and pilot tests are more "quantitative" and hence more amenable to standardized procedures, but may not help identify more fundamental design flaws. For example, responses to pretests and pilots may not uncover ways in which respondents misunderstood the CV scenario. Inviting and carefully studying respondent's verbatim comments on the survey as well as including follow-up questions designed to probe for understanding may be helpful.

Clearly, qualitative research to enhance content validity is a very important part of any CV study, particularly studies of non-use values, where respondents may lack intimate familiarity with the environmental resources being valued. Much more research is needed to build consensus on proper procedures for conducting this phase of instrument development and reporting results. In the meantime, though they lack fully standardized methods, such procedures enhance content validity.

Finally, a study that is inadequate in its econometrics would be of questionable content validity. This aspect is noted for completeness, but little more needs to be said here. Economists normally have the training to do well in this regard. To the extent that CV studies involve competent applications of econometric methods, they will have higher content validity, all else equal.

In the end, content validity cannot be proven in some objective sense. Rather, it is up to the researcher to demonstrate to his or her peers that the study is designed and executed to be as conducive as possible to revelation of WTP_t. To be sure, some evidence can be accumulated that may support the content validity of a study. Questions can be added to the survey to generate data relevant to the assessment of content validity, for example. Results from focus groups and other qualitative procedures can be called upon for support as well. Content validity, nevertheless, is ultimately a matter of professional judgment.

Actual CV studies will display differing degrees of content validity. That a given study has some apparent procedural flaws will not normally be grounds for totally dismissing its results. Still, the more such flaws are identified and the more serious they are judged to be by peer reviewers, the less credible are the estimates of value and more tenuous and tentative are any policy, damage estimates, and methodological conclusions derived from them. This is a point which has not been adequately recognized in the current literature. Instead, it is not unusual for authors to attempt to draw rather sweeping conclusions from results that many would judge as having limited content validity. While our primary purpose is to consider broad principles for assessing the validity of CV studies and not to give detailed reviews of individual studies, a couple of examples of studies from the current literature may help to clarify the sorts of problems we are concerned about.

Much has been made of the so-called embedding problem based primarily on the paper by Kahneman and Knetsch (1992). Drawing upon studies reported in their paper, Kahneman and Knetsch (1992, 58) concluded that embedding effects are "perhaps the most serious shortcoming of CVM [the contingent valuation method] . . ." Yet we have serious concerns about the content validity of the studies on which this conclusion is based. Consider their study to value improvements in the environment, disaster preparedness, and medical personnel and equipment at various levels of embeddedness. At all three levels of embeddedness, study participants were asked to value vaguely defined products under vaguely defined conditions. The reference levels of services were not defined at all and the target levels were merely described as "improvements." Nothing was said about which particular attributes would be improved, about the physical locations of the changes, about the timing of the changes, or other aspects. Instead of specific details about the terms of the proposed transaction, respondents were left with vague references to taxes, prices, and user fees to be placed in some undefined "specific fund." Given such weaknesses in content validity, how can generalizations about the shortcomings of CV be made?

Or, consider a second study. Based on several different CV treatments involving logging of wilderness areas in the western U.S., Diamond et al. (1992, 15) concluded that, in general, "whatever contingent valuation surveys are measuring, they are not measuring consumers' preferences for environmental amenities." Though not so sweeping in his conclusions, McFadden (1994) used the same data set as a basis for voicing grave concerns about the usefulness of the CV method. Does this data set have sufficient content validity to support such a far-reaching conclusion? Respondents were told that seven or eight or nine wilderness areas, depending on the treatment, would be logged somewhere, but the location was not mentioned except that at least one would be located somewhere in the respondent's home state (Colorado, Wyoming, Montana, or Idaho). Via telephone interviews, respondents were asked to value one or more specified wilderness areas, again depending on the treatment, but these areas were only roughly described in terms of size and location, and little was said about how and when the logging would be conducted or what effects it might have on environmental parameters. Given all the vagueness in the information provided, respondents may be forgiven for expressing values that were not consistent with prior expectations of the researchers. It is not surprising, for example, that respondents missed the subtleties of whether seven or eight or nine other wilderness areas were already slated for logging. In addition, most CV researchers would shy away from a telephone survey for a study involving an issue of this complexity. Qualitative research might have addressed these concerns, perhaps even demonstrating that the telephone survey was a satisfactory approach, but no such enquiry is mentioned in the written materials from the study. Given that the content validity of the Diamond et al. study is highly questionable, then surely sweeping conclusions about the efficacy of the CV method as a whole based on the study results are equally questionable.

Construct validity

Construct validity deals with the degree to which the measure under scrutiny (in our case observed WTP) relates to other measures as predicted by theory. Mitchell and Carson (1989) discuss two forms of construct validity -- convergent and theoretical. Tests of convergent validity consider the relationship between the CV measure of the good's value and alternative measures of its value. For example, convergent validity could be assessed by comparing values estimated from a CV study to values estimated using a travel cost model or an hedonic pricing model. At least at present, this approach does not appear promising in the current context, since CV is widely considered the only method capable of estimating non-use values.

Theoretical validity is often assessed by considering the relationship between a CV measure and independent variables that theory indicates may be determinants of WTP_t. Assessing the theoretical validity of a measure may involve simple contingency table analyses. Or, more sophisticated multivariate regression procedures are applied and coefficients on potentially important independent variables are scrutinized for appropriate signs, statistical significance, and relative magnitudes.

Diamond et al. (1992), among others, have recently advocated a different form of theoretical validity test. They advocate testing theory-based hypotheses about relationships between two or more contingent values. For example, one would expect levels of WTP_t to be higher the more of an environmental amenity is provided or the larger is the environmental insult that is avoided. CV estimates of values should, if they are measuring WTP_t for different levels of provision that affect consumer welfare, exhibit relative magnitudes positively related to relative levels of provision. Tests of hypotheses about expected variations in estimated values with respect to changes in the size of environmental improvements or insults have come to be known as "scope tests." Within the taxonomy being followed here, scope tests are theoretical validity tests. Theory also tells us that values should be sensitive to the availability of complements and substitutes. Hence, one might construct CV exercises to test hypotheses about such effects. Or, transitivity is one of the core assumptions about preferences and might be used to develop construct validity tests for contingent values.

A fundamental question follows: What if the results from a CV application fail to pass a theoretical validity test? Suppose, for example, that a valuation equation fails to produce a positive relationship between observed WTP and income of respondents. Should the whole study be thrown out as invalid? Surely not. Failure to get a positive coefficient on income could even be consistent with theory. The value of the environmental amenity in question may simply be insensitive to income.

Now suppose that the results fail a scope test or some other test involving contingent value comparisons. Failure of a scope test would call for even more careful scrutiny of the content validity of the study. One would want to ask, for example, whether the qualitative phases of the research succeeded in identifying dimensions of the environmental amenity in question that mattered to potential respondents. The matter of whether the survey instrument communicated well would need to be pursued with extra vigor. Careful attention to statistical issues would also be warranted. Values may be inherently highly variable, and failure of a scope test might simply reflect the noisiness of the data. In the end, CV studies that fail scope tests will have less credibility that those that pass.

Suppose a study attempts to demonstrate sensitivity of values to availability of complements and substitutes or tests for transitivity and fails. Again this may indicate flaws in study design or statistical noise. Or, more fundamental problems may be indicated. As we have already noted, the economic theory on which such tests are based is highly abstract and stylized. In other words, reality is some unknown mixture of what theory models and what we termed "other things." Failure of responses to a CV survey to conform to theory may indicate that "other things" (phenomena not considered in the theory) are having a strong influence. What these "other things" are and whether they are somehow biasing results will usually not be very clear.

The overall conclusion would be that CV studies that display strong theoretical validity ought to be considered superior to those that display weaknesses in these respects or do not include theoretical validity tests in their study design at all. This is so because studies with strong theoretical validity are more likely to be indicative of true values as defined in theory. Suspected weaknesses identified during theoretical validity testing may indicate flaws in study design that were not detected when the content validity of the study was assessed. Or, they may arise because unknown factors outside the theory used to define WTP_t are influencing results.

It seems likely that there will be wide variations in how well CV studies perform in theoretical validity testing. We propose that theoretical validity tests be divided into two categories, which we shall term rudimentary and advanced tests. Through regression analysis, contingency tables, or other such procedures, the rudimentary tests would explore whether expected theoretical relationships can be found between contingent values, on the one hand, and socioeconomic, behavioral, and attitudinal variables, on the other. Independent variables could include income, socioeconomic characteristics, and attitudes relative to the resources in question and the environmental issues more generally. Having previously visited the site, membership in environmental organizations, participation in recreational activities related to the environmental resources in question, past volunteer activities, and other such variables could also be considered in such analyses. Rudimentary tests should be feasible using data from a relatively simple survey of a single sample. They are "rudimentary" in the sense that they are relatively cheap and straightforward to perform and probably ought to be a part of all CV studies. It should be recognized from the beginning that results from a study that lacks the money and/or time to gather and analyze information on at least some such variables will likely not have much credibility.

Advanced construct validity tests involve comparisons between contingent values. Theoretical expectations relative to scope, variations in substitutes and complements, and other relationships between values are tested. Such tests may be beyond the resources available to many studies not only because they will involve more sophistication in survey design and execution, but also because they may involve costly split-sample designs.

We propose that studies be categorized into a three-level hierarchy expressing increasing degrees of construct validity. At the lowest level would be studies that either have not included any construct validity tests or have failed to pass rudimentary tests. Such studies might typically have had low budgets and/or severe time constraints and this may have limited the amount of qualitative research that could be conducted, thus limiting the content validity of the study as well. Such studies may be useful for scientific purposes or as exercises involving training of students, but should be used in policy analysis and litigation only with the heaviest caveats. The second level of the hierarchy would involve studies that have achieved a fair amount of success in the rudimentary tests, but that either do not have the budget to support advanced testing or have not succeeded in passing advanced tests. Second-level studies may be usable in cost-benefit analyses, since normally the goal of such analyses is simply to determining whether the benefits of an intervention exceed the costs. Of course, unless benefits exceed costs by a fairly wide margin or vice versa, potential imprecision in second level studies may mean that the issue of whether benefits exceed costs remains open. Second level studies may be less applicable in litigation, where relatively precise estimates of value are needed to assess damages, but they may still be useful in preliminary damage assessments. Third level studies are studies that have conducted and achieved substantial success in passing advanced tests. Provided that such studies are judged to have a high degree of content validity as well, they would have the highest level of credibility for benefit-cost analysis and litigation.

The other issue needing attention in this section is the extent to which success or failure in construct validity tests implies that CV itself is a valid or invalid procedure. Notice that the focus has changed substantially. Up to now we have been concerned about the validity of individual applications. Now the ability of the CV method in general to estimate values of WTP_t is the issue. Can construct validity testing help to address this much broader question?

The difficulties created by our inability to observe true values become painfully apparent at this point. While failure to pass construct validity tests does, as we have just seen, create some degree of doubt about individual studies, the problems thus identified may be peculiar to the study in question. Perhaps design flaws in the individual study are to blame. Such flaws may have been identified when content validity was considered, but they may also have been hidden. Perhaps the "other things" that theory ignores are more potent or play themselves out in some unusual way in the study in question. For these reasons, the temptation to draw sweeping conclusions about the validity of the CV method from one or only a few studies should be resisted. Only if a large number of seemingly high-quality CV studies consistently fail rudimentary and/or advanced tests, would a negative conclusion regarding the overall validity of the CV method in general be warranted. Likewise, if CV studies consistently pass such tests, then the validity of the method would be supported. In the intermediate case where CV studies sometimes pass such tests and sometimes fail them, a very different conclusion would be warranted. Assuming that the studies in question have a high degree of content validity, such an outcome would imply that intervening factors are sometimes, but not always, interfering in the successful application of the method. Research would be called for to identify what those intervening factors are. New content and construct validity criteria would follow. Ultimately, it may be possible to develop criteria for judging where CV can be applied with good prospects for success and where it cannot. In the meantime, the conclusion regarding the overall validity of the CV method would be that it is capable of producing results that pass validity tests under at least some circumstances. We will return to the top topic of overall validity after considering the third of the Three Cs.

Criterion validity

To assess criterion validity, Mitchell and Carson (1989, 192) point out that "it is necessary to have in hand a criterion which is unequivocally closer to the theoretical construct [WTP_t or its mean value over some population] than the measure whose validity is being assessed [the CV-based measure of value]. " The closer the contingent value is to the criterion, the more valid it is judged to be.

Given the credibility that preference expressions in markets have as indicators of true values, actual market prices would be ideal criteria to use in evaluating contingent values; however, because such market prices are rare in the environmental area and especially for non-use values, so-called "simulated market" values are perhaps a more promising alternative for judging the criterion validity of contingent values. Simulated markets involve creating situations in the field or laboratory where subjects have the opportunity to actually pay for the good or service or receive compensation for it. CV is used to estimate the value of the same good or service.

Simulated markets differ from real markets in two ways. First, each individual may be involved in only one transaction. Second, the mechanism by which the price is determined may seem somewhat artificial to participants. Bohrnstedt (1983) provides a useful distinction between two kinds of criterion validity: predictive validity and concurrent validity. Applied in the context of CV, predictive validity might be assessed by asking subjects a CV question at one point in time and later giving the same individual a chance to actually purchase the same good (see, for example, Kealy et al. 1990). For concurrent validity, the measure and the criterion against which it is to be assessed are measured contemporaneously. This could involve a split-sample design where randomly assigned subjects participate in either a CV exercise or a simulated market in which the same good can actually be bought or sold (see, for example, Bishop and Heberlein 1979).

Simulated market experiments have been conducted for both use values (Bohm 1972; Bishop and Heberlein 1979; Dickie et al. 1987; Coursey et al. 1987; Kealy et al. 1990; Bishop, et al. 1993; Neill et al. 1994) and total values where non-use values are likely to be a substantial component (Boyce et al. 1989; Kealy et al. 1990; Duffield and Patterson 1992; Seip and Strand 1992; Champ et al. 1994). It is tempting to launch into a discussion of these studies, for they provide many interesting features and results. Space and time preclude doing justice to such an exercise. It must suffice to say that the evidence is somewhat mixed, with several studies providing support for the criterion validity of CV, especially for use values. Results from simulated market experiments that have focused on total values (including non-use values) are even farther from being conclusive. Furthermore, for both use and total value studies, problems arise that are not unlike those already mentioned for construct validity. Circumstances, commodities to be valued, procedures applied, and other details vary so greatly from one study to the next, that it is difficult to generalize from the studies that exist to the method in general. For example, in Kealy et al. (1990), Duffield and Patterson (1992), Seip and Strand (1992), and Champ et al. (1994) there is substantial evidence that donation vehicles lead to overestimation of total values, but little evidence exists from simulated markets about how other payment vehicles perform. Clearly, the challenges of conducting a simulated market to estimate non-use values with a high degree of content validity are formidable.

An alternative with some promise would be to use CV to predict the share of the population that would vote in favor of propositions in actual referenda. The potential usefulness of referenda as indicators of true values was discussed above. It is worth adding that the advantages of the referendum format for CV non-use value studies are well established in the literature (Mitchell and Carson 1989; Hoehn and Randall 1987). At least one criterion validity study using this approach has already been conducted (Carson, Hanemann, and Mitchell 1986). They were able to successfully forecast the outcome of an actual referendum in California using CV, a result that supports the validity of the CV method. Though additional studies of this kind should be pursued, their disadvantage relative to simulated markets should be recognized. True values, as defined here, are monetary values. Voting in real referenda will not produce direct evidence to estimate true values that can serve as a standard of comparison for contingent values. Referenda can only produce as criteria the percentages of citizens voting for and against ballot propositions. Econometric models of CV responses would then be used to predict the vote based on survey responses. The null hypothesis to be tested is that the CV-based predicted vote equals the actual vote. Results would obviously be relevant to understanding the validity of CV, but would not be fully equivalent to comparing monetary values.

SOME FINAL THOUGHTS ON THE OVERALL VALIDITY OF HE METHOD

We might sum up the evidence on the overall validity of the CV method by saying that, in both construct and criterion validity testing, CV seems to perform well in some studies and not so well in others. Carson et al. (forthcoming) suggest a new way to try to come to grips with variety of results that are now available. They located a total of 83 studies that contained both revealed preference and contingent values for the same interventions. Some of the revealed preference results came from criterion validity studies where simulated market or actual market comparisons were feasible. Other studies involved comparisons of contingent values with hedonic price, travel-cost, and averting expenditure studies and would probably be best considered convergent validity comparisons. All the studies consulted involved WTP. Carson et al. calculated a total of 616 possible ratios of contingent values to revealed preferences from these studies. These ratios were analyzed in several different ways, but the simplest approach, which took the ratios as a data set containing 616 observations, is fairly typical. The ratios averaged 0.89 with a 95 percent confidence interval of [0.81-0.96] and a median of 0.75. The Spearman rank correlation coefficient for contingent values and associated revealed preference values was 0.78.

Caution is warranted in interpreting these results. Only where use values dominate are revealed preference values available to calculate such ratios. Non-use values may present special difficulties that were not present for use values. Also, such averages do not guarantee that any particular CV study, no matter how well or poorly is was conducted and regardless of specific circumstances, will get a value comparable to what would have been obtained had a revealed-preference study been done. Granting all that, both the closeness of this ratio to unity and the tightness of the confidence interval are impressive. It would appear that for use values at least, contingent valuation studies tend to get values that are comparable in magnitude to revealed preference values. And, if people can answer CV use value questions in ways that tend to be close to the value of the same resource from revealed-preference based studies, then this will tend to support those who argue that they can answer well-designed CV total value questions in ways that reflect their underlying economic preferences. Further favorable evidence is provided by noting that both use and total value CV studies frequently pass scope tests, as Richard Carson's paper in this volume shows. While not all studies pass rudimentary and advanced tests, enough do to conclude that CV is capable of producing results of sufficient validity to be useful in policy analysis and damage assessment.

SUMMARY

The debate over CV is a debate that can only be resolved with empirical evidence. Too often, it seems to us, the critics of CV simply speculate about what might go wrong in CV studies and then assume that those things actually do go wrong. On the other hand, CV practitioners have probably been far too willing to accept the results of their studies at face value. Carrying on the debate at this level will continue to bear little fruit.

In order to consider the empirical evidence systematically and objectively, the ground rules must be determined in advance. What is needed is a theory of measurement for CV that can guide the empirical research. To that end, we have attempted in this paper to expand on a theme that already exists in the literature on CV. The approach builds on the theory of psychological testing. It is based on the premise that true values are unobservable, so that validity must be evaluated indirectly, through drawing of inferences from a number of directions. In psychology, reliability must be carefully considered along with validity. If the data are too noisy, it will be impossible to detect biases in observations at the individual level even if the noise is simply random. Reliability is somewhat important for CV as well, but it takes on less importance because, in economics, the goal is normally to measure values for a population, and not for the individual. Individual values could be quite noisy, yet average values could be unbiased and accuracy would simply be a matter of sample size.

The Three C's--content validity, construct validity, and criterion validity--seem to us to fit the problem of evaluating the validity of CV rather well. The first step toward achieving a valid CV study--if that is possible--is to design and execute the study properly, and the goal of content validity assessment is to evaluate the study procedures. Since the goal is to measure the theoretical WTP, a well-designed study will show a close correspondence between the economic theory which is used to define the true value and the structure and wording of the CV question. Stated differently, everything that neoclassical consumers would need to formulate and reveal their true values must be present in the CV exercise. Furthermore, since normal human beings, and not theoretical consumers, will be asked to complete the survey, care must be taken to design the survey to be effective in communicating with real people. There are numerous hidden pitfalls here that may require a substantial amount of qualitative research to overcome. Furthermore, a study with high content validity will have carefully executed all phases of the survey, from population definition and sampling through coding and entry of the responses. Finally, a study with high content validity will have applied appropriate econometric procedures to arrive at values and related statistics.

For non-use valuation studies, construct validity assessment will mainly involve testing theoretically motivated prior expectation about relationships between the contingent value estimate or estimates in question and other, non-value variables (rudimentary tests) or other contingent values (advanced tests). Studies that fail to show expected relationships in rudimentary tests will have the least credibility. Such studies fall at the bottom of our hierarchy of construct validity. At the top of the hierarchy will be studies that pass a battery of rudimentary and advanced tests of theoretical validity.

Theoretical validity testing can shed some light the broader question of whether the CV method itself is valid. Because individual studies vary widely in their subject matter and content and construct validity, the weight of evidence from many studies will be required in order to judge the overall validity of CV. The temptation to reach broad conclusions on the basis of one or a few studies should be resisted. If, across a wide range of studies, it had turned out that CV consistently fails theoretical validity tests, then we would conclude that CV, at least as it has been applied in the past, is a scientific dead-end. However, as we have seen, this has not been the case. Instead, while not all studies have performed well under theoretical validity testing, many have performed quite well in both rudimentary tests and scope tests.

Criterion validity tests may be capable of casting further light on the overall validity of the method. Here, simulated market experiments--while they involve significant challenges in design and implementation--may yet turn out to be a productive avenue. Further efforts to find circumstances where simulated markets are feasible could produce rich dividends in judging the potential of the method. Here again, individual studies are unlikely to be definitive. Also, care will always be required in extrapolating conclusions from such simulated markets to specific field applications of CV. Content and construct validity will continue to play a central role in evaluating the validity of individual CV studies, with criterion validity studies hopefully helping to refine the criteria applied to individual studies.

ENDNOTES

1 Bishop is a Professor in the Department of Agricultural Economics and the Institute for Environmental Studies at the University of Wisconsin--Madison. Champ was formerly a Graduate Student in the Department of Agricultural Economics at the University of Wisconsin--Madison and is now an economist at the Rocky Mountain Forest and Range Experiment Station. Brown and McCollum are economists at the Rocky Mountain Forest and Range Experiment Station, Forest Service, United States Department of Agriculture. The research was supported by the Rocky Mountain Forest and Range Experiment Station, by the College of Agricultural and Life Sciences, University of Wisconsin--Madison, and by the Wisconsin Sea Grant Institute (under grants from the National Sea Grant College Program, National Oceanic and Atmospheric Administration, U.S. Department of Commerce, and from the State of Wisconsin; Federal grant number NA90AA-D-SG469, project number R/PS-38).

2 We shall limit the discussion to interventions that affect the environment, although everything said is directly applicable to other types of interventions.

3 Care must be taken in this sort of discussion to avoid making theory into a straw man. Economists interested in household decision making, decision making under uncertainty, and other economic problems do develop much richer theoretical models than those typically drawn upon in conceptualizing WTP_t for purposes of applied welfare analysis. Perhaps richer theories will eventually yield new insights and testable hypotheses for valuation studies, but they have yet to do so. To date, the simpler models, which intentionally leave numerous potentially important other factors out of the analysis, have dominated. discussions of WTP_t

REFERENCES

Bishop, R.C., P.A. Champ, D.J. Mullarkey. 1995. "Contingent Valuation." *Handbook of Environmental Economics*. Ed. Daniel W. Bromley. Oxford: Blackwell Publishers, pp. 629-654.

Bishop, R.C. and T.A. Heberlein. 1979. "Measuring Values of Extramarket Goods: Are Indirect Measures Biased?" *American Journal of Agricultural Economics* 61(5):926-930.

Bishop, R.C. and M.P. Welsh. 1992. "Existence Values in Benefit-Cost Analysis and Damage Assessment." *Land Economics* 68(4):405-417.

Bishop, R.C., M.P. Welsh, and T.A. Heberlein. 1993. "Some Experimental Evidence on the Validity of Contingent Valuation." Unpublished paper, Department of Agricultural Economics, University of Wisconsin--Madison.

Bohm, P. 1972. "Estimating Demand for Public Goods: An Experiment." *European Economic Review* 3:111-130.

Bohrnstedt, G.W. 1983. "Measurement." *Handbook of Survey Research*. Eds. P.H. Rossi, J.D. Wright, and A.B Anderson. New York: Academic Press, Inc.

Boyce, R.R., T.C. Brown, G.D. McClelland, G.L. Peterson, and W.D. Schulze. 1989. "Experimental Evidence of Existence Value in Payment and Compensation Contexts." Paper presented at the joint meetings of the Western Committee on the Benefits and Costs of Natural Resource Planning (W133) and the Western Regional Science Association, San Diego, CA.

Boyle, K.J., and R.C. Bishop. 1987. "Valuing Wildlife in Benefit-Cost Analyses: A Case Study Involving Endangered Species." *Water Resources Research* 23(5):943-950.

Carson, R.T., N.E. Flores, K.M. Martin, and J.L. Wright. Forthcoming. "Contingent Valuation and Revealed Preferences Methodologies: Comparing the Estimates for Quasi-Public Goods." *Land Economics*.

Carson, R.T., W. Michael Hanemann, and Robert C. Mitchell. 1986. "Determining the Demand for Public Goods by Simulating Referendums at Different Tax Prices." Manuscript, University of California, San Diego.

Champ, P.A., R.C. Bishop, T.C. Brown and D.W. McCollum. 1994. "Some Evidence Concerning the Validity of Contingent Valuation: Preliminary Results of an Experiment." Ed. R.C. Ready, W-133 Seventh Interim Report. Western Regional Research Publication, Lexington, KY.

Coursey, D.L., J.J. Hovis, and W.D. Schulze. 1987. "The Disparity between Willingness to Accept and Willingness to Pay Measures of Value." *Quarterly Journal of Economics* 102:679-90.

Deacon, R. and P. Shapiro. "Private Preference for Collective Goods Revealed Through Voting in Referenda." *American Economic Review* 65(5):943-955.

Diamond, P.A., J.A. Hausman, F.R. Johnson, R.W. Dunford, K.J. Boyle, S.P. Hudson, and K.N. Wilson. 1992. "Measuring Natural Resource Damages with Contingent Valuation: Tests of Validity and Reliability." Paper presented at the Cambridge Economics, Inc. symposium titled "Contingent Valuation: A Critical Assessment", Washington, D.C., April 2 and 3.

Dickie, M., A. Fisher, and S. Gerking. 1987. "Market Transactions and Hypothetical Demand Data: A Comparative Study." *Journal of the American Statistical Association* 82:69-75.

Duffield, J.W., and D.A. Patterson. 1992. "Field Testing Existence Values: Comparison of Hypothetical and Cash Transaction Values." Paper presented at the joint meetings of the Western Committee on the Benefits and Costs of Natural Resource Planning (W133) and the Western Regional Science Association, South Lake Tahoe, Nevada.

Fischoff, B., and L. Furby. 1988. "Measuring Values: A Conceptual Framework for Interpreting Transactions with Special Reference to Contingent Valuation of Visibility." *Journal of Risk and Uncertainty* 1:147-184.

Freeman III, M. 1993. *The Measurement of Environmental and Resource Values.* Washington, D.C.: Resources for the Future.

Hoehn, J.P., and A. Randall. 1987. "A Satisfactory Benefit Cost Indicator from Contingent Valuation." *Journal of Environmental Economics and Management* 14(3):226-47.

Kahneman, D. and J.L. Knetsch. 1992. "Valuing Public Goods: The Purchase of Moral Satisfaction." *Journal of Environmental Economics and Management* 22(1):57-70.

Kealy, M.J., M. Montgomery, J.F. Dovidio. 1990. "Reliability and Predictive Validity of Contingent Values: Does the Nature of the Good Matter?" *Journal of Environmental Economics and Management* 19:244-263.

Krutilla, J.V. "Conservation Reconsidered." *American Economic Review* 57:777-86.

Madariaga, B., and K.E. McConnell. 1987. "Exploring Existence Value." *Water Resources Research* 23(5):936-942.

McFadden, D. 1994. "Contingent Valuation and Social Choice." *American Journal of Agricultural Economics* 76(4):689-708.

Mitchell, R.C., and R.T. Carson. 1989. *Using Surveys to Value Public Goods: The Contingent Valuation Method.* Washington, D.C.: Resources for the Future.

Neill, H.R., R.G. Cummings, P.T. Ganderton, G.W. Harrison, and T. McGuckin. 1994. "Hypothetical Surveys and Economic Commitments." *Land Economics* 70:145-154.

Randall, A., and J.R. Stoll. 1983. "Existence Value in a Total Valuation Framework" in *Managing Air Quality and Scenic Resources at National Parks and Wilderness Areas.* Eds. R.D. Rowe and L.G. Chestnut. Boulder, CO: Westview Press.

Seip, K., and J. Strand. 1992. "Willingness to Pay for Environmental Goods in Norway: A Contingent Valuation Study with Real Payment." *Environmental and Resource Economics* 2(1):91-106.

Smith, V.K. 1987. "Nonuse Values in Benefit-Cost Analysis." *Southern Economic Journal* 51:19-26.

Swallow, B.M. and M. Wondyalew. 1994. "Evaluating Willingness to Contribute to a Local Public Good: Application of Contingent Valuation to Tsetse Control in Ethiopia." *Ecological Economics* 11:153-161.

4

ECONOMIC AND PSYCHOLOGICAL ASPECTS OF VALUING RISK REDUCTION

W. Kip Viscusi

INTRODUCTION

The appropriate approach to valuing risk reduction depends in large part on one's intent. In the case of government regulatory efforts, the overall objective is typically to value changes in risk. These policies have a small incremental effect in reducing risk, and the typical policy question is how much society is willing to pay for this reduction. When risks are being imposed involuntarily, the objective is often to determine how much the person bearing the risk must be compensated. This measure consequently focuses on a willingness-to-accept amount, which for small changes in risk should reflect the same tradeoff rate as the willingness-to-pay amount.

In many instances, however, the risks involved are not small. For some purposes, it is necessary to establish a value of a certain elimination or imposition of a risk. If the question being addressed is how much an individual must be compensated to be made whole after suffering an adverse risky outcome, then the appropriate compensation measure will be the implicit value of the certainty of such an outcome, where this amount will typically not be the same as the local tradeoff rate per unit risk.

An alternative certainty concept is the optimal insurance amount. In particular, how much would the individual choose to transfer to the risky outcome state if actuarially fair insurance were available? In the case of monetary losses, this amount will be the level that is needed to restore the individual's level of utility. For non-monetary outcomes, these two amounts generally will differ.

The overall metric for analyzing the value of risk reduction must also be selected. The usual economic approach is to use money as the currency of interest. What, for example, is the monetary value of a small risk reduction? Although using money has considerable appeal among economists, it is not without controversy, particularly among those who view health risk tradeoffs as being too sensitive to be put in monetary terms. For many policy purposes metrics other than money are often sufficient. For example, one might wish to establish a lives saved or a life years equivalent metric for analyzing different kinds of effects. Using such a metric, one can rate different outcomes in terms of death risk equivalents, which may be sufficient for many policy purposes.

After the particular risk reduction valuation concept has been selected, one must then determine whether the matter of interest is the actual value that individuals would place on the risk reduction if they were fully rational or their values given individual irrationality. Numerous types of biases in risk perception may distort the valuation amount, as may faulty decisions based on these risk perceptions. Survey methods that explore the nature and characteristics of these biases are often instructive in indicating the limitations of individual decisions. However, for policy purposes our objective should be to ascertain the valuations of risk reduction assuming full rationality. The objective of government programs should not be to institutionalize society's irrational responses but rather to promote the risk reduction efforts that best enhance individual welfare if individuals understood the risks they faced and responded to them rationally.

As this discussion suggests, the task of valuing risks is not a narrowly defined enterprise. Nor has the process of implementing empirical strategies proven to be straightforward. In this paper I will explore different aspects of the risk evaluation process, focusing particular attention on previous studies that explore different aspects of the risk valuations.

The discussion begins in Section 2 with an investigation of individual processing of risk information. How do individuals form risk beliefs, and how do the various biases in the nature of these perceptional responses influence the risk valuations that are elicited in surveys? Section 3 provides a brief overview of attempts to assess risk-money tradeoffs and explores the problems associated with market estimation of risk-money tradeoffs that seem to be most salient. Instead of focusing on risk-money tradeoffs, one instead could explore other types of metrics, such as a death risk metric. The death risk metric, which is the subject of Section 4, is potentially desirable not only from the standpoint of providing information that is more acceptable in policy discussions, but it also may assist individuals in determining their valuation of risk. Section 5 concludes the essay.

PROCESSING OF RISK INFORMATION

A key component of any study of the valuation risk is the character of the risk perceptions of those interviewed. Several different approaches and situations can arise. First, the researcher may assume that individuals have perfect knowledge of the risks and that some objective measure of the risk can be used in the valuation process. For example, studies of compensating differentials in the labor market often assume that the objective measures of the risk by industry and occupation correspond with individual risk beliefs. The only remaining question is what level of compensation individuals receive for bearing these risks, thus enabling one to calculate the appropriate wage-risk tradeoffs.

A variant on this situation is that in which there is also an attempt to elicit individuals' subjective perception of the risks. At a relatively crude level, one could inquire whether the job poses any hazards. More refined approaches entail the use of presenting respondents with various kinds of risk scales that they can use to categorize the degree of risk posed by their job. Rather than assuming that individuals' risk perceptions coincide with objective measures of the risk, this approach attempts to ascertain the subjective risk perceptions that are pertinent for individual decisions.

The third situation is that in which individuals are presented with risk information as part of the survey. This information may be qualitative, as in the case in which respondents are given hazard warnings from which they must infer a degree of riskiness. In other cases, the information may be quantitative. Most experimental studies of the rationality of choice under uncertainty involve the presentation of quantitative information about the probabilities associated with different lottery outcomes. Even if quantitative information is presented, however, individuals may not treat this information at face value. As will be indicated below, this is only one limiting case in which the survey information is treated as being fully informative.

The final variant of information is that in which risk information is presented to respondents and there is also an attempt to elicit from respondents their level of risk perceptions. Including a component of the survey to ascertain these risk perceptions is reasonably straightforward in the case in which respondents have been given qualitative risk information. However, if respondents have been given a quantitative risk amount, then such debriefing of subjective risk perceptions may be viewed as a memory recall or reading comprehension task. Thus, there is the danger that respondents may simply repeat the information that they have been given, as opposed to actually reflecting upon how their risk beliefs have been altered.

The conceptual approach that I have used in Viscusi (1989, 1992a) to analyze individual processing of risk information is quasi-Bayesian in nature. In particular, I assume that individuals process risk information they receive in conjunction with their prior risk beliefs. They treat information received in the survey process as being partially informative within the context of a Bayesian updating process. In the special case in which the risk information is fully informative, their risk beliefs will coincide with the information the survey presents to them. However, even in situations in which the survey researchers believe that they are providing full information, there may be a partial updating process which will generate many of the observed anomalies in the literature.

More specifically, let individuals have a prior probability of outcome ι equal to θ_i and a probability π_i of this outcome that has been communicated to them as part of the survey. Their prior beliefs have an informational content g, and the survey risk information has informational content ξ. In effect, individuals act as if they have drawn $\gamma+\xi$ balls from an urn, where γ reflects the number of balls associated with the prior beliefs and ξ reflects the number of balls associated with the new risk information. The individual's posterior probability $\Pi(\theta_\iota,\pi_\iota)$ that outcome ι will occur as given by

$$P(q_i, p_i) = (\gamma q_i + \xi p_i)/(\gamma + \xi) \qquad (1)$$

If the survey information has no effect on the individual's risk beliefs, than q_i will be the risk assessment. If the survey information is fully credible, then p_i will be the risk assessment. In the usual instance in which there is a partial weight to both forms of information, the risk perception will be a weighted average of the prior and the new risk information.

In many instances, individuals bring to the survey context specific knowledge of the risks based on their past experience. Surveys that deal with risks posed by jobs, the environment, cigarette smoking, and other familiar hazards address issues for which the prior informational weights are likely to be substantial. In other cases, such as laboratory experiments or studies considering hypothetical lotteries that are not context-specific, respondents may not have specific information regarding the particular lottery outcomes. However, they may nevertheless treat the experimentally provided information as being partially informative. In this instance, I have hypothesized that individuals use as their prior risk beliefs the probability 1/n, where there are n possible outcomes. Thus, the perceived probability function P will update the stated probability given to the respondent in a Bayesian manner following

$$P(1/n, p_i) = [\gamma(1/n) + \xi p_i]/(\gamma + \xi) \qquad (2)$$

What is pertinent from the standpoint of analyzing risk tradeoffs is not the Bayesian tradeoff involving the stated risk p_i but rather the tradeoff involving the individual's perceived risk $P(1/n, p_i)$. Only if the experimentally provided information is fully credible or in the case in which p_i equals 1/n will the two be equal.

The final stipulation pertains to the treatment of certain outcomes. In the case in which there is no probabilistic element, this formulation assumes that.

$$P(1/n, 0) = 0 \text{ and } P(1/n, 1) = 1 \qquad (3)$$

Thus, probabilities associated with non-stochastic events are treated at face value.

In terms of the character of the risk beliefs, this formulation is consistent with the relationship indicated in Figure 1. Stated probabilities are indicated on the horizontal axis, and perceived probabilities appear on the vertical axis. The perceived probability exceeds the stated probability for low probability events, and is below it for high probability events. The perceived probability-stated probability relationship is linear, with a positive intercept. Moreover, the theory precisely predicts the intersection point between perceived and stated probabilities, which in the symmetric reference point case in which q_i equals 1/n is given by 1/n.

Elsewhere in Viscusi (1989, 1992a) I have elaborated on this formulation and have applied it to analyze many widely observed phenomena in the literature. The noteworthy aspect of this approach is that this quite simple structure has a model that *predicts* many anomalies. Thus, this formulation does not simply make it feasible to reconcile the anomalies that have been observed in the literature with a suitably structured model. Rather, this model predicts that these aberrations will necessarily take place if individuals are expected utility maximizers, where the probabilities involved have been transformed in a manner consistent with equations 1-3.

The range of behavior that can be predicted by this theory is quite extensive. This theory predicts, for example, Kahneman and Tversky's (1979) "general principle underlying substitution axiom violations," which is that any given ratio of two probabilities will be viewed as more similar the smaller is the value of the two probabilities. For example, the value 0.3/0.6 will be viewed by respondents as being much smaller than the value of .003/.006, as the latter ratio will appear to be closer to 1.0. Similarly, the theory predicts the overweighting of low probability outcomes,[2] the premiums associated with certain elimination of the risk, and other phenomena in the literature, including the representativness heuristic (Tversky and Kahneman, 1974 and Grether, 1980), the Allais paradox (Allias, 1953), the isolation effect (Tversky and Kahneman, 1979), and the Ellsberg paradox (Ellsberg, 1961). For purposes here, my formulation will be used only to provide a framework for thinking about how risk beliefs are formulated.

It is useful to review some of the different ways in which risk perceptions may be flawed, particularly as these may affect how individuals respond to surveys pertaining to risk valuations. Not all of these deficiencies are necessarily pertinent in every context, but they do represent concerns that researchers should attempt to address as part of their study design.

One of the most well established biases is that individuals exhibit a tendency to overestimate the risks associated with low probability events. As was indicated above with respect to the characterization in Figure 1, small probabilities tend to be overestimated and large probabilities underestimated. To the extent that individuals approach different events with no knowledge, thus establishing an equal probability 1/n to all possible outcomes, the result will be an overestimation of all events with below-average probability and underestimation of the risk of all events with an above-average probability. As the individual's information pertaining to the specific risks increases, then the perceived risk line in Figure 1 rotates from an initial horizontal position to being closer to the 45 degree line in which stated probabilities and perceived probabilities are identical. This phenomenon of overestimating low probability events and underestimating larger risks has been extensively documented in the psychology literature.

In Viscusi (1992a), I report on different sets of empirical estimates in which the prospective reference theory model has been fitted to various risk belief data in a manner that is consistent with this formulation. For example, this approach has been used both to estimate the underlying risk perception functions for the mortality risk data used in the original study by psychologists, and it has also been used to assess the formulation of job hazard risk beliefs within a survey context in which individual workers report their prior risk beliefs, receive a hazard warning, and then report their posterior risk beliefs. In this situation, it is possible to estimate two of the key parameters affecting the formulation of risk beliefs. Table 1 reports on the estimates of two components of equation 1 for labels for four different chemicals: sodium bicarbonate, chloroacetophenone, asbestos, and TNT. The implicit risk p_i being communicated by each of these labels appears in the first column of Table 1, where its value ranges from 0.038 for the relatively safe substance sodium bicarbonate to a high of 0.317 for TNT. It is also possible to estimate the relative informational content associated with the warning information. In the case of chloroacetophenone, a not particularly well known chemical, the hazard warning had informational content roughly comparable to that of the individuals' prior beliefs. However, in the case of TNT, the informational content was over 31 times as great as that associated with the prior risk beliefs.

TABLE 1: RISKS AND INFORMATIONAL CONTENT OF WARNING LABELS

	Implicit Risk p_i	Relative Informational Content ξ/δ
Sodium Bicarbonate	.038	3.72
Chloroacetophenone	.239	1.29
Asbestos	.289	6.43
TNT	.317	31.36

Source: Viscusi (1992a).

A somewhat different problem associated with low probability events is that it may be difficult for people to process information regarding small probabilities. As was indicated above, very low probabilities often pose substantial problems for individual risk assessments. When we confront probabilities such as an annual risk of one in a million or perhaps a lifetime risk of one in one million we know that these risks are small, but refined distinctions tend to be blurred. People generally have had very limited experience in drawing millions of balls from an urn in an effort to find the one red ball among a sea of black balls, whereas we have a much better grasp of probabilities involving risks of 1/100 or greater. Errors in decision making as well as the aforementioned biases are likely to be much more prevalent when dealing with very small probabilities.

Highly publicized events often also pose particular difficulties. In many instances, the media provide information regarding body counts and risk consequences, which is information regarding the numerator of the risk. Seldom is comparable information provided pertaining to the denominator. As has been widely observed by psychologists such as Fischhoff, et al. (1981), particularly dramatic events such as tornadoes are much more likely to be associated with risk overestimates than less prominent events. Similarly, the risks associated with cigarette smoking, for which body counts have been widely publicized, also appear to be overestimated (see Viscusi (1992b)), as do events that have received prominent newspaper coverage.

The character of the risk also may be consequential. If individuals have control of the risk, they may be overoptimistic with respect to how they will fare when facing the risk and under-assess its value even in the presence of risk information. This phenomenon which has been observed with respect to driving behavior by Svenson (1979) and with respect to bicycle and power mower risks by Rethans (1979). It is also apparent in contexts in which individuals are provided with risk information. In Viscusi and Magat (1987), we found that even after being provided with risk information pertaining to the chemical hazards associated with drain opener and bleach, respondents tended to believe that their risks were below average. Table 2 summarizes these results for the drain opener and bleach samples and for the four types of injuries examined. In every case, no more than three percent of the sample viewed themselves as living in a household with an above average risk. From 32 percent to 57 percent believed that they faced average risks associated with the product and 40 to 65 percent of the sample believed that their risks were below average. There is a clear asymmetry in terms of how people are distributed.

TABLE 2: DISTRIBUTION OF RISK ASSESSMENTS (PERCENTAGES) RELATIVE TO THE REST OF THE POPULATION

Risk	Above Average	Average	Below Average
Drain Opener			
Hand Burns	3	46	51
Child Poisoning	3	32	65
Bleach			
Chloramine Gas	3	50	46
Child Poisoning	2	57	40

Source: Viscusi and Magat (1987), Table 5.2.

There are two possible factors that may be at work. First, individuals may in fact underassess the risks associated with events over which they have some control. Second, when the risk perception questions are asked in relative risk terms as opposed to a scale in which they can score the risks on a continuous basis, they may be more prone to responding in a manner that does not place them at a disadvantage relative to their peers in terms of risk responsibility.

Another feature of the risks that is consequential is the ambiguity of the risk. Since the original paper by Ellsberg (1961), economists have noted that individuals treat subjective probabilities differently from objective probabilities. In the case in which there are losses associated with the risks, such as environmental damage, it has been documented in Viscusi and Magat (1992) that individuals will display an aversion to risks for which there is risk ambiguity as compared with risks that are more precisely understood. This aversion will affect the valuations individuals report so that we will be measuring not only the valuation of the risk but also the valuation of the precision with which the risk is understood.

A more general phenomenon that is perhaps most fundamental is that it is difficult for people to process probabilistic information. Many researchers who have undertaken studies to value risk have devoted substantial time to educating respondents so that they would think probabilistically. At the very least, it is essential to present the risk information in a manner that can be readily understood and processed.

RISK-MONEY TRADEOFFS

The most prevalent approach to valuing health risks in the literature has been an examination of wage-risk tradeoffs. Using data on worker wages and linking these data to worker characteristics and job characteristics, including job risks, economists have estimated the wage premiums workers receive for risk.

The overall implication of these studies, which are surveyed in Viscusi (1992a, 1993), is that on average the estimated rates of tradeoff based on labor market studies tend to cluster in the range of $3 million to $7 million per statistical life.

The validity of such estimates hinges on the rationality of the underlying job decisions. The substantial literature on choice under uncertainty has documented the difficulties that risky decisions pose. Actual market risk have an advantage over studies of survey risks in that respondents have an incentive to think seriously about real risks to their lives. Many of these problems are likely to affect the valuations elicited within a survey context, unless particular care is exercised in the design of the survey instrument. Thus, in many instances what one may be measuring may not be so much the rational valuation of risk but rather how people respond to risks given their cognitive limitations. The character of these responses is not uninteresting, but if our purpose is to establish benefit values for policy analysis, one would like to purge these responses of their irrational aspects.

The first potential difficulty is that many risky decisions involve relatively small probabilities, and these pose particular problems for individual choice. Overall, there is evidence that small probabilities tend to be overestimated, thus inflating the valuation amounts that will be elicited. However, simply noting that this bias is a potential concern does not convey the full extent of the problems that may be encountered.

Many of the risks that we face and which are the target of government regulation are quite small. The average fatality rate for blue-collar workers in the United States is 1/10,000. In many instances, a frequent threshold for government regulation is a lifetime risk of 1/1,000,000, based on an assumed lifetime of 70 years. Such substances may pose an annual fatality risk of 1/70,000,000 -- a probability so negligible that few respondents can make reliable judgements pertaining to its value.

Striking evidence of the effect of small probabilities on the valuation responses is provided by two studies involving an identical health outcome but different probabilities of the hazard. The study by Viscusi and Magat (1987) analyzed respondents' willingness to pay for improved safety of insecticides and toilet bowl cleaner, where the risks were small risks per 2,000,000 households. In contrast, the risks examined in Viscusi, Magat, and Huber (1987) pertain to larger risks per 10,000 households. The effect of individuals' overestimation of small probabilities is apparent in the implausibly large valuations elicited in the first of these studies. The health consequences associated with the risks posed by bleach and drain opener are associated with implicit values of $0.65 million to $1.78 million in the first study, whereas the health impacts associated with insecticide or toilet bowl cleaner have values ranging from $744 to $3,489 in the second study.

More pertinent is that one of the health outcomes is identical in each instance. If one mixes bleach and toilet bowl cleaner, chloramine gas forms, where the resulting chloramine gassing is the leading non-suicidal cause of poisonings among U.S. adults. When this outcome is valued within the context of willingness to pay for safer bleach, the implicit value per chloramine gassing is $1.78 million. In contrast, when the outcome is valued within the context of willingness to pay for safer toilet bowl cleaner, for which the denominator is 10,000 households rather than 2,000,000 households, the implicit value per statistical gassing is $1,113. In the case of the study with the 2,000,000 million household denominator, the risk change was in the range of 25/2,000,000 to 70/2,000,000, whereas in the latter study the risk change was 15/10,000. The risk increments consequently differed by a factor of about 100, and the valuation amounts differ by a factor of 1,600. There is consequently very little sensitivity of the willingness-to-pay amount with respect to the denominator, and indeed respondents may be more sensitive to the number of injuries than the associated risk probability.

A second class of difficulties pertains to the asymmetry between the willingness-to-pay and willingness-to-accept values. Nonmarket studies often yield high willingness to accept amounts. Although this phenomenon has been observed in a variety of non-stochastic contexts, in our study of valuation of risky products, we found that this phenomenon was particularly acute. Moreover, individuals' valuations displayed other forms of irrationality as well, such as the presence of certainty premiums. Risk decreases that diminish very low probabilities to a value of zero will lead to a discontinuous risk jump that far exceeds the actual risk change involved.

The practical consequences of these phenomena are exhibited in the result in Table 3. Respondents initially confronted the possibility of purchasing risk increment decreases for insecticide and toilet bowl cleaner on the order of 5/10,000 per risk increment, where the base risk was 15/10,000. From an economic standpoint, there should be diminishing willingness-to-pay for successive incremental risk reductions. The results in Panel A of Table 3 indicate that this phenomenon holds for the first two incremental reductions of risk, but for the final risk reduction that leads to a zero risk level, there is a marked jump in the incremental willingness-to-pay value, which is at the highest value observed for each of the four injury pairs examined. This jump reflects the certainty premium associated with completely eliminating the risk.

TABLE 3: MARGINAL VALUATIONS OF RISK DECREASES AND INCREASES

Panel A: Marginal Valuations of Reducing Both Risks by 5/10,000

Incremental Willingness To Pay ($/Bottle)				
Starting Risk (Injuries/10,000 Bottles)	Inhalation-Skin Poisoning	Inhalation-Child Poisoning	Gassing-Eyeburn	Gassing-Child Poisoning
15	1.04	1.84	0.65	0.99
10	0.34	0.54	0.19	0.24
5	2.41	5.71	0.83	0.99

Source: Viscusi and Magat (1987), Table 3.4.

TABLE 3: MARGINAL VALUATIONS OF RISK DECREASES AND INCREASES (cont.)

Panel B: Marginal Valuations of (+1,+1) Risk Increase[a]

Injury Pair	Percentage for Whom Product is Too Risky to Purchase	Mean Value ($/Bottle) of Positive Responses
Inhalation-Skin Poisoning	77.2	2.86

Inhalation-Child Poisoning	68.1	3.19
Eyeburns-Gassing	61.5	5.52
Gassing-Child Poisoning	74.3	1.28

[a]This question asked subjects what price discount they would require on the new product to accept an additional risk of 1/10,000 for both injuries, starting with risks of 15 injuries per 10,000 bottles sold for both injuries.
Source: Viscusi, Magat, and Huber (1987), p. 477.

The marginal willingness-to-pay for small incremental reductions in risk should equal the price reduction that is necessary to give consumers if there is a small increase in the product riskiness. To explore this phenomenon, we first examined the price reductions necessary for respondents to purchase a product posing a risk increase of five injuries per 10,000 bottles, or the risk increase counterpart of Panel A in Table 3. In the pre-testing of these risk changes, all respondents indicated an unwillingness to purchase the product at any price. As a result, the survey focused on a much more modest risk increase of 1/10,000. The responses to this shift are indicated in Panel B of Table 3. For the injury pairs, from 62 percent to 77 percent of the sample are unwilling to purchase the product at any price, even if they would be given the product free and be paid to use it. Moreover, for the few consumers who were willing to continue purchasing the product, the mean value of the amount of compensation they required for this very modest incremental increase in the risk far exceeded their willingness to pay for much larger risk decreases. This asymmetry, which reflects a phenomenon that we have designated the "reference risk effect," suggests that even though theoretically the willingness-to-pay and willingness-to-accept values should be equal, there may in fact be a marked disparity between the two. Because of this disparity, which may be due in part to respondents' fundamental distrust of the veracity of the risk claims once having learned that their product has become riskier, it appears preferable to rely on willingness-to-pay amounts even if the appropriate policy measure pertains to a willingness-to-accept value.

A third important feature of the risk valuation studies is that it is essential to detail enough of the consequences of the health outcome and the implications of this outcome for respondents' lives for them to be able to make meaningful judgements with respect to these outcomes. For this reason, our surveys have included extensive information pertaining to the health outcome as well as a lengthy series of questions intended to engage respondents in thinking about the implications of these health outcomes for their well being. Perhaps in part because of this extensive health outcome information, the estimates of the valuations we have obtained of the risk of chronic bronchitis in Viscusi, Magat, and Huber (1991) -- $516,000 based on risk dollar tradeoffs using a random sample -- are similar to the values for respondents who know people who have experienced the disease. The range of estimates obtained by Krupnick and Cropper

(1992), for subjects all of whom had experienced chronic lung disease, ranged from \$496,800 to \$691,200.

In contrast, some other health outcome valuation surveys that have been undertaken by other researchers have often been very terse (e.g., "The vaccine may have a side effect of causing brain damage," where this outcome is noted but characterized in no other way). The minimalist approach to conveying the consequences associated with the health outcomes is not adequate. Subjects may bring to bear quite different characteristics of the outcome to be valued. To obtain reliable and meaningful responses, it is essential to convey the complex set of implications that are the focus of the valuation and to lead respondents to think carefully about the implications of these consequences for their lives.

If individuals do in fact process risk information in the manner sketched in Figure 1, then in effect there will be a flattening out of the risk increments that respondents believe have been achieved except in the cases in which there is a shift to a non-probabilistic outcome of either no risk or a certain risk, in which case the risk change will be exaggerated. Suppose that individuals with utility function U in good health and V in ill health (where $U(x) > V(x)$, $U' > 0$, and U'', V'' £ 0) and that there is a probability q that the risky outcome imposing a monetary loss L will occur. Let this risk be perceived by the respondent as being P(q), so that the expected utility U_0 of the individual facing such a risk is given by

$$U_0 = [\,1 - P(q)][\,U(Y)\,] + [\,P(q)\,]\,[\,V(Y - L)\,] \qquad (4)$$

The key question is how the role of risk perceptions as opposed to accurate risk beliefs alters the tradeoff between the amount of compensation Y required in response to changes in the magnitude of the loss. This value can be calculated by totally differentiating equation 4, leading to the result that

$$dY / dL = [\,P(q)\,V'\,] / [\,1 - P(q)\,]\,[U' + P(q)\,V'\,] > 0 \qquad (5)$$

Even with risk perception biases, higher loss levels necessitate the provision of greater levels of compensation to lead people to bear greater risks. However, perceptional biases are consequential as well. For the points in Figure 1 for which P(q) exceeds q (i.e., to the left of the intersection of two curves), dY/dL will be higher because of the biases in risk perceptions. Consequently for very small risks, the perceptional biases will increase the tradeoff rate. At very high risk levels to the right of this intersection, the required compensation amounts will be decreased by the perceptional biases. The effect of risk perceptions in distorting observed tradeoff amounts consequently varies depending on the level of the risk and the character of the perceptional bias.

THE DEATH RISK METRIC

A major class of concerns pertains to the metric that will be used to assess the valuation of the risk reduction. It is convenient to use the familiar monetary metric. However, this metric often offends the sensitivities of non-economists and may seem a bit inappropriate to respondents who may not be comfortable in thinking about making such tradeoffs. Another approach that can be utilized is to use a risk metric in which two different classes of risk are traded off.

Although the risk-money tradeoff approach is the most common, it is also possible to use other metrics to value risk. The approach we have used to value cancer, nerve disease, and chronic bronchitis has utilized reference lotteries involving automobile accident risks. Thus, instead of giving respondents pair-wise choices involving money and health outcomes, the outcome pairs involve automobile accident deaths and the risk in question. Should one then choose to convert an automobile accident death risk metric to a monetary metric, one can either use automobile accident-money tradeoffs elicited within the survey or else use implicit value-of-life estimates based on the literature. Moreover, in some contexts it is not be necessary to make such a conversion. Policy analyses in which the critical concern is the cost per life saved do not require the establishment of a benefit value, as one can simply compare the cost per life saved amount with various reference points for policy acceptability. In the standard benefit-cost case, this reference point would be the implicit value of life, but few government agencies in the United States appear to be constrained in this manner.

The use of the death lottery metric in survey contexts has a variety of practical advantages. Most important is that it avoids the explicit presentation of money-risk tradeoffs to respondents. Many policymakers and, indeed, many respondents may be averse to making tradeoffs between cost of living and lives saved or similar kinds of choices. Use of two different risk attributes can alleviate these specialized sensitivities.

A particularly important dividend of utilizing risk-risk tradeoffs is that this approach may be less prone to criticisms that respondents are dealing with hypothetical interview currency. In situations in which respondents are asked their willingness-to-pay amounts for risk reduction, there may be a tendency to exhibit substantial willingness-to-pay that may not in fact be evidenced once confronted with real choices. Hypothetical expenditures do not run up against the same rigid budget constraints as do actual expenditures. Use of two different risk attributes makes both of the consequences involved pertinent to the respondents' well-being, and they are likely to elicit more honest and meaningful answers than would be yielded through hypothetical contingent valuation currencies.

Wholly apart from the special problems posed by the outcomes such as life and health, the death approach presents subjects with commodities that may be more commensurable. As a result, it may be easier for respondents to conceptualize tradeoffs since the attributes of the commodities are more similar.

Death risk metric studies imply that nerve disease, fatal lymphoma, and non-fatal lymphoma all are associated with implicit values of more than $1 million per statistical health outcome. Severe cases of chronic bronchitis are less highly valued, as they are tantamount to roughly one chance in three of death. In contrast, cancer is viewed as being tantamount to death by the respondents.

By utilizing two different risk tradeoffs, it is also possible to normalize the denominators associated with the risks being faced. It may be that the risks in question are truly rare events, on the order of 1/1,000,000. Respondents can then be asked what the equivalent automobile accident risk per 1,000,000 would be, thus enabling them to focus on the relative severity of the two different health outcomes involved as opposed to attempting to comprehend the subtleties of the small probabilities being presented to them.

Although there has been much less experience with the risk-risk approach than with the various risk-money contingent valuation methodologies, the technique does offer substantial potential advantages, particularly in contexts in which respondents will be better able to deal with the risk tradeoffs in a more meaningful manner.

CONCLUSION

The economic literature on the valuation of risk is still in a very formative stage. There has been a considerable literature utilizing market-based evidence to value job risks, particularly those associated with fatalities. There has also been an emerging literature utilizing surveys to address a wide range of other risks, ranging from non-use damages associated with environmental impacts to severe health consequences such as cancer. In many respects the subsequent literature utilizing surveys seems to have been constrained by attempting to provide a survey-based counterpart of what is achievable through market studies. An orientation to the market and an attempt to replicate market contexts is laudable particularly to the extent that it will make the experimental design more credible to respondents and elicit more meaningful estimates of the tradeoff values. However, economists have seldom taken full advantage of the flexibility that surveys can offer.

As indicated in my review of this literature to date, surveys offer more than just a potential to address risk consequences other than those estimatable using market data. In particular, one can utilize metrics other than risk-money tradeoffs to establish measures of risk. Perhaps chief among these is the potential use a death risk metric for assessing the severity of the risk. This metric not only offers potential advantages in terms of eliciting reliable survey responses, but it also may lead to benefit estimates that are sufficient for policy purposes and avoid many of the controversies surrounding the risk-money tradeoffs.

A recurring theme throughout a review of the analyses of valuation of risk is that the behavioral irrationalities associated with risky decisions also may confound our attempts to elicit the valuations that individuals would have if they were responding rationally to risks they face. Aberrations in choice under uncertainty are often of considerable intellectual interest, and these have spawned a considerable recent literature that has been preoccupied with different perceptional biases and failures of irrationality. These intriguing anomalies may, however, serve to undermine the validity of the estimates of risk valuation that are obtained in survey contexts if our purpose is to assess how individuals would value risks if they understood the risks and could make rational decisions with respect to them. The continuing task for those undertaking such surveys will be to structure studies in a manner that will not be contaminated by these behavioral anomalies.

ENDNOTES

1 See Fischhoff, et. al. (1981) and Lichtenstein, et. al. (1978) for documentation of this phenomenon.

REFERENCES

Allais, M. (1953), "Le comportement de l'Homme Rationnnel Devant le Risque:Critque des Postulats et Axioms de l'Ecole Americane," *Econometrica* 21:503-546.

Ellsberg, D. (1961), "Risk, Ambiguity, and the Savage Axioms," *Quarterly Journal of Economics* 75: 643-669.

Fischhoff, Baruch et al. (1981), *Acceptable Risk* (Cambridge: Cambridge University Press).

Grether, D. (1980), "Bayes Rule as a Descriptive Model: The Representativeness Heuristic," *Quarterly Journal of Economics* 95: 537-557.

Kahneman, Daniel and Amos Tversky (1979), "Prospect Theory: An Analysis of Decision under Risk," *Econometrica* 47: 263-291.

Krupnick, Alan J. and Maureen L. Cropper (1992), "The Effect of Information on Health Risk Valuations," *Journal of Risk and Uncertainty* 5(1): 29-48.

Lichtenstein, S. et al. (1978), "Judged Frequency of Lethal Events," *Journal of Experimental Psychology* 4: 551-578.

Magat, Wesley A., W. Kip Viscusi, and Joel Huber (1991), "The Death Risk Lottery Metric for Health Risks: Cancer and Nerve Disease," Duke University Working Paper.

Rethans, A. (1979), "An Investigation of Consumer Perception of Product Hazards," Doctoral Dissertation, University of Oregon-Eugene.

Svenson, O. (1979), "Are We All Among the Better Drivers?" Unpublished Manuscript, Department of Psychology, University of Stockholm.

Tversky, Amos and Daniel Kahneman (1974), "Judgement under Uncertainty: Heuristics and Biases," *Science* 185: 1124-1131.

Viscusi, W. Kip (1979), *Employment Hazards: An Investigation of Market Performance*, Cambridge: Harvard University Press, 1979.

Viscusi, W. Kip (1989), "Prospective Reference Theory: Toward an Explanation of the Paradoxes," *The Journal of Risk and Uncertainty* 2(3): 235-264.

Viscusi, W. Kip (1992a), *Fatal Tradeoffs: Public and Private Responsibilities for Risk*, New York: Oxford University Press.

Viscusi, W. Kip (1992b), *Smoking: Making the Risky Decision*, New York: Oxford University Press.

Viscusi, W. Kip (1993), "The Value of Risks to Life and Health," *Journal of Economic Literature* XXXI(4): 1912-1946.

Viscusi, W. Kip and William Evans (1990), "Utility Functions that Depend on Health Status: Estimates and Economic Implications," *American Economic Review* 80(3): 353-374.

Viscusi, W. Kip and Wesley A. Magat (1987), *Learning About Risk: Consumer and Worker Responses to Hazard Information*, Cambridge: Harvard University Press, 1987.

Viscusi, W. Kip and Wesley A. Magat (1992), "Bayesian Decisions with Ambiguous Belief Aversion," *Journal of Risk and Uncertainty* 5(4): 371-387.

Viscusi, W. Kip, Wesley A. Magat, and Anne Forrest (1988), "Altruistic and Private Valuations of Risk Reduction," *Journal of Policy Analysis and Management* 7(2): 227-245.

Viscusi, W. Kip, Wesley A. Magat, and Joel Huber (1987), "An Investigation of the Rationality of Consumer Valuations of Multiple Health Risks," *Rand Journal of Economics* 18(4): 465-479.

Viscusi, W. Kip, Wesley A. Magat, and Joel Huber (1991), "Pricing Environmental Health Risks: Survey Assessments of Risk-Risk and Risk-Dollar Tradeoffs for Chronic Bronchitis," *Journal of Environmental Economics and Management* 21(1): 32-51.

Viscusi, W. Kip, and Charles O'Connor (1984), "Adaptive Responses to Chemical Labeling : Are Workers Bayesian Decision Makers?" *American Economic Review* 74(5): 942-956.

5

CONSTRUCTING MEASURES OF ECONOMIC VALUE

Raymond J. Kopp and
V. Kerry Smith

INTRODUCTION

Few principles are more central to economic analysis than the sovereignty of consumer choice. Nonetheless economists' acceptance of consumer choice has sometimes been suspended. The most recent example of this response to choices that does not adhere to simple economic models concerns peoples' decisions involving environmental and natural resources elicited with contingent valuation (CV) surveys.[1] Ignoring consumer sovereignty in these situations has been explained as necessary because the underlying choices are inconsistent with rational behavior.[2] This argument overstates the power of economic theory to explain choices. Tests of the internal consistency of choices require auxiliary assumptions in addition to the simple axioms underlying revealed preference theory to formulate empirical hypotheses. As a consequence, these consistency tests actually evaluate composite hypotheses (the internal consistency condition plus the relevant auxiliary assumptions). Behavior judged as inconsistent based on an internal consistency condition could also arise from a violation in one or more of the required additional assumptions for the test. For example, testing internal consistency of choices using a subset of the commodities a household consumes requires that one assume separability of preferences.[3]

This argument is not new. Moreover, it is not intended to suggest that virtually any type of choice behavior can be considered rational.[4] Rather our objective is to recognize that there are limits to the properties that can be expected to be displayed in choices alone.

The purpose of this paper is to consider efforts to evaluate the consistency of choices and the implications they have for measures of economic value derived from choice. The next section outlines the general approaches used in measuring economic values and how they relate to individual choice. It also relates these arguments about choices to contingent valuation and the measurement of economic values for non-marketed environmental resources. Following that discussion, we examine two tests for internal consistency based on willingness to pay (WTP) functions that have been proposed for evaluating contingent valuation (CV) estimates.[5] Our analyses suggest that specific properties of WTP functions require additional assumptions beyond rational choice. The third section summarizes the evidence from two scope tests. The last section discusses a paradox that arises in imposing internal consistency requirements imposed on CV choices as an exclusive criteria for evaluating the method's reliability.

CHOICE AND ECONOMIC VALUE

Background

Traditional analysis of consumer behavior begins with a specification of a preference relation. That relation, along with the budget constraint, is used to describe consumer choices. Our reason for reconsidering the *choice function to preferences* approach follows from a desire to use the vocabulary of revealed preference analysis in understanding the assumptions implicit in the economic models used for valuation.

Consider the following vocabulary that describes the *elements* of a choice. They are the *object of choice* and the *circumstances of choice.* An object of choice can be anything. We do not have to be able to specify units of measurement to have an object of choice that is consistent with the conventional theory underlying the definition of economic values. The object of choice can be associated with a straightforward quantity measure, such as an apple or a loaf of bread. Alternatively, it can be something difficult to quantitatively measure, for example, a medical treatment to cure a chronic disease. It can be intangible like enjoying a scenic vista or knowing that the habitat for a rare species will be preserved. What is important to recognize is that economically relevant objects of choice do *not* have to be specified in neatly divisible units.

The circumstances of choice relate to all the factors that describe the assignment of rights, timing, degree of certainty, and consequences of a choice. To interpret choices so that economic values can be derived from them, a clearly defined object of choice must be specified *and*, preferably one consequence that results from a decision about that object. In the simple case, the choice implies the object is at least as good (or as valuable) as what was given up. When a choice is made, the consequence related to the most important foregone alternative defines a lower bound for the economic value of the object selected.

Conventional Valuation Concepts and Measurement Methods

The comparison envisioned in our discussion of choice is readily described using an indirect utility function, v(.), expressed in equation (1) as a function of individual income, m, the prices of marketed goods, P, and a vector of non-marketed environmental resources, S. When an individual is offered the opportunity to obtain a change in S, say dS, (the object of choice), in exchange for a one-time payment of the amount w (the alternative foregone), the choice is assumed to be based on the comparison given in equation (1).

$$v(m - w, P, S + dS) \gtreqless v(m, P, S) \qquad (1)$$

The economic value of dS is defined by the maximum willingness to pay and is realized by solving (1) for the value of w, say w*, that would lead the individual to be indifferent between (a) obtaining the object of choice, dS, and foregoing w, or (b) remaining with the status quo.

Early discussions of the issues associated with measuring w* emphasized the inability to recover full information about v(.) from income constrained choices. This led to a focus on the importance of income effects for the distinctions between Marshallian and Hicksian measures of the economic value of dS.[6] Unfortunately, this literature reduced the attention given to substitution effects. To illustrate how the general concept of substitution bears on current discussions of measures of w*, we will adopt a quasi-linear specification for the indirect utility function (i.e., v(.) = m + h(S)) and thereby assume that income effects are unimportant.[7] In this context, w* for dS is defined by equation (2).

$$w* = h(S + dS) - h(S) \qquad (2)$$

It is clear from (2) that, ignoring income effects, w*'s response to changes in the size of dS depend on both the level of S and the size of dS. There is something else in equation (2) that is implicit in the definition of a metric for S. By defining a way to continuously measure S, as well as the changes in it (i.e., the dS), the analysis implicitly assumes these increments provide a resource that is a perfect substitute for what we already have. If this were not the case, then the new level of S could not be written as S+dS. In practice, the actual task of measuring w* is more complex because we do not know the metric that should be used for S. Moreover, we don't observe choices that are as simple as the choice used to define WTP in equation (1).

To illustrate the importance of the perfect substitution relationship between S and dS, consider a simple characterization of the information conveyed by each of the three nonmarket valuation techniques: (1) travel cost demand; (2) hedonic property value; and (3) contingent valuation models. The development used to describe each method relies on a variation of the quasi-linear model we used to specify w* above. For the first of these models, associated with a travel cost demand framework, assume that S is a resource contributing to an individual's well-being. In addition, assume that there are different levels of quality for S available to each individual denoted by s. In general, S and s would not be perfect substitutes (i.e., additive) in their contributions to individual well-being.

This description is broadly compatible with several different forms of the travel cost model, including one that envisions consumer choice as recreationists adjusting the location and number of trips they take in response to differences in site quality.[8] Thus, if t designates the travel cost per trip and V(s) the number of trips to obtain a quality level, s, then the choice of trips to sites to acquire's can be represented as maximizing (3) with respect to s.

$$v(m,\ P,\ S,\ s) = m - t \cdot V(s) + h(S,\ s) \tag{3}$$

This implies the imputed price of a trip, at the margin, will equal the economic value of quality derived per trip as in equation (4).

$$t = \frac{h_2}{V_s}, \quad where: \ h_2 = \frac{\partial h}{\partial s} \tag{4}$$

In other words, the measure of economic value we derive from these choices requires both a specification of how s enters preferences (in relation to the other aspects of a recreation site's contribution to individual well-being) and assumptions that link s and trips to a recreation site. These are maintained assumptions that form the basis for the travel cost demand model's interpretation of recreation behavior. They are also conditions embodied in the measures of economic value developed from those choices. Thus, our measure of the value of the marginal trip, assumed observable through the imputed price, t, also reveals the value of quality. This conclusion follows from the model's assumptions. Trips and quality are linked through the V(s) function. Moreover, the model "tells a story" of recreationists adjusting the sites they visit until the desired quality is matched to what they can afford to pay. This substitution process is what allows t to "reveal" the marginal value of the quality conveyed by the marginal trip.

Consider now a second example using the hedonic property value model. This framework imposes a similar, but slightly different structure on the interpretation of choices. In a hedonic model, one would replace the product of t and V(s) by a price function r(S), that is assumed to describe a market equilibrium. For example, housing prices are assumed to be a function of the characteristics of the house and of its location.[9] In this case, there are many different assumptions that could be used. We could, for example, interpret S, as the characteristics of each location, such as the level of air quality, and s as policies to control emissions or more directly change air quality. Under these assumptions, we would redefine the indirect utility function as in equation (5):

$$v(m - r\,,\, P,\, S,\, s) = m - r(S) + h(S,\, s) \tag{5}$$

Within this framework, a person is assumed to maximize v(.) with respect to S through the process of selecting a housing location. These decisions provide information about how the S at each location contributes to well-being. In this model, people are assumed to know how S changes with location. If we now want to evaluate a policy that is intended to change that distribution of values for S there are no assurances that people will interpret the policy as equivalent to a changed level for S. For example, policies intended to control mobile sources of air pollution through vehicle inspections do not guarantee a change in the distribution implied by S. These could be defined as changing an argument, s, that is perceived by people as a substitute for S. In this situation, then, we do *not* learn about an individual's incremental value of the proposed policy from the hedonic price function. To do so requires some assumption about the relationship (e.g., degree of substitution) between S and s. This is illustrated by the marginal condition for a maximum as given in equation (6).

$$r_s = h_1(S,\, s) \quad where\ h_1 = \frac{\partial h}{\partial S} \tag{6}$$

The slope of the hedonic price function (under ideal conditions) measures the incremental value for changes in the site attribute. This could be air quality, but it does not assure that the price function provides information about the incremental value of what can be influenced by the policy (i.e. in this case - s).

Finally, for the third example, we come to contingent valuation. Most current applications have changed the framing of choice questions from the use of "hypothetical" changes in environmental resources to provide more context for how the proposed change would occur. This change involves the use of a "plan or program" as the source of a proposed change in the environmental resource. This strategy encourages respondents to interpret the CV choice as comparable to an actual choice. There is an important by-product of this approach. The framing combines the resource change that analysts seek to evaluate (i.e., the ds) with the plan for accomplishing the change. Thus, the role for S and s in an individual's preference relation closely parallels the distinction argued to be part of interpreting the hedonic model. An important difference is that CV choice questions describe both S and s, but usually offers changes in s. The choice reveals information about the value attached to a change in just s. However, often the desired focus of the estimates is only estimating a value for a change in S.

To illustrate how this distinction can make a difference to CV estimates, consider the expression for the WTP for a program proposing to change S from an initial to a final level. It is conveyed as providing an imperfect substitute for a larger S and thus would be represented in our model by a change in s. This strategy can be found in the Alaska study (see Carson et al. [1995]). Survey respondents were offered a program to protect Prince William Sound against injuries arising from *future* spills, not an opportunity to do away with the injuries arising from the actual Exxon Valdez spill. In the expression for w*, the change from s_o to s_1 is distinguished from the actual level or from a change in the level of S.

$$w* = h(S, s_1) - h(S, s_0) \tag{7}$$

Note the level for S can correspond to anything. S could be a measure of the total resource available and s to be increments in that level. What is important to our argument is the assumption that S is not automatically displaced by the amount, $s_1 - s_0$, from the respondent's perspective. Respondents' perceptions of the CV plan's effectiveness will influence the relationship between S and s. Indeed, in most situations, a realistic description of some method to alter the resource will itself introduce a difference between S and s. In the Carson et. al [1995] example of natural resource damages due to the Exxon Valdez oil spill, background information about the program described the likelihood of a spill over the time horizon relevant for the plan as approximately one. In this case, the object of choice in the CV question and the resources' injuries to be valued are different.

There are several common themes that connect our arguments about interpreting the results from these three methods for measuring economic values. First, all measures of economic value require that the full circumstances of the choice and the intended object of choice be reconstructed in order to interpret the valuation information inherent in the observed or stated choice. In the travel cost model, for example, this process required specifying a continuous measure for the aspect of environmental quality (e.g., water quality) to be valued; relating that measure to something the analyst can observe recreationists doing, such as going to different recreation sites a different number of times; and assuming the process of substituting among alternative sites at different locations (travel costs) leads to an "ideal", incremental allocation of time and monetary resources. Because contingent valuation controls these circumstances of choice, most of the discussion of reliability issues has focused on how these circumstances influence CV estimates.

Second, the metric used for measuring the object of choice is more important to the indirect methods (e.g., travel cost, hedonic, and averting behavior) than for CV. For the most part, the indirect models rely on continuous adjustment so that they must interpret choices as providing measures of marginal values.[10] To use them in efforts to measure the economic value of a change in an environmental resource requires a well-defined metric for the quantity of the resource (object of choice). This requirement contrasts with what is provided by CV estimates.

Finally, to increase respondents' belief in the situation that is described to them, current CV practice describes the manner in which the object would be delivered. Thus, the object of choice for a CV survey is a plan or program to change the resource. A key focus in the framing of a CV question involves isolating characteristics of a plan that might provide separate reasons for being in favor (or opposed) to it. While the ability to evaluate these elements in qualitative and quantitative terms is unique to CV, it is important to acknowledge that a comparable set of assumptions is made implicitly with the indirect methods when analysts assume a connection between what can be observed and what is valued. Our specification of the h(.) function with different arguments was a simple way of illustrating how these assumptions impact the conclusions drawn from these methods.

GAUGING THE RELIABILITY OF MEASURES FOR ECONOMIC VALUE

While the reliability of measures of economic value derived from travel cost and hedonic models have been debated in the literature, the primary focus of current discussions of reliability (and internal consistency of choices) has focused on CV. Natural resource damage litigation heightened the interest in the reliability of CV. The prospect of large damage cases led the National Oceanic and Atmospheric Administration (NOAA) to convene an expert panel co-chaired by Kenneth Arrow and Robert Solow to critically evaluate the reliability of CV.[11]

One of the important conclusions of the Arrow-Solow panel was a suggested test for the internal consistency of CV choices based on available economic theory. The panel observed:

> Rationality in its weakest form requires certain kinds of consistency among choices made by individuals. . . . Usually, though not always, it is reasonable to suppose that more of something regarded as good is better so long as an individual is not satiated. This is, in general, translated into a willingness to pay somewhat more for more of a good, as judged by the individual. Also, if marginal or incremental willingness to pay for additional amounts does decline with the amount already available, it is usually not reasonable to assume that it declines very abruptly. (Arrow et. al. [1993] p. 4604)

The panel then stated:

> Until such time as there is a set of reliable reference surveys, the burden of proof of reliability must rest on the survey designers. They must show

> through pretesting or other experiments that their survey does not suffer from the problems that these guidelines are intended to avoid. Specifically, if a CV survey suffered from any of the following maladies, we would judge its findings "unreliable".

One of the specified maladies was described as "Inadequate responsiveness to the scope of the environmental insult." This requirement has since been described as a *scope* test. The *scope* test requires that WTP estimates derived from CV surveys should be related to the "size" of the object of choice.

Recently Diamond [1994, 1995] and Diamond and Hausman [1994] have argued that more stringent conditions should be used in assessing the reliability of CV estimates. Diamond's scope test considers a situation where there is a level of an environmental resource (e.g., a population of some species) and the WTP is for a plan to avoid losses to that resource. In this case, with a quasi-linear utility specification, he derives an in equality for evaluating the relative size of the WTPs for different sized losses (say s and $\bar{s}$, as shown in equation (8)).

$$w^*(s) > \left(\frac{s}{\bar{s}}\right) w^*(\bar{s}) \quad \textbf{(8)}$$

A second consistency condition is also due to Diamond, Hausman, Leonard and Denning [1993]. It has been referred to as an adding-up test. To develop the test each change, such as dS from equation (2), would be partitioned into two (or more) parts with $dS = dS_1 + dS_2$. The test is based on the argument that the sum of the WTP's for each part should equal the WTP for the whole change. Equations (9a) through (9d) illustrate the logic with our quasi-linear specification:

$$w^*(dS_1) = h(S_0+dS_1) - h(S_0) \quad \textbf{(9a)}$$

$$w^*(dS_2|dS_1) = h(S_0+dS_1+dS_2) - h(S_0+dS_1) \quad \textbf{(9b)}$$

$$w^*(dS_1+dS_2) = h(S_0+dS_1+dS_2) - h(S_0) \quad \textbf{(9c)}$$

$$w^*(dS_1)+w(dS_2|dS_1) = h(S_0+dS_1)-h(S_0)+h(S_0+dS_1+dS_2)-h(S_0+dS_1) \quad \textbf{(9d)}$$

The first and the last terms on the right side of equation (9d) cancel. Thus, comparing equation (9d) to (9c) illustrates how the adding-up result can be derived for preferences without income effects. Diamond also suggests that, for conventional specifications of individual preferences (i.e., without the assumption of quasi-linearity), the income effects will be small:
With a WTP on the order of $30, a household income level of $30,000, and income elasticity of WTP of one, the deviation from strict adding-up would be $0.03.[12]

TABLE 1:COMPARISON OF SCOPE, ADDING-UP AND CALIBRATION CONDITONS WITH VARYING DEGREES SUBSTITUTION

$\sigma^{b} = \frac{1}{(1-\alpha)}$	$\frac{w^{*}(s)}{w^{*}(\bar{s})}$	$\frac{w^{*}(s_1+s_2)}{w^{*}(s_1)+w^{*}(s_2)}$	$\frac{w^{*\prime}(S)}{w^{*\prime}(s)}$
100.0	95.5	.99	.97
25.0	83.1	.98	.87
5.0	39.5	.89	.51
2.0	9.2	.72	.18
1.5	3.5	.61	.10
1.2	1.2	.51	.06

The computations in this table are based on a variation to Desvousges et. al. [1992] bird example using S = 3 million, s = 100,000 and $\bar{s}$= 1,000. The overall conclusions are not sensitive to these parameters and the sensitively of scope, adding-up, and marginal conditions to the assumed substitution can be confirmed over a wide range of values for S and s. [b] σ is the elasticity of substitution between S and s.

It is not necessary to consider the role of income in questioning the implications of these auxiliary assumptions maintained by these two tests. Once we introduce the role of a plan to change the resource -- whether avoiding losses or improving the overall condition of a resource, the arguments we developed in the previous section for comparing travel cost, hedonic, and CV methods become relevant for these internal consistency tests. To illustrate, consider one specific form of the quasi-linear preferences that has been used by Smith and Osborne [1995] to evaluate scope and adding-up tests. Let $h(S,s)=(S^{\alpha}- s^{\alpha})^{1/\alpha}$. In this case, the parameter, α, controls the elasticity of substitution between what the plan describes as losses (s) that will be avoided and how a potential respondent interprets the relationship of those losses to the original resource (S).

Diamond's scope relationship is now an exact multiple, given in equation (10), and the relationship between w*(s) and w*($\bar{s}$) depends on the degree to which the plan, for avoiding losses provides a perfect substitute for original resource.

$$w^*(s) = \frac{S-(S^{\alpha}-s^{\alpha})^{1/\alpha}}{S-(S^{\alpha}-\bar{s}^{\alpha})} \cdot w(\bar{s}) \qquad \textbf{(10)}$$

The second column in Table 1 illustrates how important the prospects for substitution can be to Diamond's proposed bound. His bound is relevant for the case of high levels of substitution (i.e., $\sigma = 100$), but it has no power to gauge reliability when the elasticity is between one and two.

$$w^*(s_1+s_2) = S-[S^{\alpha}-(s_1+s_2)^{\alpha}]^{1/\alpha} \qquad \textbf{(11c)}$$

$$w^*(s_2) = (S-s_1) - [(S-s_1)^{\alpha}-s_2^{\alpha}]^{1/\alpha} \qquad \textbf{(11a)}$$

$$w^*(s_1) = S-[S^{\alpha}-s_1^{\alpha}]^{1/\alpha} \qquad \textbf{(11b)}$$

The adding-up condition faces a comparable outcome, once imperfect substitution is admitted. In this case, the equivalent of the equations (9a), (9b) and (9c) would be given as equations (11a) through (11c). The third column in Table 1 considers the ratio $w^*(s_1+s_2)$ relative to $w^*(s_1) + w^*(s_2)$. Once again the larger the substitution between S and s, as provided by the plan to avoid changes in S, the closer the adding up condition comes to being strictly satisfied. However, as this substitution declines to a σ between 1 and 2, use of the adding-up condition is unlikely to offer a credible gauge of reliability.[13]

Finally, it is important to recognize that these limitations are not unique to evaluating the internal consistency of CV based estimates. If we return to the hedonic framework and our discussion of the potential for differences in location specific levels of environmental quality that contribute to housing prices (and the measurements of marginal WTP based on these price functions) versus estimates of the marginal value of avoiding deteriorations in these conditions, the same types of arguments would apply. That is, if we assume a plan to avoid the deterioration plays a role comparable to the distinction between S and s in our analysis of the scope and adding up conditions, then the question posed for hedonic models is the relationship between the marginal value that is measured for the level of site-specific amenities (S) versus what we would like to measure for the program intended to avoid proposed deteriorations in those amenities (s). The difference between these measures will also depend on σ, as illustrated by the ratio of the absolute value of the marginal willingness to pay calculated for a change in S relative to s and given in the fourth column of Table 1. These ratios are evaluated at S = 3,000,000 and s = 100,000. As in the case of the scope and adding-up conditions, the behavior of this ratio depends on σ and is relatively insensitive to the assumptions we make about the specific values of S and s. Our results suggest that strict adherence to the scope and adding-up conditions (of the Diamond *et al*, type) as internal consistency tests for CV estimates is inappropriate, even in cases where we ignore income effects.

TWO EXAMPLES OF SCOPE TESTS

In what follows, we present the results of two different types of scope tests. One indicates that WP is responsive to the scope (or size) of the object of choice, as perceived by respondents. The second provides suggestive evidence, but would not be regarded as definitive. As a result, it illustrates the difficulty in evaluating how subtle differences in an environmental resource will be understood by people comprising a survey. These studies are reviewed to illustrate the general points developed in the previous section. We have not attempted to include a review and evaluation of other research that could be used in judging the overall evidence on responsiveness of CV estimates to scope. Equally important, we have not considered tests of the Diamond adding-up condition.[14]

Using Visual Perceptions of Marine Debris for a Scope Test

A crude scope test can be developed from an effort attempting to estimate and distinguish the use and nonuse values for marine debris. This study was undertaken by Smith, Zhang, and Palmquist [1995]. It included a complex design that varied the type of resource, payment mechanism, and location of the population being sampled. The study had an overly ambitious design that limited the sample available for a scope test. We selected one aspect of their study, whether respondents interpreted differences in the debris represented using four sets of two color photographs of beach conditions in the same area (Mustang Island, Texas) as distinctive amounts of impairment to beaches.[15] To evaluate scope effects, we must consider whether their choices for a plan to clean up debris imply WTP estimates that would vary consistently with the size of the impairments depicted with debris.

The questionnaire design was derived from limited preliminary research -- three focus groups and a modest pretest. A telephone-mail-telephone survey format was used. This approach involves using a random digit dialed sample for areas surrounding New Jersey beaches and a comparable sample for North Carolina beaches. Each respondent was first interviewed to request their participation in a second stage interview concerned with controlling marine debris. Before asking for a respondent's co-operation, information about that person's attitudes and demographic characteristics was collected. During a ten to fourteen day period between the two interviews, an eight-page information booklet, along with one of eight sets of color photographs, were sent to each participating individual. Our analysis focuses on the questions that involved an annual income tax surcharge for programs to control marine debris along beaches in North Carolina (for the North Carolina subsample) and in New Jersey (for the New Jersey sub-sample).

TABLE 2 : CROSS TABULATIONS FOR CHOICE PLANS TO CONTROL MARINE DEBRIS

	Photo of Debris Conditions			
Sample	A	B	C	D
Full Sample		$\chi^2_{(3)}$=3.38		(p-value=.337)
Not for Control Plan	63 (56.8)	47 (58.8)	60 (60.0)	47 (70.2)
For Plan	48 (43.2)	33 (41.2)	40 (40.0)	20 (29.8)
North Carolina Sample		$\chi^2_{(3)}$=0.22		(p-value=.975)
Not for Control Plan	41 (62.1)	26 (59.1)	34 (63.0)	21 (63.6)
For Plan	25 (37.9)	18 (40.9)	20 (37.0)	12 (36.4)
New Jersey Sample		$\chi^2_{(3)}$=6.32		(p-value=.097)

TABLE 2 : CROSS TABULATIONS FOR CHOICE PLANS TO CONTROL MARINE DEBRIS				
		Photo of Debris Conditions		
Sample	A	B	C	D
Not for Control Plan	22 (48.9)	21 (58.3)	26 (56.5)	26 (76.5)
For Plan	23 (51.1)	15 (41.7)	20 (43.5)	8 (23.5)

Source: Smith, Zhang, and Palmquist [1995]

The response rates for this survey are much lower than with the Carson et. al. analysis. The Phase I survey realized a 52.6% response rate, interviewing 1,773 respondents. 58.9% of these people were re-interviewed in the second stage sample for a combined response rate of about 39.1%.[16] Table 2 presents three approaches for testing the effects of differences in the amount of debris presented in photos describing the conditions proposed to characterize beaches in North Carolina and New Jersey without a debris cleanup program. The first test computes a cross-tabulation of the responses receiving the annual tax for each of the four photos reporting those not for and those for a program to control and cleanup debris (the specific text of the question is in Appendix A). There is not a significant difference in the decisions for and against the plan with the photos used to describe baseline conditions. Sub-sampling to distinguish the North Carolina and New Jersey samples, based on the argument that the later group may have had more experience with conditions similar to the photos, does indicate that there may well be differences with the photo used to describe the baseline conditions.

However, there are also a number of other factors changing in the responses presented in these four columns. The most important of these is the different tax amounts assigned to respondents. Because this process was random, we would expect an approximately uniform distribution of values across the four sub-samples. We expect that the tax amount should have the same directional effect on choice regardless of the photo received. As a result, one way to control for the effects of tax amount while testing for the effect of debris conditions is the Cochran-Mantel-Haenszel statistic (see Snedecor and Cochran [1980]). In this case, using the general association alternative hypothesis, the χ^2 statistics (with 3 degrees of freedom) was 6.577. This has a p-value of .087, implying that at the 10 percent level we would conclude there were differences in the effects of the debris conditions. This conclusion is reinforced if we selected the most extreme photos (i.e. A and D). Using the simple chi square test, the choices in this case would have been judged significantly different at a .075 p-value (without taking account of amount of charge). The New Jersey sample would also have rejected the null hypothesis at a .013 p-value.

Nonetheless, the survey does provide evidence of a scope response when the choices for those receiving the photo depicting the most serious example of debris are compared with the least serious (i.e., a scene with only kelp or natural debris on the beach). Given the limited sample size and the prospect for a selection effect, this comparison was developed using a Weibull survival function that included an inverse Mills ratio as an adjustment for selection effects (based on a probit model estimated from the demographic information of respondents to the Phase I survey). These results are reported in Table 3. Two estimated functions are reported - one that treats the errors in the survival model as homoscedastic and a second that specifies a multiplicative heteroscedastic model related to the inverse Mills ratio.[17] Our overall conclusion is not altered by this adjustment, but the significance of the test for differences in the photos is reduced.

TABLE 3: WTP FOR CONTROLLING MARINE DEBRIS: A SURVIVAL MODEL

		Weibull Survival Models	
	Estimated Median[b]	Homoscedastic	Heteroscedastic
Intercept		9.38 (6.11)	12.60 (5.97)
Photo A	$72.18 [34.20-152.32]	1.35 (2.31)	1.02 (1.87)
Photo B	$40.97 [11.72-143.23]	.64 (1.02)	.38 (0.65)
Photo C	$63.21 [29.63-139.83]	.80 (1.37)	.66 (1.21)
Photo D	$21.38 [5.71-80.02]	-	-
Inverse Mills Ratio[c]		-12.83 (-3.47)	-20.58 (-3.87)
Pseudo R^2	-	0.075	-
log (L)	-	-193.43	-189.76
n	-	348	348

TABLE 3: WTP FOR CONTROLLING MARINE DEBRIS: A SURVIVAL MODEL			
Weibull Survival Models			
	Estimated Median[b]	Homoscedastic	Heteroscedastic
<u>ln(σ)</u> α_0	-	.96 (7.18)	-.82 (-1.12)
Inverse Mills Ratio (IMR)	-	-	4.21 (2.36)

The numbers in parentheses below the estimated parameters for the homoscedastic and heteroscedastic survival functions are the ratios of the coefficients to their estimated asymptotic standard errors.

These estimated medians are derived from models treating each photo as a separate sub-sample, including only the inverse Mills ratio to adjust for selection effects. With the subsample for Photo A, the model rejected the null hypothesis of homoscedasticity. With all other sub-samples, this hypothesis was not rejected. The specific models to derive these results are given as follows:

In the first column, we report the estimated median WTP from separate Weibull models applied to each sample individually. As the table indicates, these estimates display wide confidence intervals. Nonetheless, the overall ordering of the point estimates is consistent with our test results.

Overall, these results offer suggestive evidence that a larger, more focused survey would be likely to yield WTP estimates exhibiting responses to scope. At the same time, they highlight the difficulties posed (with limited research budgets) in evaluating how people's choices are affected by subtle changes in the characteristics of complex, multi-dimensional environmental resources.

Using Meta Analysis for a Scope Test

The second example of a scope test illustrates a case involving scenic views in national parks. There has been a substantive research record indicating that changes in the distance associated with visible range provide a reasonably good approximation to describe how people perceive visibility changes (see Stewart, Middleton and Ely [1983] and Stewart, Middleton, Downton, and Ely [1984]). To exploit this consistent link between perceptions and the visible range, Smith and

Osborne [1995] selected five contingent valuation studies of visibility and the scenic vistas using photos to describe the visibility changes at specific national parks.

They composed a sample consisting of the estimates of WTP for visibility change based on the original estimates from each study. Each observation in their summary is a sample mean, computed over a subset of each total sample, with the subset defined by the proposed visibility change or another design feature of each study. The estimates were converted to monthly payments and expressed in 1990 dollars (using the Consumer Price Index).

Table 4 reports three models from the Smith-Osborne summary. Equations (1) and (2) in the table report their results with semi-log models expressing the log of WTP as a function of the proportionate change in the miles of visibility, a measure distinguishing visibility's effects on Eastern versus Western parks and a variety of qualitative variables describing how each survey in their sample, was implemented.[18] Equation (3) drops the observations associated with visibility changes at Eastern park sites. The key result from the perspective of testing scope effects is the statistically significant, positive, coefficient for the measure used to describe the amount of the "commodity" serving as the object of choice. As all the equations indicate, this finding is not impacted by including other variables taking account of the question format. Inclusion of use related attributes of the interview variables to account for the format of survey questions, or dropping the observations associated with visibility at Eastern park sites do not change this basic conclusion.

TABLE 4: SMITH-OSBORNE TEST OF SCOPE EFFECTS IN WTP FOR VISIBILITY

Independent Variables	Mean Values		Models	
		(1)	(2)	(3)
Intercept		0.916 (4.31)	1.326 (5.67)	0.919 (4.41)
Proportionate change in visibility[b]	.709	1.127 (2.39)	1.127 (2.41)	1.112 (2.30)
East*proportionate change in visibility	.156[c]	-0.843 (-2.57)	-0.814 (-2.52)	-
Iterative bidding (=1)	.052	-	0.116 (0.76)	0.571 (1.85)

TABLE 4: SMITH-OSBORNE TEST OF SCOPE EFFECTS IN WTP FOR VISIBILITY				
Independent Variables	Mean Values		Models	
Direct question (=1)	.078	-4.206 (-20.37)	-4.616 (-14.42)	-4.196 (-19.92)
Direction of change (=1)	.302	1.335 (1.32)	.395 (1.74)	.402 (1.38)
Asked region (=1)	.661	-	-0.468 (-1.86)	-
Park interview (=1)	.096	-	-0.621 (-4.88)	-0.693 (-9.08)
Question framed for visibility change at revisit to site (=1)	.174	-0.849 (-1.87)	-1.041 (-2.14)	-0.558 (-1.64)
Entrance fee	.198	-	0.289 (5.36)	-
Sample composed of residents	.261	-	0.148 (1.00)	-
n R^2	-	115 0.703	115 0.7255	97 0.725

Numbers in parentheses are ratios of coefficients to Huber-White consistent variance estimates. This variable is scaled by 100 for these estimates so it is the proportionate change in the miles of visibility in absolute magnitude -- [revised - initial]/initial. Fraction of observations for visibility changes at eastern sites.

Thus, these results would suggest that in some cases, where there are relatively clear perceptions by respondents of differences in the "amount" of an environmental resource, responsiveness to scope can be detected with simple models. The models parallel the types used elsewhere in economics in that a simple measure of the amount of the change in the commodity that CV questions attempted to convey to respondents is positively related to willingness to pay.

IMPLICATIONS

There is an interesting paradox in some economists' negative reactions to using contingent valuation choices as a source of information about economic values. Economic values are constructed from people's choices. Economists interpret a person's choice together with information about what an individual has given up (or could have given up) to acquire the object of interest to define a lower bound for that object's economic value. The paradox posed by CV arises because it is the *only* method that offers the economist control over these circumstances of choice through the framing of CV questions. For all the other revealed preference or indirect methods, measures of economic values require the analyst to specify either what must have been the circumstances facing those individuals observed to make choices, or to make a series of simplifying assumptions that restrict the form specified to describe their preferences. In each of these cases, we have no direct basis for evaluating the appropriateness of these assumptions, yet they are central elements to the measures of economic values.

To date, the most stringent tests proposed to evaluate CV's reliability are efforts to impose the same types of prior restrictions required by revealed preference on the choices obtained from CV analyses. These restrictions are not requirements for rational choice, but instead are the conditions that have been essential to using the indirect methods to construct measures of economic values. Thus, the paradox arises when we impose restrictions on methods that don't require them, because these methods do not strictly conform to a set of prior beliefs that stem from adopting those restrictions because of incomplete information.

ENDNOTES

1 This has also been true of people's choices involving situations with uncertain outcomes. Economists have been reluctant to accepted uncritically choices involving lotteries. For example, Lucas [1986] argues that:

"Economics has tended to focus on situations in which the agent can be expected to 'know' or to have learned the consequences of different actions so that his observed choices reveal stable features of his underlying preferences. We use economic theory to calculate how certain variations in the situation are predicted to affect behavior, but these calculations obviously do not reflect or usefully model the adaptive process by which subjects have themselves arrived at the decision rules they use. Technically, I think of economics as studying decision rules that are steady states of some adaptive process, decision rules, that are found to work over a range of situations and hence are no longer revised appreciably as more experience accumulates" (p. S402).

His arguments have been used to explain violations in expected utility theory. See the Hogarth and Reder [1986] introduction in the same special issue for further discussion.

2 Diamond and Hausman [1994] conclude their critique of contingent valuation in very general terms, calling into question people's actual choices involving environmental resources. Indeed, their arguments bear a strong resemblance to the general line of argument developed by Lucas in commenting on people's behavior with *actual* lotteries. Diamond and Hausman state:

"It is impossible to conclude definitely that surveys with new methods for the latest survey that has been done) will not pass internal consistency tests. Yet, we do not see much hope for such success. This skepticism comes from the belief that *internal consistency problems come from an absence of preferences, not a flaw in survey methodology. That is, we do not think people hold views about individual environmental sites (many of which they have never heard of)* . . . This absence of preferences shows up as inconsistency in responses across surveys and implies the survey responses are not satisfactory bases for policy" (p. 63, emphasis added).

3 As Varian observed, there are limits to what can be inferred from tests of the implications of revealed preference, even within the simplified framework used to evaluate market choices. Indeed, in a capstone essay on this line of research, he observed that:

"The sad fact of the matter is that the restrictions imposed by the optimization hypothesis only apply when we have observed the entire choice set. Hence, the normal sorts of tests for consistency of observed choice must be interpreted instead as tests for separability of the observed choices from other variables in the utility function rather than test of maximization *per se*". (Varian [1988] pp 184).

4 Harrison [1990] developed a comparable line of argument in criticizing the experimental tests of the expected utility hypothesis.

5 These tests have been termed *scope* (see Arrow et al, 1993) and *adding-up,* see Diamond [1995].

6 See Freeman [1993] for a discussion of these relationships and Mohring [1971] and Morey [1984] for early and more recent reviews of the development of applied welfare economics.

7 Because a quasi-linear specification maintains a constant marginal utility of income, it is generally regarded as an unusual specification for preferences. Nonetheless, we adopt it here for three reasons: to isolate and focus on substitution effects; to simplify the analysis; and to be compatible with Diamond's [1995] discussion of scope tests.

8 To derive this indirect utility function, we start with direct utility function:

$$U = x + h(S,s)$$

and budget constraint $m = Px + t \cdot V(s)$

Let P = 1, then a "partial indirect utility, (e.g. one that does not describe how s is chosen) is given as:

$$V = m - t \cdot V(s) + h(S,s)$$

We use this result in equation (3) and a comparable derivation for the hedonic price function in equation (5).

This framework is comparable to what would be used in describing the varying parameter model for conventional travel cost demand models that allow for variations in site characteristics (see Smith and Desvousges [1986]) and to what is implied by the random utility model (see Bockstael, McConnell and Strand [1991]). In both cases, the analysis envisions an individual selects a "best" site for the recreational choice consistent with the time horizon of the model.

9 See Palmquist [1991] and Freeman [1993] for a review of the model.

10 The random utility model does not require this assumption. However, it does require some quantitative measure of the characteristics of distinctive recreation sites to estimate the probabilities individuals would select those sites.

11 See Portney [1994] for a description of the context for the NOAA Panel's activities. The Panel included: Kenneth Arrow, Robert Solow, Roy Radner, Edward Leamer, Paul Portney, and Howard Schuman.

12 Diamond [1995] p. 8.

13 See Carson [1995] for a review of the available research evaluating responsiveness to the scope of the directly or indirectly CV estimates of WTP's responsiveness to the scope of the environmental resource.

14 There are two reasons for this second omission. The first is straightforward. To our knowledge, there is only one test (Diamond, Hausman, Leonard, and Denning [1993]) and the questions used in that study did not explain the choices in ways that were consistent with the hypothesis being tested. As a result, it is difficult to know how to interpret its findings. Second, and equally important, the difficulties with this first implementation of the test highlight the general problems in using the test. Decomposing an object of choice into components requires that the circumstances of choice be as understandable and as plausible to respondents when they are described in parts as they are when the object of choice is treated as a whole. Otherwise, the test is confounded. Differences in the implementation change what is being evaluated.

15 The photos were made available to the authors by Professor Tony Amos of the University of Texas. They were selected based on focus group evaluations (see Smith et. al. [1995]).

16 The Phase I sample was completed September 18, 1992 and the Phase II interviewing finished by November 1992.

The allocation of the sample between New Jersey and North Carolina was designed to attempt to gauge the importance of users from outside each state. This was done by constructing RDD samples for New Jersey (577) and North Carolina (445) as stand alone entities. Additional observations were added from additional states based on records from the Public Area Recreation Visitors Surveys of beaches in the two states. A total of 880 respondents were interviewed in the Phase I survey of New Jersey and 893 for North Carolina. The distribution is given as follows:

<u>New Jersey Sample</u>	<u>Observation</u>	
New Jersey	577	
Philadelphia Area		151
New York City Area	102	
Delaware	50	
<u>North Carolina Sample</u>		
North Carolina		445
Eastern Virginia/Maryland		93
Midwestern States	179	
Pennsylvania and New Jersey	176	

17 The rationale for this strategy follows from White's [1982] development of the asymptotic properties of quasi-maximum likelihood estimators. Including the inverse Mills ratio in the estimated hazard model allows the model to take account of selection effects. While not theoretically consistent (with the different assumed distributions), it is an approximate method for controlling for these effects. We also use the model's ability to deal with multiplicative heteroscedasticity as a method to test for the importance of non-spherical errors that arise from estimates of the selection term.

18 Four variables describe the commodity, complementary resources, and descriptive information contained in the survey we hypothesized would influence respondents' interpretation of information presented in each CV survey. The first is the absolute value of the proportionate change in visible range offered (proportionate change in visibility). The second interacts this measure with a qualitative variable that identifies surveys involving Eastern sites. Some surveys posed CV questions to avoid a decline as compared with an improvement. These are identified as a "direction of change." The fourth identifies whether the change was offered for one park or the region.

The remaining variables in the model identify the question format (i.e., iterative bidding or direct question); the payment mechanism (i.e., as an entrance fee or not); the location of the interview (at park site or not); whether the respondent lived in the state or not (residents) and whether the question is framed as a visibility change for a re-visit to the site at a future time.

REFERENCES

Bishop, Richard C. and Thomas A. Heberlein, 1980. "Simulated Markets, Hypothetical Markets, and Travel Cost Analysis: Alternative Methods of Estimating Outdoor Recreation Demand" Working Paper No. 187, Department of Agricultural Economics, University of Wisconsin, Madison, December.

Bockstael, Nancy E., Kenneth E. McConnell, and Ivar Strand, 1991. "Recreation" in *Measuring the Demand for Environmental Commodities*, edited by J. Braden and C. Kolstad, (Amsterdam: North Holland), 227-270.

Carson, Richard T., 1995. "Contingent Valuation Surveys and Tests of Insensitivity to Scope," Department of Economics, University of California, San Diego, unpublished paper, January.

Carson, Richard T., Robert C. Mitchell, W. Michael Hanemann, Raymond J. Kopp, Stanley Presser and Paul A. Ruud, 1995, "Contingent Valuationn and Lost Passive Use: Damages from the Exxon Valdez." discussion paper. Quality of the Environment Division, Resources for the Future.

Carson, Richard T., Nicholas E. Flores, and W. Michael Hanemann, 1991. "On the Nature of Compensable Value in a Natural Resource Damage Assessment." Working paper. The American Economic Association meeting, New Orleans, LA, January.

Carson, Richard T., Jennifer Wright, Anna Alberini, Nancy Carson and Nicholas Flores, 1994. *A Bibliography of Contingent Valuation Studies and Papers*, Natural Resource Damage Assessment, Inc., La Jolla, Ca., March.

Carson, Richard T. and Robert Cameron Mitchell, 1995. "Sequencing and Nesting in Contingent Valuation Surveys," *Journal of Environmental Economics and Management* (in press).

Desvousges, William H., F. Reed Johnson, Richard W. Dunford, Kevin J. Boyle, Sara P. Hudson, K. Nicole Wilson, 1992. *Measuring Nonuse Damages Using Contingent Valuation: An Experimental Evaluation of Accuracy*, RTI Monograph 92-1 (Research Triangle Park, N.C.: Research Triangle Institute, June).

Diamond, Peter A., 1994. *Comments on the Proposed Rules for Natural Resource Damage Assessments: A Submission to the National Oceanic and Atmospheric Administration*, September 16.

Diamond, Peter, 1995. "Testing the Internal Consistency of Contingent Valuation Survey" unpublished paper, Dept. of Economics, Massachusetts Institute of Technology, January.

Diamond, Peter A., Jerry A. Hausman, Gregory K. Leonard and Mike A. Denning, 1993. "Does Contingent Valuation Measure Preferences? Experimental Evidence" in J.A. Hausman editor *Contingent Valuation: A Critical Assessment* (Amsterdam: North Holland).

Diamond, Peter A. and Jerry A. Hausman, 1994. "Contingent Valuation: Is Some Number Better Than No Number," *Journal of Economic Perspectives*, Vol. 8 (Fall): 45-64.

Freeman, A. Myrick III, 1993. *The Measurement of Environmental and Resource Values: Theory and Methods* (Washington, D.C.: Resources for the Future).

Hanemann, W. Michael, 1991. "Willingness to Pay and Willingness to Accept: How Much Can They Differ?" *American Economic Review Vol. 81 (June): 635-647.*

Harrison, Glenn, 1990. "Expected Utility Theory and the Experimentalists," Department of Economics, University of South Carolina, working paper, No. 90-04, September.

Hogarth, Robin M. and Melvin W. Reder, 1986. "Editors Comments: Perspectives from Economics and Psychology," *Journal of Business Special Supplement, The Behavioral Foundations of Economic Theory*, edited by R.M. Hogarth and M.W. Reder, Vol. 59 (October): PPS185-S208.

Kreps, David M., 1990. *A Course in Microeconomic Theory* (Princeton, N.J.: Princeton Univ. Press).

Lucas, Robert E. Jr., 1986. "Adaptive Behavior and Economic Theory" *Journal of Business Special Supplement, The Behavioral Foundations of Economic Theory*, edited by R.M. Hogarth and M.W. Reder, Vol. 59 (October): 5401-5426.

Mohring, Herbert, 1971. "Alternative Welfare Gain and Loss Measures," *Western Economic Journal* (December) 349-368.

Morey, Edward R., 1984. "Confuser Surplus," *American Economic Review*, Vol. 74 (March) 163-173.

NOAA Panel on Contingent Valuation, 1993. Report, Federal Register, Vol. 58, No. 10, January 15, 4602-4614.

Palmquist, Raymond B., 1991. "Hedonic Methods" in *Measuring the Demand for Environmental Quality*, edited by J. Braden and C. Kolstad (Amsterdam: North Holland): 7-120.

Portney, Paul R., 1994. "The Contingent Valuation Debate: Why Economists Should Care," *Journal of Economic Perspectives*, Vol. 8 (Fall): 3-18.

Samuelson, Paul A., 1938. "A Note on the Pure Theory of Consumer's Behavior," *Economica*, Vol. 5, 61-71.

Smith, V. Kerry and William H. Desvousges, 1986. *Measuring Water Quality Benefits* (Boston: Kluwer Nijhoff).

Smith, V. Kerry and Laura Osborne, 1995. "Do Contingent Valuation Estimates Pass a 'Scope' Test? A Meta Analysis." Center for Environmental and Resource Economics, Duke University, unpublished paper, revised, November.

Smith, V. Kerry, Xiaolong Zhang, and Raymond B. Palmquist, 1995. "The Economic Value of Controlling Marine Debris," in J. Coe and D. Rodgers, editors *Marine Debris* (New York: Springer Verlag, forthcoming).

Snedecor, G. W. and W. G. Cochran, 1980, *Statistical Methods*, 7th edition (Ames, Iowa: Iowa State University Press).

Stewart, T.K., P. Middleton, and D. Ely. 1983. "Judgments of Visual Air Quality: Reliability and Validity." *Journal of Environmental Management* 3: 129-145.

Stewart, T.K., P. Middleton, M. Downton, and D. Ely. 1984. "Judgments of Photographs Versus Field Observations in Studies of Perception and Judgment of the Visual Environment." *Journal of Environmental Psychology* 4: 283-302.

Varian, Hal R., 1988. "Revealed Preference With a Subset of Goods," *Journal of Economic Theory*, Vol. 46 (October): 179-185.

White, Halbert, 1982. "Maximum Likelihood Estimation of Mispecified Models" *Econometrica*, Vol. 50 (January):1-76.

6

CONTINGENT VALUATION SURVEYS AND TESTS OF INSENSITIVITY TO SCOPE

Richard T. Carson

INTRODUCTION

The central claim made by critics of contingent valuation (CV) is that respondents to a CV survey are inherently unresponsive to the characteristics of the good being valued.[1] In particular, it is alleged that respondents are not willing to pay more for more of a particular good; in economic jargon, respondents are insensitive to the scope of the good offered in the valuation exercise.[2] The focus of this debate is not whether CV results showing insensitivity to scope are obtainable, a point readily conceded by CV practitioners, but rather whether this result is generally avoidable with appropriate survey design, pretesting, and administration.

In the first section of the paper, I provide a historical sketch of the scope insensitivity debate. In particular, I discuss the claim of generic scope insensitivity in CV surveys and the evidence used to support this claim. I examine some of the tangential claims about respondents' behavior in CV surveys which can be seen to provide interpretations as to why the phenomenon of scope insensitivity may be observed. I also look at some of the subtle interplay between cognitive psychology and economics which underlies the scope insensitivity debate.

In the second section, I advance arguments and indirect evidence which suggest that the hypothesis that CV survey results will typically exhibit scope insensitivity is unlikely to be true. First, drawing upon the literature on surveys of public policy questions, I investigate whether there is evidence that respondents are insensitive to differences in the way policies are described. Next, turning to the CV literature, I argue that there are various ways in which scope insensitivity would likely be reflected if one looks across and within CV studies.

In the third section, I examine the formal CV tests of the scope insensitivity hypothesis which have been conducted using two or more independent samples. In contrast to assertions by Diamond and Hausman (1994) that few tests of scope insensitivity which use independent samples exist, other than those conducted by Exxon and Kahneman, I show that there are over 30 such tests which provide evidence on this point. Because some CV critics, such as Desvousges *et al.* (1993) draw a distinction between goods with principally direct use values and those with substantial passive use values, while others do not (Kahneman and Knetsch, 1992a), I address whether the results from this literature suggest that a distinction should be drawn.

SCOPE INSENSITIVITY: ORIGINS AND FREQUENTLY CITED EVIDENCE

The notion that CV survey results are likely to be insensitive to the scope of the good being valued originated with Kahneman (1986).[3] Kahneman argued (on the basis of a graph he presented) that respondents' willingness to pay (WTP) for cleaning-up all of the lakes in the Canadian Province of Ontario was not much larger than cleaning-up all of the lakes in Muskoka, a small part of the Province. He also offered an explanation for the phenomena: respondents were expressing ideological rather than economic values. Further, Kahneman argued that CV researchers had not observed the result because the experiments which varied the scope of the good being valued were with-in subject designs.

Kahneman's argument received considerable attention for four reasons. First, he claimed to have presented empirical evidence that CV results violate the simple economic maxim that people should be willing to pay more for more of something they want. Second, he provided an explanation for this occurrence which sounded, to many CV critics, like an argument that people were not really willing to pay the amount they stated. Third, he provided a simple explanation of why CV researchers had missed the scope insensitivity effect. Fourth, Kahneman was well respected in the research community and known for his interesting work on human behavior and response effects.

Contingent valuation researchers took the possibility of scope insensitivity seriously but attributed it to survey design and administration problems rather than to fundamental cognitive difficulties. Mitchell and Carson (1989) devoted considerable attention to different survey problems which might produce an apparent insensitivity to the characteristics of the good being valued.[4] They emphasized that respondents may confuse the good being valued with either a larger or smaller good (part-whole bias), that a poorly described good may be perceived as symbolic of a larger good (symbolic bias), that the researcher could be defining the good in a different metric than that used by respondents (metric bias), and that respondents might be skeptical that the good would actually be provided (probability of provision bias). In all of these cases, the solution was to present a more understandable description of the good and a more plausible provision context. Fischoff and Furby (1988) interpreted the problem similarly by emphasizing that respondents would tend to fill in any of the key aspects of the good or provision context not explicitly provided by the CV scenario.

Another problem, which can give the appearance of scope insensitivity, occurs when the researcher believes one good encompasses another, but respondents find the two goods offered indistinguishable. For example, suppose an ecosystem which provides habitat for five endangered species is at risk. As a scope test, the researcher informs one sample that the habitat will be purchased to protect the five species and then informs another sample that the habitat will be purchased to protect only two species.

Respondents in the second sample may reason that protecting the habitat will provide protection for all five species and are therefore paying for the same good as that offered to the first sample. Economists call this joint production. From a CV perspective, it is simply a case where the survey designer is either unaware of the problem (and therefore, a form of part-whole bias) or a case where respondents refuse to accept the clear counter-factual in formulating their response.[5]
As a rule, economists do not traffic in motives with this principal enshrined as respect for consumer sovereignty. As a result, Kahneman's notion of ideological values did not go very far on its own. Unexpected findings often result in a questioning of the adequacy of the assumed economic theory and provoke a search for alternative explanations.[6] Kahneman and Knetsch (1992a) interpret contingent valuation responses as follows: "Contingent valuation responses reflect the willingness to pay for the moral satisfaction of contributing to public goods, not the economic value of these goods." However, from an economic perspective, motives are of little importance as long as the agent would actually pay for the good rather than do without it.[7] The fact that the good is a public good further imposes an obligation on the government (or the survey designer) that people clearly understand what they are paying for. Insensitivity to scope suggests that one of these two conditions is being violated.

As a postscript on the origins of the scope insensitivity hypothesis, it is interesting to note that Kahneman and Knetsch (1992a) repeat the earlier Kahneman (1986) assertion:

> "A finding that we obtained some time ago illustrates the embedding effect: the expressed willingness of Toronto residents to pay increased taxes to prevent the drop in fish populations in all Ontario lakes was only slightly higher than the willingness to pay to preserve the fish stocks in only a small area of the province [Muskoka]."

This finding is now typically attributed to Kahneman and Knetsch (1992a), rather than Kahneman (1986), where it was actually introduced. The new results contained in Kahneman and Knetsch (1992a) which pertain to scope are inconsequential and have received little attention. However, the Ontario lakes example is cited throughout the recent benefit-cost literature (*e.g.*, Zerbe and Dively, 1994) and in the decision science literature (Kleindorfer, Kunreuther, and Schoemaker, 1993), both as a "fact" and as the most telling criticism of contingent valuation. What is unfortunate about this turn of events is that no statistical test of this claim was ever presented in either Kahneman (1986) or Kahneman and Knetsch (1992a). The graph in Kahneman (1986), however, can be used to obtain an approximate estimate of willingness to pay for all Ontario lakes and the Muskoka lakes. Performing this exercise shows that WTP for all Ontario lakes is 50% higher than for the Muskoka lakes. While it is possible to argue about what the magnitude of the difference should be, the difference is clearly not "only slightly higher," and experiments incapable of detecting a 50% difference seem pointless to conduct.

The actual story in Kahneman and Knetsch (1992a) is, for the most part, quite different from that of scope insensitivity, and instead, involves the sequence in which public goods are offered. Because this issue continues to caused a great deal of confusion, I now turn to it.

Economic theory behind the tests of sequence and scope

Kahneman's argument was quickly embraced by economists advocating industry's position with regard to the use of CV, as well as those generally opposed to benefit-cost analysis. However, many economists have been reluctant to accept Kahneman's story for two primary reasons. One reason is the *ad hoc* nature of Kahneman's story; more pointedly, his story is not based on a behavioral model but rather on an isolated explanation. For example, in his comment in *Valuing Environmental Goods* (Cummings, Brookshire, and Schulze, 1986), Kahneman draws the distinction between CV studies of use values and CV studies of passive use values. The former appear to be for economic values and the latter for ideological values. From a theoretical perspective, Kahneman's story is very much like Robert Louis Stevenson's Dr. Jekyll and Mr. Hyde. For goods with use values, agents exhibit all of the selfish virtues of *homo economicus*. However, for goods with substantial passive use values, agents are transformed from *homo economicus* into idealogues whose responses are suddenly stripped of any economic content.[8] Kahneman's story fails to provide any link between these two beasts. No appeal to any special or unusual conditions is necessary in order to offer an economic explanation for much of Kahneman's empirical evidence. The ability and willingness to grasp the economic story, however, is influenced by the filters through which one views the evidence. For the economist, the economic story does not offer a surprise ending. However, for the cognitive psychologist looking for evidence against economic theory, the story resembles a black comedy for which missing the ending comes as no great loss.

The recent articulation of the Kahneman critique in Kahneman and Knetsch (1992a) presents two lines of criticism. The first of which is not relevant to scope, but rather argues that economic values may be subject to a "regular embedding" effect.[9] Although the quality of the Kahneman and Knetsch study which provided the evidence in support of this criticism has been severely criticized (Smith, 1992), the claim is one with which Smith and most other economists would not disagree, as economic theory predicts this result.[10]

The second line of criticism is a repackaging of the ideological values criticism found in the Kahneman (1986) comment and is directly related to scope. The name is changed from ideological values to a catchier phrase, the "purchase of moral satisfaction." Kahneman and Knetsch use another term, "warm glow" borrowed from Andreoni (1990), to describe what they believe individuals actually gain when responding to contingent valuation surveys.[11] According to Kahneman and Knetsch, individuals are only basking in their warm glow and will pay basically the same for any good for which they are asked to value. That is to say, they are economically insensitive to the scope of the good they are asked to value.[12] In their reply to Smith, Kahneman and Knetsch refer to this phenomenon as "perfect embedding."

Predictions from economic theory: nested goods[13]

In this subsection, I look at valuing sequences of public goods and the theoretical structure of the tests involving sequencing and nesting of such goods. To help make the discussion more concrete, I define three different valuation sequences in Table I, each of which is to be given to a different but equivalent (in a statistical sense) subsample. The valuation sequences (and subsamples) are denoted I, II, and III. Three different goods are offered: **A**, **B**, and **C**. The order in which the goods are offered in the sequence is denoted by a subscript, 1, 2, or 3. It is important to note that economic theory says little about the relationship between the elements of the three valuation sequences without specifying more about the nature of the three goods including their relationships to each other. I will make two assumptions: (1) all of the goods being considered are normal goods, a reasonable assumption for most environmental goods, and (2) all goods in the set of interest are individually and in any group Hicksian substitutes for each other. This latter assumption, while frequently made, is probably less generally true than the former normality assumption. These two assumptions cause the income and substitution effects to work in the same direction in a WTP valuation sequence.[14]

TABLE I: STRUCTURE OF VALUATION SEQUENCES

Subsample I	Subsample II	Subsample III
A_I^1		
B_I^2	B_{II}^1	
C_I^3	C_{II}^2	C_{III}^1

Under these conditions, it can be shown that two external WTP tests of economic theory are possible: (1a) $\mathbf{B}_I^2 \le \mathbf{B}_{II}^1$ and (1b) $\mathbf{C}_I^3 \le \mathbf{C}_{II}^2 \le \mathbf{C}_{III}^1$. Tests of the hypotheses represented by equations (1a) and (1b) will be termed *embedding effect tests*, in that they look at the effect of embedding a good farther down in a specific valuation sequence. If we make the further assumption that the respondent will always get positive utility from possessing any of these goods regardless of whether the respondent already possesses any or all of the other goods at issue, the weak inequalities above can be replaced with strong inequalities. Economic theory does not say anything *a priori* about comparisons between different goods, e.g. $(\mathbf{B}_j^i, \mathbf{C}_j^i)$.

Nested goods, where ***B*** is a proper subset of ***A*** and ***C*** is a proper subset of ***B***, are a special case of conventional goods so that (1a) and (1b) hold if we make the same assumptions. To get the strong inequality in the nested goods case, one must assume for (1a) that respondents still get positive utility from **B** after they possess its complement **B*** and, for (1b), that respondents still get positive utility for **C** after they possess **C***. Testing a null hypothesis of equality in an embedding effect test is essentially testing for consistency with a flat utility function with respect to further increases in the good (*e.g.*, WTP(**B**), conditional on having **B***, is zero). Note that, although a flat utility function with respect to **B** (or **C**) conditional on possessing **B*** (**C***) might not be considered well behaved, it is not ruled out by economic theory assuming local nonsatiation does rule out such behavior.

The nesting property also allows predictions about other possible comparisons the first of which are internal tests using top-down or bottom-up sequences.[15] Here, since a top-down valuation sequence is used, it can be shown that: (2a) $\mathbf{A}_{I}^{1} \geq \mathbf{B}_{I}^{2} \geq \mathbf{C}_{I}^{3}$ and (2b) $\mathbf{B}_{II}^{1} \geq \mathbf{C}_{II}^{2}$. A variant on (2a) and (2b) using a bottom-up approach can be written as: (2c) $\mathbf{C}_{I}^{1} \leq \mathbf{B}_{I}^{2} \leq \mathbf{A}_{I}^{3}$, and (2d) $\mathbf{C}_{II}^{1} \leq \mathbf{B}_{II}^{2}$. It is important to note that the willingness-to-pay amounts for the goods in the top-down and bottom-up valuation sequences will, in general, not be the same. This is because of the differences respondents perceive in the choice set implied to be available (initially large or broad depending on the type of nesting in the top-down sequence, and initially small or narrow in the bottom-up sequence) and because of differences in whether the respondent believes he or she already possesses the complement of the good being valued (the top-down case) or has just purchased it (the bottom-up case).[16] The (2a) and (2b) results follow from monotonicity assumptions. Again, the weak inequalities may be replaced by strong inequalities if it is assumed that respondents get utility from the complement of the element being valued. Tests of the hypotheses represented by these equations will be called *nested sequence tests*.

Another comparison which can be made is along the diagonal of Table I: (3) $\mathbf{A}_{I}^{1} \geq \mathbf{B}_{II}^{1} \geq \mathbf{C}_{III}^{1}$. I will term this comparison a *test of component sensitivity*. It is the type of *scope insensitivity hypothesis test* generally implemented in recent CV surveys. This test looks at whether respondents are sensitive to differences in levels of the good (quantitative nesting) or the level of inclusion (categorical nesting) in a way that should change its value. It is the external test version of equation (2) and has the same theoretical properties as in (2).[17]

It is important to note that this test does not say anything about the magnitude of the difference that should be observed. Some CV critics, such as Diamond (1993), have proposed theoretical tests which they claim allow one to test not only the direction of the difference but also the magnitude. Thus far, the validity of such tests depends crucially on a set of strong auxiliary assumptions which seem unlikely to be satisfied for the types of goods usually valued with contingent valuation surveys.[18]

Kahneman and Knetsch scope and sequence test

Table II displays the results from Kahneman and Knetsch's (1992a) embedding test which was implemented using a short telephone survey. Drawing on Table I and the discussion of it, going across the rows provides a test of the embedding effect and the results are in accord with economic theory. Looking down the columns, one finds the nested sequence effect tests. These results are also in accord with economic theory. Down the diagonal, one finds the test of component sensitivity which is the hypothesis test for scope insensitivity. A comparison of the first two diagonal elements suggests scope insensitivity; however, there was little reason for Group I respondents to think that the long description of improved disaster preparedness that was read to the Group II respondents was actually contained in their description of the environmental services that would be delivered (Smith, 1992; Harrison, 1993).[19] Looking at the second two diagonal elements, one observes again the expected result.

TABLE II: WILLINGNESS TO PAY FOR SELECTED CLASSES OF GOODS AND ALLOCATIONS OF TOTALS TO LESS INCLUSIVE GROUPS

Public Good		Group I (N=66)	Group II (N=78)	Group III (N=74)
Environmental Services	Mean Median	$135.91 $50.00		
Improve Disaster Preparedness	Mean Median	$29.06 $10.00	$151.6 $50.00	
Improve Rescue Equipment Personnel	Mean Median	$14.12 $1.00	$74.65 $16.00	$122.64 $25.00

The Exxon scope experiments

Along with the Kahneman studies, the Exxon-sponsored scope experiments in the Hausman volume (1993)—Diamond *et al.*, Desvousges *et al.*, Schkade and Payne—are usually cited as the principal evidence supporting the contention that contingent valuation estimates are not responsive to the nature of the good being valued.[20] Indeed, it is often asserted that these are basically the only studies which have looked at the issue. For instance, Diamond and Hausman in their 1994 *Journal of Economics Perspectives* symposium paper on contingent valuation make the following remarks with respect to the embedding effect (insensitivity to scope) which they call the "main contingent valuation anomaly":[21]

> "With a pattern of results that are inconsistent with the usual economic assumptions, two interpretations are always possible: the surveys were defective or the contingent valuation method as currently practiced does not measure preferences with accuracy. One should consider all the surveys that attempt to test for consistency in order to judge which interpretation is likely to be correct. The studies we have described [Kahneman and Exxon's] have been criticized as not done well enough to be an adequate test. However, they are the only quantitative tests we are aware of. No comparable comparison tests have been done by proponents of the accuracy of contingent valuation, although the embedding effect has long been recognized." [bracketed material added for clarity]

Diamond et al.

Diamond *et al.* (1993) use a number of split-samples to ask respondents about programs involving different wilderness areas. Here I will only address their scope test which is labeled as Hypothesis I and operationalized as a test of whether willingness to pay for each of three different wilderness areas was equivalent.[22] They hypothesized further that WTP should vary by the size of the wilderness area: Selway Bitteroot (1.3 million acres), Bob Marshall (1.0 million acres), and Washakie (0.7 million acres).

Diamond *et al.* (1993) tested this hypothesis on a cleaned data set using a non-parametric Kruskall-Wallis test which ignores the size ordering of the three wilderness areas. They report a p-value of 0.42 for the hypothesis test and consider this result as evidence that respondents are insensitive to the scope of the good being valued.

Carson and Flores (1993) fit the following model in order to test Hypothesis I:

$$Y = \alpha + \beta \text{ ACRES} + \epsilon ,$$

where the p-value reported for β in Table III is from the one-sided test indicated by (1a).

TABLE III: LINEAR REGRESSION ESTIMATE USING DIAMOND *ET AL.* DATA

Parameter	Estimate	t-statistic	p-value
α	-17.834	-0.643	0.52
β	58.782	2.187	0.01*

Using a likelihood ratio test one can further look at the hypothesis, $\alpha=0$. This null hypothesis is accepted ($\chi_1^2=0.421$, p-value=0.52). Following this result, Carson and Flores (1993) then fit the model without a constant ($\beta=41.866$; $t_\beta=6.60$). Figure 1 displays the difference between the regression line fit by Carson and Flores and the null hypothesis accepted by Diamond *et al.*

A further test of the scope insensitivity hypothesis is available by noting that Diamond *et al.* also asked about willingness to pay for Selway with no wilderness areas developed and about developing all 57 wilderness areas. This comparison clearly rejects the scope insensitivity hypothesis at $p < 0.001$.[23]

Desvousges et al.

Desvousges *et al.* (1992; 1993) performed two scope experiments, one involving preventing birds from being killed in oil ponds in the Rocky mountain states and the other involved protecting coastal areas from oil spills, which provide results suggesting insensitivity to scope. Both were self-administered surveys in Atlanta shopping malls and had a high fraction of young respondents and both show little ability to explain the WTP responses. The oil spill experiment is marred by the fact that the larger good invoked a different (and lower) probability of success of preventing a large spill than had been used in the second treatment, thereby providing a significant confounding factor. The bird study used three treatments: saving 2000 birds, 20,000 birds, and 200,000 birds. These treatments were also labeled "much less than 1% of the population," "less than 1% of the population" and "about 2% of the population." The mean estimates for the three treatments were \$80, \$78, and \$88, respectively, with the median for all three treatments equal to \$25. A careful look at the data suggests a number of outliers in the right tail. Table IV shows a regression using the 10% trimmed mean data displayed in the appendix to their 1992 monograph. This result suggests that there is a significant relationship between the treatments. However, even the trimmed data is not monotonically increasing in the number of birds saved and, if one is willing to accept evidence from a quick shopping mall intercept survey, Desvousges *et al.* should probably be counted as supporting the hypothesis that CV results are insensitive to scope.

TABLE IV: DESVOUSGES *et al.* (1992) BIRD STUDY

10% Trimmed Data Regression Analysis — $WTP = \alpha + \beta$ (% BIRDS SAVED) + ϵ

Parameter	Estimate	t-Statistic	p-value
α	47.476	13.088	
β	8.484	3.073	0.001

Schkade and Payne

Schkade and Payne (1993; 1994) use the Desvousges *et al.* bird questionnaire with the same three treatments in the third Exxon scope experiment. This experiment uses a "think aloud" technique from psychology called verbal protocol analysis. In it, Schkade and Payne attempt to delve into what people are thinking and what motivates their responses. I do not address those issues here; rather, I note that the slower pace of the think-aloud technique and the presence of an interviewer in the room at the marketing research firm provide a situation more like that of an in-person interview than did those in the Desvousges *et al.* self-administered mall-intercept surveys.[24]

In the Exxon conference version of the paper (1993), Schkade and Payne report a p-value of 0.42 for an analysis of variance test of the scope insensitivity hypothesis using willingness to pay as the response variable. The journal version of the paper (1994) presents an additional analysis of variance test of the hypothesis using the log of willingness to pay as the response variable and reports a p-value of 0.18 for the test and notes that the WTP data looks log-normal.

In my reanalysis of Schkade and Payne's data, it is useful to make two key points. First, the hypothesis Schkade and Payne tested does not correspond to the theoretical argument they claimed to want to test. Schkade and Payne test a more general hypothesis, and as a result of their small samples sizes, they lack almost any statistical power because the models estimated do not incorporate information that the treatments (and the economic hypothesis) are monotonically ordered. It is possible to show that simply regressing the log of willingness to pay on the number of birds results in a rejection of the null hypothesis that WTP is not monotonically increasing in the number of birds valued at $p < 0.05$ using a one-sided t-test.[25] The other problem with the data is that much of the value is driven by a small number of very large outliers. The results of dropping the largest two outliers and the largest six outliers are displayed in Table IV along with the original Schkade and Payne results.[26] This analysis suggests that dropping out just the two highest observations eliminates the apparent violation of the economic restriction that WTP increase monotonically with increases in the level of the good. Dropping these two observations also results in a substantial reduction in the estimates of the standard error of the mean for the first and third treatments. Dropping the next four largest observations does not change the relative rankings of WTP for the three treatments, but as one would expect, does further reduce the standard errors.

TABLE V: SCHKADE AND PAYNE BIRD EXPERIMENT DATA				
2,000 BIRDS (MUCH LESS THAN 1% OF POPULATION TREATMENT)				
SAMPLE	MEAN	S.E. MEAN	MEDIAN	N
ALL OBS	$84.23	$34.70	$25	28

OBS ≤ $1000	$53.70	$17.06	$25	27
OBS ≤ $500	$38.31	$7.61	$25	26
20,000 BIRDS (LESS THAN 1% OF POPULATION TREATMENT)				
ALL OBS	$62.47	$18.82	$30	29
OBS ≤ $1000	$62.47	$18.82	$30	29
OBS ≤ $500	$45.13	$7.57	$30	28
200,000 BIRDS (ABOUT 2% OF POPULATION TREATMENT)				
ALL OBS	$121.82	$39.51	$50	30
OBS ≤ $1000	$88.13	$21.28	$50	29
OBS ≤ $500	$60.67	$10.03	$50	27

SCOPE SENSITIVITY: SUPPORTING ARGUMENTS AND EVIDENCE

Before undertaking the task of looking at other direct tests of scope insensitivity, I believe it is useful to ask the question: is there survey evidence from other sources that is likely to shed light on how plausible this hypothesis is likely to be? The answer, of course, is yes. At one level, a contingent valuation survey can simply be thought of as a very in-depth survey which elicits a respondent's views on a specific government policy. As such, there is a large body of evidence to draw upon to ascertain whether responses to survey questions on public policy issues are generally sensitive to the specifics of the policy question asked and the societal conditions at the time the question is asked. With respect to contingent valuation itself, there are a very large number of studies which may provide indirect evidence which tends to either contradict or support the general proposition of scope insensitivity. This evidence falls into a number of different categories. I first look at whether there is substantial variation in contingent valuation estimates across commodities as the scope insensitivity hypothesis suggests a lack of such variation. Second, I look at the correlation between CV and revealed preference (RP) estimates for the same good when it is possible to use these two different valuation approaches. The scope insensitivity hypothesis suggests that one will not see a strong correlation unless RP estimates are also insensitive to the scope of the good valued. Next, I will look at whether CV estimates tend to systematically vary with respondent characteristics. Then, I will look at whether CV estimates are sensitive to non-scope characteristics of the good, such as the payment vehicle used and the cost stated when the binary discrete choice elicitation method is used. Finally, using an example from a recent study, I will look at internal tests of scope and argue that these tests are not as uninformative as Kahneman contends.

Survey research on policy issues

Much survey research over the last 50 years has been devoted to showing how, and understanding why, small differences in question wording can lead to substantial differences in the results obtained (Payne, 1951; Schuman and Presser, 1981; Sudman and Bradburn, 1983; Krosnick and Fabrigar, forthcoming). If anything, one gets the impression reading such works, as well as the standard fare of articles in journals such as *Public Opinion Quarterly*, that responses to survey questions are perhaps too sensitive to question wording and that this can often create problems in the interpretation of policy questions (Schuman and Scott, 1987) by those unaware of the nuances of the question that was asked.

Two interesting examples of this come from split-sample experiments described in Stanley Payne's 1951 classic, *The Art of Asking Questions*. In the first experiment, 82% of the sample receiving the question, "Do you think anything *should* be done to make it easier for people to pay doctor or hospital bills?" responded positively, while 77% of sample receiving the word "*could*" rather than "*should*" responded positively, while only 63% of the sample responded positively when the word "*might*" replaced "*should.*" In a second experiment, 92% of the sample responded positively to the statement, "Some people have a kind of insurance for which *they* pay a certain amount each month to cover any hospital care *they* or *their* families may have in the future," but only 66% of the respondents agreed with the statement when it was framed in terms of taking the action personally. None of these differences is at all surprising once it is realized that fundamentally different questions were asked. More importantly, though, these differences suggest respondents *can* pay close attention to subtle differences in question wording. Payne's experiments are in no sense isolated examples. For instance, large differences in the percentage favoring a government policy toward abortion have long been observed based on whether or not that policy includes federal funding for abortion (NORC, 1991). Support for welfare programs is highly sensitive to whether the program requires able bodied participants to work (Smith, 1987). In more recent times, one sees large differences in the percentage in favor of supporting United Nations peace-keeping efforts in places like Bosnia, Somalia, Rwanda, and Haiti based on whether committing U.S. ground troops is part of the proposal. Support for environmental protection has been shown to be dependent on whether it simply involves higher costs or substantial unemployment effects (Dunlap and Scarce, 1991).

One can also look at responses to the same survey question over time and ask whether the public and policy makers are sensitive to changes in economic and social conditions over time. Here Page and Shapiro (1990) have provided substantial evidence that public opinion on national expenditures and policy actions tend to track each other fairly closely, sometimes following and sometimes leading as one might expect in a democracy.[27] For environmental expenditures, the National Opinion Research Center's General Social Survey demonstrates that an increase of 1% in the perception that the country is "spending too little on the environment" tends to be followed by a 1.3% increase in the government's rate of spending on the environment. Mueller (1985; 1994) documents how military actions in Vietnam and Kuwait were highly sensitive to responses to public opinion questions.[28] Knowledge on issues such as the greenhouse effect can be shown to steadily increase with the continual flow of information, with the percentage of "don't knows" falling from 36% to 11% over the course of seven years (Dunlap and Scarce, 1991). In another interesting example, the percent saying that oil companies were doing a poor job protecting coastal areas, which had been stable over time, more than doubled when the question was asked six months after the Exxon Valdez spill (Dunlap and Scarce, 1991).

Unless there is something fundamentally different about asking people for their willingness to pay for a particular project, there does not appear to be anything in the survey research literature which suggests that people are inherently unable to recognize and respond to differences in the scope of the good they are asked about. What the survey literature does point out is that one must take great care to ensure that respondents understand what the researcher is describing. It is often difficult and frequently time consuming to ask questions in a manner which the vast majority of the public can comprehend. Respondents will try to answer whatever question is put to them. They often do not realize that the researcher is asking a different question than the one they heard and, even when they are confused about what the question is asking, they frequently do not ask for clarification. This reason is usually found to lie behind most of the aberrant results in the survey research literature, not some fundamental inability of the respondent to deal with the question the researcher really wanted answered.[29]

Variation in CV estimates

The most extreme variant of the scope insensitivity argument is that CV respondents are always willing to pay the same amount irrespective of the good being valued. A frequent assertion by CV critics is that all CV studies provide estimates of approximately $30. Other CV critics (*e.g.*, Cummings, 1989; Note, 1992) suggest different amounts. Most are in the $10 to $60 range, but all seem to fall in the range of $10-$120. While a $10-$120 range is broad and would cover a large fraction of the non-grocery store purchases made by consumers, even that range can easily be shown to be false. Thompson (1986), interviewing a sample of respondents suffering from rheumatoid arthritis found that they were willing to pay on average $5000 for a particular arthritis treatment. Randall and Kriesel (1990) found American households willing to pay almost $700 on average for large improvements in several national environmental programs. Brookshire *et al.* (1985) found respondents to be willing to pay $4650 more for the same house in the Los Angeles area if it is located outside an earthquake zone. Mitchell and Carson (1993) found respondents willing to pay on average $275 for a very large improvement in national water quality. In contrast, Milon *et al.* (1993) found Florida fishermen willing to pay on average only $0.65 for a management plan which would increase the allowable harvest of the Pompano fish, while Carson *et al.* (1992) found households willing to pay less than $1 to improve 10 days of bad visibility in the Grand Canyon in the winter. Thayer (1981) finds respondents willing to pay about $2.50 more per trip to prevent geothermal development in the Jemez Mountain area of New Mexico while Boyle and Bishop (1987) respondents were willing to pay about $5 to protect an endangered species. While these examples, and any sort of systematic inspection of the estimates from CV studies, suggests that any argument that all CV estimates fall in any sort of narrow range is clearly specious, a formal statistical test (Neil, 1992) of the hypothesis based on collecting datasets from a number of CV survey rejects it.

Perhaps even more telling are two meta-analysis which have been done of CV estimates for specific classes of goods. Walsh, Johnson and McKean (1992) look at CV studies valuing outdoor recreation trips. While they find a mean value of $34 from the 287 studies, the individual studies produced estimates ranging from $4 to $220. Moreover, the differences in the estimates were systematically related to the characteristics of the trips. Smith and Osborne (1994) look at visibility estimates for national parks and find that they systematically vary with the scope of the change looked at and show that the estimates from the various studies are largely consistent with each other.

Comparisons between CV and RP estimates

For quasi-public goods, it is sometimes possible to use both contingent valuation and revealed preference approaches, such as hedonic pricing and travel cost analysis, to estimate willingness to pay for the good. If respondents in a CV survey for such a good were insensitive to its scope, one would not expect to see much of a correlation between CV and RP estimates for such goods unless actual behavior is also largely insensitive to the scope of the good being valued. Carson *et al.* (1994) have recently performed a meta-analysis looking at 616 comparisons of CV and RP estimates for the same approximate good from 83 studies spanning almost 30 years and 6 continents. They find the correlation between the CV and RP estimates ranges between 0.83 and 0.98 depending upon the whether the full, trimmed or weighted sample is used. This suggests that, at least for quasi-public goods, CV estimates are roughly as sensitive to scope as are estimates obtained from techniques based on observed behavior.

Systematic relationships between CV estimates and respondent characteristics

If one assumes the scope insensitivity hypothesis, then one would expect that willingness to pay *in general* would not vary with respondent characteristics. This proposition is easy to examine because it is common practice to estimate valuation functions in analysis of contingent valuation data. Looking at this large body of evidence, it is quite apparent that CV estimates usually vary in a systematic and expected way with various covariates. Such variation is taken as a sign of construct validity (Mitchell and Carson, 1989) whereas the lack of such relationships (*e.g.,* in the Desvousges *et al.* bird study) should be taken as a sign of potential problems with the study as a whole or as an indicator of gross outliers in the data.

As it would be possible to write a lengthy book discussing the various valuation functions found in contingent valuation studies, I simply note here some of the more frequently found or interesting relationships between WTP responses and various covariates. With respect to standard demographic variables one often finds that income is a significant predictor of willingness to pay, particularly in studies where the mean WTP estimate is fairly high. Consistent with economic theory, a large number of contingent valuation studies have found a positive and statistically significant relationship between income and WTP (*e.g.*, Cocheba and Langford, 1978; Walsh, Miller and Gilliam, 1983). This relationship tends to be stronger for studies valuing large changes (Thompson, 1986; Randall and Kreisel, 1990; Carson and Mitchell, 1993). Age is often significantly (and usually negatively) related to WTP, particularly for preservation issues (*e.g.*, Hoehn, 1991, Loomis 1987, Whitehead and Blomquist, 1991). Education is often positively related to WTP, particularly for development and risk issues (*e.g.*, Bergstrom, Dillman and Stoll, 1985; John, Walsh and Moore, 1992; Loomis and duVair, 1993) as well as for some of the more exotic forms of outdoor recreation (*e.g.*, Cicchetti and Smith, 1976; Daubert and Young, 1981).

As one might expect, strong environmentalists are usually willing to pay more for an environmental good than other respondents (*e.g.*, Bergstrom *et al.* 1990; Hanley and Craig, 1991; Carson *et al.* 1992). Specific environmental attitudes, particular those closely tied to the good being valued, are also usually good predictors (*e.g.*, Randall and Kriesel, 1990; Carson, Wilks and Imber (1994); Carson *et al.*, 1992).

Starting with Knetch and Davis' well-known 1966 study of outdoor recreation in the Maine woods, a number of authors have found statistically significant relationships between past recreational experiences and WTP for future recreation (*e.g.*, Johansson, 1990; Karou, 1993; Loomis, Creel and Park, 1991). A number of studies have found a negative relationship between a respondent's distance from the site and his or her willingness to pay for it (*e.g.*, Gramlich, 1977; Sutherland and Walsh, 1985; Bateman *et al.*, 1992). Researchers have typically found that direct users of a resource are willing to pay substantially more than passive users (Barrick and Beazley, 1990; Carson and Mitchell, 1993).

Sensitivity of CV estimates to important non-scope characteristics

If respondents in a CV survey are insensitive to the scope of the good they are asked to value, one might reasonably expect to see insensitivity to other important characteristics of the good such as the payment vehicle used and its price. Sensitivity to the payment vehicle was observed more than a decade ago using split-sample designs quite early on by CV researchers (*e.g.*, Brookshire, Randall, and Stoll, 1980; Greenley, Walsh, and Young, 1981) and continues to be documented (*e.g.*, Duffield, 1992).[30]

Bishop and Heberlein (1979) in their seminal paper on eliciting CV responses using a binary discrete choice framework observed considerable sensitivity to the price of the good the respondent was asked about. This result was extremely robust and, given the large number of binary discrete choice CV studies which have been conducted, I have not located a single clear example of insensitivity to price.[31]

With-in subject tests of scope insensitivity

Sensitivity to scope can be tested internally within subjects or externally between subjects, with the same restriction from economic theory being tested in both cases. Internal tests of scope, where the same respondent is asked about willingness to pay for different levels of the good of interest, have a long history in contingent valuation (*e.g.*, Randall, Ives, and Eastman, 1974). This should not be surprising, since curves defined over levels of the good of interest—not a single point estimate—are the standard tools of benefit-cost analysis. It is much easier (and cheaper) to ask a single respondent about several levels of a good than to ask several respondents about a single level of the good and one almost always finds that respondents are sensitive to the different levels of the good. From an economic perspective, it is often interesting to observe different patterns of declining marginal valuation (often going to zero) for respondents with different attributes. The information from such questions can be incorporated into a valuation function and, in the statistical estimation of the valuation function, the level of the good is almost always a highly significant WTP predictor (*e.g.*, Carson and Mitchell, 1993).

Having consistently observed internal tests of the scope insensitivity hypothesis being rejected in samples of any size, one might reasonably expect to see this hypothesis rejected in external tests. The typical argument by CV critics against the large number of internal tests of scope sensitivity having any bearing on external tests of scope sensitivity is that when a respondent gets asked about multiple levels of a good they try to act in an internally consistent way by simply valuing higher levels higher. Essentially this is an argument that more always costs more and is better, and hence, respondents are still not necessarily paying much attention to the actual level of the good. This need not be the case, as is shown in the following example from a study Michael Hanemann designed for the California Water Resources Control Board on Mono Lake (Jones and Stokes, 1993). In that study, respondents were asked to value three changes in the water level of Mono Lake with the cost of purchasing additional water being the driving force behind the need to determine willingness to pay for the changes. Respondents valued the first change in the water level quite highly, the second change more highly than the first, but the third change much less than either the first or the second; and indeed, the third change appears to be not much preferred to the base condition. What was the cause of this result since the lake level clearly kept rising over the change as did the perceived cost of buying water to fill the lake? What happened was that the first two lake level changes involved clear environmental improvements to the respondents. The third rise in lake level did not; it toppled a significant fraction of the tufa towers the lake is famous for and, while providing substantially more habitat for some species, it displaced others. Obviously, respondents were paying attention to the details and not simply saying more water is better because it cost more.

Direct tests of the hypothesis

Part of what has lent credence to those asserting the validity of the scope insensitivity hypothesis is their claim that only a few tests of this hypothesis have been conducted and that those tests almost uniformly show scope insensitivity. This claim can easily be shown to be false by searching the CV literature for split-sample comparisons which allow one to test the scope insensitivity hypothesis. In most instances, these split-sample tests were designed to look at different project configurations rather than to formally test the scope insensitivity hypothesis. Often the justification behind the use of such split samples was that the elements of one possible project configuration might influence respondent views about other project configurations with different characteristics. The advantage of these studies is that they tended to receive much more developmental work than did the Kahneman and Exxon surveys and they tended to use larger samples and better modes of survey administration.

Studies rejecting scope insensitivity hypothesis

Table VI presents a list of studies, appearing since Kahneman's original 1984 presentation, which contain a rejection of the scope insensitivity hypothesis at $p < 0.10$.[32] Most of the studies contain rejections at $p < 0.05$ and many contain rejections at better than $p < 0.001$. Studies where passive use is thought to be important are marked with a dagger (†).

TABLE VI: STUDIES WITH SIGNIFICANT SCOPE EFFECTS	
STUDY	GOOD VALUED
Bowker & Didychuk (1994)†	Preservation of different numbers of acres of agricultural land in Canada

TABLE VI: STUDIES WITH SIGNIFICANT SCOPE EFFECTS	
Boyle, Welsh, & Bishop (1993)	Different water flow levels of the Grand Canyon River
Brown, Layton, & Lazo (1994)†	Different options for policies on the Pacific Northwest old growth forests and Northern spotted owls
Buzby, Ready, & Hu (1994)	Reductions in risks associated with pesticides on grapefruits
Carson & Mitchell (1991)	Four scenarios for avoiding urban water shortages
Carson, Mitchell, & Ruud (1989)	Combinations of air pollution visibility & health effects
Carson & Mitchell (1993)†	National versus regional water quality
Carson, Wilks, & Imber (1994)†	Comparison of two different impact scenarios for Australia's Kakadu Conservation Zone
Carson *et al.* (1994)†	Comparison of two different natural resource injury accelerated recovery plans
Diamond *et al.* (1992) as reanalyzed†	Comparisons of different wilderness areas in four Rocky Mountain states
Duffield & Neher (1991)	Comparison of Montana waterfowl hunting trips differing by number of birds hunted
HBRS, Inc. (1994)†	Different impacts on downstream resources from Glenn Canyon Dam operations
Hoevenagel (1994)†	Package of six environmental programs versus specific components (acid rain, greenhouse effect)
Jakus (1992)	Two different Gypsy moth control programs in Pennsylvania and Maryland

TABLE VI: STUDIES WITH SIGNIFICANT SCOPE EFFECTS	
Krieger (1994)	Sport fishing toxics information programs
Loomis, Lockwood, & DeLacy (1993)†	Forest area protection program of Southeastern Australia and two smaller portions of the same area
Magnussen (1992)†	Comparisons of various Norwegian pollution control programs with emphasis on water pollution and the North Sea
McDaniels (1988)	Avoidance of different numbers of automobile deaths
Mitchell & Carson (1986)	Comparison of different levels of drinking water risk reduction
Navrud (1989)†	Comparison of different acid rain programs
Propper (1990)	Different National Health Service waiting times
Ready (1990)†	Preserving different percentages of Kentucky Horse Farms
Römer & Pommerehne (Forthcoming)	Different hazardous waste risk reductions
Rowe *et al.* (1991)†	Multiple versus single Pacific Northwest oil spills
Schkade & Payne (1994) as reanalyzed†	Preventing different numbers of birds from being killed in oil ponds
Smith & Zhang (1994)†	Cleaning-up different levels of marine debris on distant beaches
Tolley & Babcock (1986)	Comparison of different number of days of light health symptoms; comparison of two different variations of Angina
Veisten, *et al.* (1993)†	Environmental programs including biodiversity in Norwegian forests

TABLE VI: STUDIES WITH SIGNIFICANT SCOPE EFFECTS	
Whitehead (1992)†	Different probabilities of North Carolina Sea turtle extinction
Whitehead & Blomquist (1991)†	Different Kentucky wetland programs
Wu (1991)†	Different improvement programs at Ohio's Big Darby Creek

It would take a great deal of space to discuss each of these studies in any detail. A few highlights, however, are likely to be useful. First, the scope insensitivity hypothesis is strongly rejected ($p < 0.001$) by two large recent in-person contingent valuation studies, Carson, Wilks and Imber (1994) and Carson *et al.* (1994), which used extensive visual aids and very clean experimental designs to value goods thought to have substantial passive use considerations. Second, other very recent studies of goods thought to have substantial passive use considerations such as increasing the probability of preserving spotted owls (Brown, Layton and Lazo, 1994) and cleaning-up marine debris on distant beaches (Smith et al., 1994), show respondent sensitivity to very subtle changes in split-sample tests.

The Desvousges *et al.* version of the scope insensitivity hypothesis is stark — one should rarely observe significant differences between the WTP estimates of equivalent subsamples which vary with respect to the scope of the good they are asked to value if that good involves substantial passive use considerations. Table VI, however, shows 19 studies valuing goods thought to have substantial passive use considerations where the hypothesis that respondents are inherently insensitive to differences in scope can be rejected. In contrast, studies where the uniform acceptance of the Desvousges *et al.* hypothesis appears to be indicated are few in number. Kahneman and Knetsch's version of the hypothesis is even more stark and implies that CV results will almost always be insensitive to the scope of the good being valued irrespective of the nature of the good. Here Table VI shows over 30 rejections of Kahneman and Knetsch's hypothesis and very few instances where it is not rejected. From these results I conclude that either version of the hypothesis that scope insensitivity is inevitable in CV surveys is clearly rejected by the large number of available studies which directly address the issue.

This conclusion should not, however, be taken as a statement that there are not potential problems with the results from a particular CV survey. The most plausible alternative hypothesis which is consistent with the data is that there are isolated instances of scope insensitivity which are related to the particular survey design and administration problems noted earlier. One of those deserves special note here because there are a few studies listed in Table VI (*e.g.*, Ready; Magnussen; Loomis;

Lockwood and DeLacy) which do not show significant scope effects with respect to the largest program they valued. This is most noticeable in Ready where preservation of 100% of Kentucky horse farms is actually valued less than 75%. Ready argues, and probably correctly so, that respondents found the 100% preservation plan implausible. Fischoff *et al.*'s experiments suggest the likely reason: the probability of provision of very large programs tends to be seen as less than that of smaller programs.[33] A closely related type of difficulty may arise when respondents already have a clear idea of what a policy will accomplish and refuse to accept the depiction presented in the CV scenario (Carson, Wilks, and Imber, 1994).

It should also be noted that some of the initial CV work on valuing reductions in food safety risks (*e.g.*, Lin and Milon, 1993) does not seem to show responsiveness to the size of the risk being valued. Whether this is due in this particular case to the use of a short telephone survey, general difficulties in conveying small risk reductions, or a lack of an adequate means of conveying the risk reduction and a plausible means of delivering it is unclear. On this last point, it should be noted that Krieger's (1994) original pilot study did not show a difference between a complete and a partial sport fishing toxics risk information program but did show a difference after the survey instrument was redesigned to be more understandable.[34] Finally, for completeness, I should also note that there are also a few instances where using one elicitation method rejects lack of sensitivity to scope while, using another elicitation method, the scope insensitivity hypothesis cannot be rejected.[35] While there does not seem to be any clear pattern here, there may be interactions between the informational content of elicitation formats and their incentive properties which need to be explored.

CONCLUDING REMARKS

The conclusion that should be drawn from the large body of direct and indirect evidence seems clear: any hypothesis of generic respondent insensitivity to the scope of the good being valued should be rejected. There are over 30 studies with direct split-sample tests of the scope insensitivity hypothesis which reject it. In contrast, there are only a handful of studies in which the hypothesis is not clearly rejected. These studies tend to suffer from (a) small sample sizes, (b) poor survey design (c) shifts in the probability that the good would be provided between subsamples and/or (d) the use of a mode of survey administration, such as the telephone or shopping mall intercepts, which do not encourage respondents to pay close attention to the questions being asked. The large number of available split-sample CV tests do not suggest any difference in scope sensitivity between goods with substantial direct use values and those with substantial passive use values.

In retrospect, it is surprising that the scope insensitivity hypothesis ever gained any currency since the general survey finding is that respondents often pick up on small nuances in question wording. A closer examination of the scope insensitivity hypothesis suggests a number of other patterns which CV data should exhibit if this hypothesis were true. An examination of a very large body evidence shows that such patterns do not generally exist. Once the confusion over the term embedding was sorted out into a test of sequence effects and a test of scope insensitivity (across the rows and down the diagonal, respectively), it became clear that all a test of scope insensitivity required was a split-sample test where one subsample valued a good that was larger than the good valued by the other subsample. Realizing this, it became apparent that there were a fairly large number of existing split-sample CV studies existing in the literature which provided direct evidence rejecting the scope insensitivity hypothesis. Studies conducted subsequent to the Kahneman and Knetsch paper (1992) and the Exxon-sponsored conference (Hausman, 1993) have only tended to confirm this conclusion.

Rejection of generic insensitivity to scope in CV surveys should not be taken to imply that one cannot design a CV questionnaire and administer it in such a way as to find scope insensitivity. Indeed this can be done fairly easily. The remedies for the problem are straightforward in concept but often difficult and expensive in practice to implement.[36] The respondent must (i) clearly understand the characteristics of the good they are asked to value, (ii) find the CV scenario elements related to the good's provision plausible, and (iii) answer the CV questions in a deliberate and meaningful manner.

ENDNOTES

1 Examples of such criticisms can be found in *Contingent Valuation: A Critical Response*, the collection of Exxon-sponsored research on CV (1993; J.A. Hausman ed.) and testimony on behalf of several oil and chemical companies by Peter Diamond, William Desvousges, Jerry Hausman, Daniel Kahneman, Daniel McFadden, Steven Shavell and others before the NOAA Blue Ribbon Panel on Contingent Valuation co-chaired by Kenneth Arrow and Robert Solow.

2 We use the term "scope" rather than "embedding" because scope is the term used in the recommendation section of the NOAA Blue Ribbon Panel (Arrow *et al.*, 1993) and is a well-defined economic concept. In contrast, embedding (Kahneman and Knetsch, 1992a) has been used to describe a variety of different phenomena, some of which represent violations of economic theory and some of which are predicted by it (Smith, 1992; Carson and Mitchell, forthcoming).

3 Kahneman's original presentation was at a 1984 U.S. Environmental Protection Agency workshop. A written account can be found in Cummings, Brookshire, and Schulze (1986).

4 Kahneman's results had come from a short telephone survey with very little description of the good or how it would be provided. Mitchell and Carson (1989) informally compared estimates of willingness to pay from two very similar surveys, one valuing national water quality changes and the other valuing regional water quality changes, noting the large difference in estimates. A formal statistical test of this comparison is provided in Carson and Mitchell (1993).

5 CV researchers became aware of this problem in the context of valuation of air quality improvements where the U.S. Clean Air Act does not allow the U.S. Environmental Protection Agency to assess health benefits in dollar terms but allows non-health benefits such as visibility improvements to be assessed in dollar terms. See Carson, Mitchell and Ruud (1990), Fischoff and Furby (1986), and McClelland *et al.* (1991) for discussions and empirical applications.

6 See, for instance, Hanemann's (1991) theoretical demonstration that the tight link between willingness to pay and willingness to accept for price changes need not hold for imposed quantity changes.

7 Harrison (1992), in a now famous line, responds with the standard economic position: "I call my utility `jolly.' What you choose to call your utility is, as far as I am concerned, your business. What Kahneman and Knetsch want to call it is, of course their business. To be blunt, this hypothesis is `meaningless' in the standard methodological sense. To paraphrase Samuelson (1947, p. 92), it places no definite restrictions on observable behavior, even under ideal observational conditions."

8 Kahneman has since reversed his position and now condemns almost all contingent valuation values.

9 In their original paper, Kahneman and Knetsch refer only to embedding. They draw a distinction between regular embedding and perfect embedding in their reply (1992b) to Smith's (1992) comment.

10 Indeed, the recent Flores (1994) analysis shows that because one is effectively dealing with an inverted quantity constrained demand system, large sequence effects are likely to be the rule not the exception.

11 Andreoni's (1990) theory of warm glow offers an explanation of the confounding empirical evidence against the neutrality hypothesis. This hypothesis states that government expenditures on public goods will perfectly crowd out charitable donations for the provision of these same goods. The theory of warm glow presents a model in which government provision is an imperfect substitute for private donations because individuals receive a warm

glow from the act of giving not available when the same level is provided through lump sum taxes. Two qualifications of the adoption of the "warm glow" term by CV critics are in order. First, Andreoni's model does not specify a warm glow for anonymous payment of taxes, which is perhaps the most common payment mechanism used in contingent valuation surveys. Second, with multiple public goods, the warm glow must come from the simple act of paying taxes irrespective of whether the government provides anything in return.

12 Kahneman and Knetsch do advance an argument that differences in more satisfaction, not economic motivations, may drive differences in WTP. However, it is unclear what Kahneman and Knetsch believe is and is not a legitimate economic motive, as they fail to provide a list of acceptable economic motivations. See Samuelson (1993) for a recent restatement of the neoclassical economic position which rejects the notion that some motives are not legitimate determinants of economic behavior.

13 This section is largely taken from Carson and Mitchell (forthcoming).

14 These two assumptions work in the opposite direction in a willingness to accept compensation valuation sequence (Carson, Flores, and Hanemann, 1994).

15 We define a top-down sequence as essentially asking, "How much less are you willing to pay for **A** if **B** is not part of **A**?" and a bottom-down as, "How much more are you willing to pay for **A** given that you have just paid for **B**?"

16 It is of course possible to define top-down and bottom-up sequences which, from theoretical perspective, ask the same thing. However, the implementation of one of the two sequences will almost always involve asking respondents to "forget" the choice information they have previously been given, something which survey respondents generally do not do (Schwarz and Strack, 1991). This problem is avoided with the test described in equation (3) below.

17 Note that this test has quite different statistical properties because it is a between sample test rather than a within sample test. Between sample tests will generally require substantially larger sample sizes for the same level of precision in the estimate of the difference between WTP estimates for different goods. Three other factors can also substantially reduce the statistical power of tests of (3). The first is to ignore the known relationship between the goods being valued if there are more than two goods. The second is to conduct the test in a situation where there are a large number of respondents who do not value any level of the good. The third is to use a two-sided hypothesis test when (3) clearly calls for a one-sided test.

18 For instance, Smith and Osborne (1994) and Hanemann (1994) show that Diamond's assumption in the example he uses from the Desvousges *et al.* (1992) bird study is equivalent to assuming that people are indifferent between a government program which would keep some number of birds from being killed by oil and one which would simply increase the bird population by the same number. More generally, Smith and Osborne (1994) show by moving from Diamond's quasi-linear utility function to something as simple as a CES utility function, the adding-up condition proposed by Diamond need no longer hold.

19 It should also be noted that respondents are usually suspicious that much will actually be provided by paying for vaguely defined improvements in a broad aggregate commodity. This probability of provision effect with large goods (Fishchoff *et al.*, 1993) can lead to situations where the less inclusive good is actually valued more highly.

20 The fourth reported Exxon experiment, Kemp and Maxwell (1993), looked at different valuation sequences but not at scope, and as a result, is not discussed here.

21 Diamond and Hausman say "An example of embedding would be a willingness-to-pay to clean up one lake roughly equal to that for cleaning up five lakes, including the one asked about individually. The embedding effect is usually thought to arise from the non-existence of individual preferences for the good in question and from the failure of survey respondents, in the hypothetical circumstances of the survey, to consider the effects of their budget constraints." Much of Diamond and Hausman's actual discussion concerns sequencing effects and here, after dismissing the importance of income and substitution effects, they conclude: "If a survey question reveals a true valuation, it should not matter whether the question is asked by itself or with other questions, nor if asked with any other questions, what the order of questioning is."

22 Carson and Flores (1993) discuss the Diamond *et al.* experiments in detail. In particular, they show that finding Hypothesis I (stated WTP to Protect Each of the Three Areas [Selway Bitterroot, Washakie, and Bob Marshall] is the same) was true is crucial to the validity of each of the additional hypotheses that Diamond *et al.* attempt to test.

23 Selway Bitterroot, which was one of the largest wilderness areas with approximately 10% of the total acreage, has a mean WTP of $28.54 with a standard error of the mean of $4.84 (N=286) while the 57 wilderness areas as a group have a mean of $78.90 with a standard error of $13.18 (N=297). This

hypothesis test (t=3.53) turns out to be the only one in the Diamond *et al.* paper which does not require an assumption about which wilderness areas had already been slated for development (Carson and Flores, 1993).

24 Indeed Schkade and Payne, Desvousges *et al.*, and Diamond and Hausman all argue that since the Schkade and Payne and the Desvousges *et al.* willingness to pay estimates are similar in magnitude, and both show insensitivity to scope, that the mode of survey administration makes no difference to their claim of scope insensitivity.

25 The estimate equation is log(WTP)=3.0704 + .0034*(BIRDS/1000) where the t-statistics on the constant and BIRDS variable are 13.72 and 1.80, respectively.

26 The Schkade and Payne data have a very long right tail with two obvious breaks in the data: 2 observations above $600 (1 at $1000 and 1 at $1200) and 4 additional observations above $200 (3 at $500 and 1 at $600).

27 See Ferris (1983) for a more economic based approach to this use of survey data.

28 One of the more interesting examples with respect to military action was the Reagan administration's commission of a survey posing various policy options toward Libya. The most popular option with the public, bombing Qaddafi, was quickly thereafter implemented (Anderson and Van Atta, 1988).

29 One of the most striking recent examples occurred on a recent Roper survey commissioned by the American Jewish Federation. Twenty-two percent of the respondents appeared to be saying that they believed that the holocaust never happened and 12% were not sure. This was of great concern to the sponsor and at odds with several other survey questions on this issue. The problem was traced back to a confusing double-negative in the question. Roper reworded the question so as to avoid the double-negative and refielded the survey. The percentage then dropped to 1% who believed that the holocaust never happened and 8% were unsure, a response in line with other well-known surveys on the issue. See Morin (1994) for an account.

30 This sensitivity initially bothered some environmental economists lacking a public choice background. In that tradition, public preferences for particular tax structures has long been an area of research by both economists and political scientists and a subject of interest to bureaucrats and politicians. See the discussion on this point in Cummings, Brookshire and Schulze (1986). Those who tend to see "value" as something which should be context independent are still troubled when two substantially different estimates of willingness to pay are obtained using two different payment vehicles. See Mitchell and Carson (1989) for an extensive discussion of the role of payment vehicles in CV surveys.

31 This remark should not be taken to imply that there are no violations of the restriction from economic theory that the percent willing to pay should not increase as the price increases at particular design points. Such violations are, however, generally small in number and well within what one might expect from sampling theory. No doubt there is a demand curve in some CV study which is not downward sloping, the results of which would clearly be questionable.

32 There are several earlier CV studies which effectively used a split sample by obtaining willingness to pay estimates under a variety of different congestion conditions. For example, McConnell (1977) asks respondents for their WTP for the beach day they have just experienced and finds that the level of beach congestion on the day of the interview is a highly significant predictor of WTP. Cicchetti and Smith (1976) obtained willingness to pay for wilderness hiking days for both the day of the interview and under alternative congestion scenarios pooling these sources to obtain an estimate of the value of congestion effects.

33 What one would obviously like to do is change the scope of the good without changing the perceived probability of provision as that change will generally work against the likelihood that a significant scope effect is observed. It may be possible to improve the power of scope tests by taking steps to help ensure that the probability of provision is held constant across subsamples receiving different goods.

34 Tolley, Brian, and Fabien (1988) had a similar finding in an early air pollution study where their initial study showed a lack of sensitivity to fairly large differences in air quality improvements whereas changing the presentation of the two programs to make their key elements clearer to respondents resulted in different (plausible) valuations.

35 Loomis, Lockwood, and DeLacy (1993) find significant differences between all three changes they examined using a dichotomous choice format but only between two of the three changes using an open-ended format. Buzby, Ready, and Hu (1994) find differences using a payment card but do not find a significant difference with a dichotomous choice. Navrud's (1989) results tend to show significant differences between different acid rain programs using a bidding game but not using a payment card.

36 Robert Mitchell and I discuss different aspects of this issue at length in Mitchell and Carson (1989), Carson and Mitchell (1993), Carson and Mitchell (forthcoming), and Mitchell and Carson (forthcoming).

REFERENCES

Anderson, Jack, and Dale Van Atta. "The Secret Polls Behind the Libya Raid." *Washington Post*, 29 February 1988.

Andreoni, James. "Giving with Impure Altruism: Applications to Charity and Ricardian Equivalence." *Journal of Political Economy* 97, no. 6 (1989): 1447-1458.

------. "Impure Altruism and Donations To Public Goods: A Theory of Warm-Glow Giving." *The Economic Journal* 100 (1990): 464-477.

Arrow, Kenneth, Robert Solow, Paul R. Portney, Edward E. Leamer, Roy Radner, and Howard Schuman. "Contingent Valuation Methodology Report (Report of the NOAA Panel on Contingent Valuation)." *Federal Register* 58(15 January 1993): 4602-4614.

Barrick, Kenneth Andrew, and Ronald I. Beazley. "Magnitude and Distribution of Option Value for the Washakie Wilderness, Northwest, Wyoming, USA." *Environmental Management* 14, no. 3 (1990): 367-380.

Bergstrom, John C., B.L. Dillman, and John Raymond Stoll. "Public Environmental Amenity Benefits of Private Land: The Case of Prime Agricultural Land." *Southern Journal of Agricultural Economics* 17, no. 1 (1985): 139-149.

Bishop, Richard C., and Thomas A. Heberlein. "Measuring Values of Extra-Market Goods: Are Indirect Measures Biased?" *American Journal of Agricultural Economics* 61, no. 5 (1979): 926-930.

Blomquist, Glenn C., and John C. Whitehead. *The Effect of Alternative and Reclaimed Areas on the Value of Wetlands*. Final report OSM 597 to the U.S. Department of the Interior. Office of Surface Mining Reclamation and Enforcement, 1990.

Bowker, J.M. and D.D. Didychuk. "Estimation of the Nonmarket Benefits of Agricultural Land Retention in Eastern Canada." *Agricultural and Resource Economics Review* 23, no. 2 (1994): 218-225.

Boyle, Kevin J., and Richard C. Bishop. "Valuing Wildlife in Benefit-Cost Analyses: A Case Study Involving Endangered Species." *Water Resources Research* 23, (1987): 943-950.

Boyle, Kevin J., Michael P. Welsh, and Richard C. Bishop. "The Role of Question Order and Respondent Experience in Contingent Valuation Studies." *Journal of Environmental Economics and Management* 25, no. 1 (1993): 45-55.

Brookshire, David S., Alan Randall, and John Raymond Stoll. "Valuing Increments and Decrements in Natural Resource Service Flows." *American Journal of Agricultural Economics* 62, no. 3 (1980): 478-488.

Brookshire, David S., Mark A. Thayer, John Tschirhart, and William D. Schulze. "A Tesonmental and Resource Economists. Stockholm, June, 1991.

Carson, Richard T., Robert C. Mitchell, W. Michael Hanemann, Raymond J. Kopp, Stanley Presser, and Paul A. Ruud. *A Contingent Valuation Study of Lost Passive Use Values Resulting from the Exxon Valdez Oil Spill.* Report to the Attorney General of the State of Alaska. Natural Resource Damage Assessment, Inc., November, 1992.

Carson, Richard T., Robert Cameron Mitchell, and Paul A. Ruud. "Valuing Air Quality Improvements: Simulating a Hedonic Pricing Equation in the Context of a Contingent Valuation Scenario." In *Visibility and Fine Particles*, edited by C.V. Mathai, 639-646. Pittsburgh: Air and Waste Management Association, 1990.

Carson, Richard T., Leanne Wilks, and David Imber. "Valuing the Preservation of Australia's Kakadu Conservation Zone." *Oxford Economic Papers* 46 (1994) 727-749.

Cicchetti, Charles J., and V. Kerry Smith. *The Costs of Congestion: An Econometric Analysis of Wilderness Recreation.* Cambridge, MA: Ballinger, 1976.

Cocheba, Donald J., and William A. Langford. "Wildlife Valuation: The Collective Good Aspect of Hunting." *Land Economics* 54. no. 4 (1978): 490-504.

Cummings, Ronald G. Comment submitted to the Office of Environmental Project Review, Department of the Interior, in response to ANPR Concerning Type B Natural Resource Damage Assessments (54 FR 183, September 22, 1989). 1989.

Cummings, Ronald G., David S. Brookshire, and William D. Schulze. *Valuing Environmental Goods: An Assessment of the Contingent Valuation Method.* Totowa, NJ: Rowman and Allanheld, 1986.

Daniel, Terry C., Thomas C. Brown, David A. King, Merton T. Richards, and William P. Stewart. "Perceived Scenic Beauty and Contingent Valuation of Forest Campgrounds." *Forest Science* 35, no. 1 (1989): 76-90.

Daubert, John T., and Robert A. Young. "Recreational Demands for Maintaining Instream Flows: A Contingent Valuation Approach." *American Journal of Agricultural Economics* 63, no. 4 (1981): 666-676.

Desvousges, William H., Alicia R. Gable, Richard W. Dunford, and Sara P. Hudson. "Contingent Valuation: The Wrong Tool for Damage Assessment." *Choices*, no. 2 (1993): 9-11.

Desvousges, William H., F. Reed Johnson, Richard W. Dunford, Kevin J. Boyle, Sara P. Hudson, and K. Nicole Wilson. *Measuring Nonuse Damages Using Contingent Valuation: An Experimental Evaluation of Accuracy*. Research Triangle Park, NC: Research Triangle Institute, 1992.

Desvousges, William H., F. Reed Johnson, Richard W. Dunford, Kevin J. Boyle, Sara P. Hudson, and K. Nicole Wilson. "Measuring Natural Resource Damages with Contingent Valuation: Tests of Validity and Reliability." In *Contingent Valuation: A Critical Assessment*, edited by Jerry A. Hausman. Amsterdam: North Holland Publishers, 1993.

Diamond, Peter A. "Testing the Internal Consistency of Contingent Valuation Surveys." Working paper 93-1, Department of Economics, Massachusetts Institute of Technology.

Diamond, Peter A., and Jerry A. Hausman. "Contingent Valuation: Is Some Number Better than No Number?" *Journal of Economic Perspectives* 8 (1994), 45-64.

Diamond, Peter A., Jerry A. Hausman, Gregory K. Leonard, and Mike A. Denning. "Does Contingent Valuation Measure Preferences? Experimental Evidence." In *Contingent Valuation: A Critical Assessment*, edited by Jerry A. Hausman. Amsterdam: North Holland Publishers, 1993.

Duffield, John W., and Chris Neher. *Montana Waterfowl Hunting: A Contingent Valuation Assessment of Economic Benefits and Hunter Attitudes*. Report to Montana Department of Fish, May, 1991.

Dunlap, Riley, E., and Rik Scarce. "Environmental Problems and Protection." *Public Opinion Quarterly* 55 (1991): 651-672.

Farkas, Steve, Robert Y. Shapiro, and Benjamin I. Page. *The Dynamics of Public Opinion and Policy*. Presented at American Association for Public Opinion Research Meeting, 1990.

Ferris, James M. "Demands for Public Spending: An Attitudinal Approach." *Public Choice* 40 (1983): 135-154.

Fischhoff, Baruch, and Lita Furby. "A Review and Critique of Tolley, Randall *et al.*: `Establishing and Valuing the Effects of Improved Visibility in the Eastern United States'." Eugene Research Institute, Eugene, October, 1986.

------. "Measuring Values: A Conceptual Framework for Interpreting Transactions with Special Reference to Contingent Valuation of Visibility." *Journal of Risk and Uncertainty* 1 (1988): 147-184.

Fischhoff, Baruch, M.J. Quadrel, M. Kamlet, R. Dawes, P. Fischbeck, S. Klepper, J. Leland, and G. Loewenstein. "Embedding Effects: Stimulus Representation and Response Modes." *Journal of Risk and Uncertainty* 6 (1993): 211-234.

Flores, Nicholas. "The Effects of Rationing and Valuation Elasticities." Unpublished paper. Department of Economics, University of California, San Diego, November 1994.

Gramlich, Frederick W. "The Demand for Clean Water: The Case of the Charles River." *National Tax Journal* 30, no. 2 (1977): 183-194.

Greenley, Douglas A., Richard G. Walsh, and Robert A. Young. "Option Value: Empirical Evidence from a Case Study of Recreation and Water Quality." *Quarterly Journal of Economics* 96, no. 4 (1981): 657-672.

Hanemann, W. Michael. "Willingness to Pay and Willingness to Accept: How Much Can They Differ?" *American Economic Review* 81, no. 3 (1991): 635-647.

Hanley, Nicholas D., and Stephen Craig. "The Economic Value of Wilderness Areas: An Application to the Krutilla-Fisher Model to Scotland's' Flow Country." In *Environmental Policy and the Economy*, edited by F. Dietz, R. van der Ploeg and J. van der Straaten, 95-115. Amsterdam: North Holland Publishing Company, 1991.

Harrison, Glenn W. "Valuing Public Goods with the Contingent Valuation Method: A Critique of Kahneman and Knetsch." *Journal of Environmental Economics and Management* 23, no. 3 (1992): 248-257.

Hausman, Jerry A., ed. *Contingent Valuation: A Critical Assessment*. Contributions to Economic Analysis. Amsterdam: North Holland Publishers, 1993.

HBRS, Inc. "Pilot Test, Nonuse Value Study Glen Canyon Environmental Studies," Draft report, Madison, WI, July 1994.

Hoehn, John P. "Valuing the Multidimensional Impacts of Environmental Policy: Theory and Methods." *American Journal of Agricultural Economics* 73, no. 2 (1991): 289-299.

Hoevenagel, Ruud. *The Contingent Valuation Method: Scope and Validity*, Dissertation, Vrije Universiteit te Amsterdam, 1994.

Jakus, Paul M. *Valuing the Private and Public Dimensions of a Mixed Good: An Application to Pest Control.* Dissertation. North Carolina State University, 1992.

Johansson, Per-Olov. "Willingness to Pay Measures and Expectations: An Experiment." *Applied Economics* 22 (1990): 313-329.

Jones & Stokes Associates, Inc. *Environmental Impact Report for the Review of Mono Basin Water Rights of the City of Los Angeles.* Draft report to California State Water Resources Control Board. 1993.

Kahneman, Daniel. "Comments." In *Valuing Environmental Goods: An Assessment of the Contingent Valuation Method*, edited by Ronald G. Cummings, David S. Brookshire and William D. Schulze. Totowa, NJ: Rowman and Allanheld, 1986.

Kahneman, Daniel, and Jack Knetsch. "Valuing Public Goods: The Purchase of Moral Satisfaction." *Journal of Environmental Economics and Management* 22 (1992a): 57-70.

------. "Contingent Valuation and the Value of Public Goods: Reply." *Journal of Environmental Economics and Management* 22, no. 1 (1992b): 90-94.

Kaoru, Yoshiaki. "Differentiating Use and Nonuse Values for Coastal Pond Water Quality Improvements." *Environmental and Resource Economics* 3(May 1993): 487-494.

Kemp, Michael A., and Christopher Maxwell. "Exploring a Budget Context for Contingent Valuation Estimates." In *Contingent Valuation: A Critical Assessment*, edited by Jerry A. Hausman. Amsterdam: North Holland Publishers, 1993.

Knetsch, Jack L., and Robert K. Davis. "Comparisons of Methods for Resource Evaluation." In *Water Research*, edited by Allen V. Kneese and Stephen C. Smith. Baltimore, MD: Johns Hopkins University Press for Resources for the Future, 1966.

Krieger, Douglas J. *Economic Value of Environmental Risk Information: Theory and Application to Michigan Sport Fishery*. Dissertation. Michigan State University, 1994.

Krosnick, J.A., and L.R. Fabrigar. *Designing Questionnaires to Measure Attitudes: Insights from Cognitive and Social Psychology*. New York: Oxford University Press, Forthcoming.

Lin, C.T.J. and J.W., Milon. "Contingent Valuation of Health Risk Reductions for Shellfish Products," Presented at U.S.D.A. NE-165 Workshop on Foodsafety and Nutrition, 1993.

Loomis, John B. "Balancing Public Trust Resources of Mono Lake and Los Angeles Water Rights: An Economic Approach." *Water Resources Research* 23, (1987): 1449-1456.

Loomis, John B., Michael Creel, and Timothy Park. "Comparing Benefit Estimates from Travel Cost and Contingent Valuation Using Confidence Intervals for Hicksian Welfare Measures." *Applied Economics* 23, no. 11 (1991): 1725-1731.

Loomis, John B., and Pierre duvair. "Evaluating the Effect of Alternative Risk Communication Devices on Willingness to Pay: Results from a Dichotomous Choice Contingent Valuation Experiment." *Land Economics* 69, no. 3 (1993): 287-298.

Loomis, John, Michael Lockwood, and Terry DeLacy. "Some Empirical Evidence on Embedding Effects in Contingent Valuation of Forest Protection." *Journal of Environmental and Economics Management* 25, no. 1 (1993): 45-55.

Madden, Paul. "A Generalization of Hicksian Substitutes and Complements with Application to Demand Rationing." *Econometrica* 59, no. 5 (1991): 1497-1508.

Magnussen, Kristin. "Valuation of Reduced Water Pollution Using the Contingent Valuation Method - Testing for Amenity Misspecification." In *Pricing the European Environment*, edited by Ståle Navrud. Oslo, Norway: Scandinavian University Press, 1992.

McClelland, Gary H., William D. Schulze, Donald Waldman, D. Schenk, J. Irwin, T. Stewart, L. Deck, and M. Thayer. *Valuing Eastern Visibility: A Field Test of the Contingent Valuation Method - Innovative Approaches for Valuing Perceived Environmental Quality*. Report to the U.S. Environmental Protection Agency Cooperative Agreement, 1991.

McConnell, Kenneth E. "Congestion and Willingness to Pay: A Study of Beach Use." *Land Economics* 53, no. 2 (1977): 186-195.

McDaniels, Timothy L. "Comparing Expressed and Revealed Preferences for Risk Reduction: Different Hazards and Question Frames." *Risk Analysis* 8 (1988): 593-604.

Milon, J. Walter, Eric M. Thunberg, Charles M. Adams, and C.T. Jordan Lin. *Recreational Anglers' Valuation of Near-Shore Marine Fisheries in Florida.* Report prepared for the Florida Marine Fisheries Commission, 1993.

Mitchell, Robert C., and Richard T. Carson. *Valuing Drinking Water Risk Reductions Using the Contingent Valuation Method: A Methodological Study of Risks from THM and Giardia.* Report to the U.S. Environmental Protection Agency, 1986.

------. *Using Surveys to Value Public Goods: The Contingent Valuation Method.* Washington, DC: Resources for the Future, 1989.

------."Current Issues in the Design, Administration and Analysis of Contingent Valuation Surveys." In *Current Issues in Environmental Economics*, edited by P.O. Johansson, B. Kriström and K.G. Mäler. Manchester University Press, forthcoming.

Morin, Richard. "That Misleading Holocaust Survey: A Flawed Poll Overstated the Public's Skepticism." Washington Post, p. C3, March 20, 1994

Mueller, John E. *Policy and Opinion in the Gulf War.* Chicago: University of Chicago Press, 1994.

------. *War, Presidents, and Public Opinion.* Lanham: University Press of America, Inc., 1985.

National Opinion Research Center. *General Social Surveys, 1972-1991: Cumulative Codebook.* Chicago: NORC, University of Chicago, 1991.

Navrud, Ståle. "Estimating Social Benefits of Environmental Improvements from Reduced Acid Rain Deposition: A Contingent Valuation Survey." In: Valuation Methods and Policy Making in Environmental Economics, edited by Folmer, H. and E. van Ierland, Elsevier Science Publishers, 1989.

Neill, Helen Rosemary. *Valuing Public Goods with the Contingent Valuation Method: Three Essays.* Dissertation. Department of Economics, University of New Mexico, July, 1992.

Note. "Ask a Silly Question..: Contingent Valuation of Natural Resource Damages." *Harvard Law Review* 105, no. 8 (1992): 1981-2000.

Payne, Stanley L. *The Art of Asking Questions*. Princeton: Princeton University Press, 1951.

Propper, Carol. "Contingent Valuation of Time Spent on NHS Lists." *The Economics Journal* 100, no. 400 (1990): 193-199.

Randall, Alan, Berry C. Ives, and Clyde Eastman. "Bidding Games for Valuation of Aesthetic Environmental Improvements." *Journal of Environmental Economics and Management* 1 (1974): 132-149.

Randall, Alan, and W. Kriesel. "Evaluating National Policy Proposals by Contingent Valuation." In *Economic Valuation of Natural Resources: Issues, Theory, and Applications*, edited by R.L. Johnson and G.V. Johnson. Boulder: Westview Press, 1990.

Ready, Richard C. *The Value to Kentuckians of the Kentucky Equine Industry: A Contingent Valuation Study*. Preliminary report Lexington Chamber of Commerce, 1990.

Römer, Anselm U., and Werner W. Pommerehne. "Valuing Reductions of Public Risks: The Case of Hazardous Waste." In *Models and Measurement of Welfare and Inequality*, edited by Peter Eichhorn. Springer, Heidelberg, Forthcoming.

Rosenthal, Donald H., and Richard G. Walsh. "Hiking Values and the Recreation Opportunity Spectrum." *Forest Science* 32 (1986): 405-415.

Rowe, Robert D., Edward R. Morey, William D. Schulze, and William S. Breffle. *Compensable Natural Resource Damage Determination for the Upper Clark Fork River NPL Sites*. Report to the State of Montana, December, 1993.

Rowe, Robert D., William D. Schulze, W.D. Shaw, L.G. Chestnut, and D. Schenk. *Contingent Valuation of Natural Resource Damage Due to the Nestucca Oil Spill*. Final report to the British Columbia Ministry of Environment, June, 1991.

Samuelson, Paul A. "Alturism as a Problem Involving Group Versus Individual Selection in Economics and Biology." *American Economic Review*, 83, no. 2 (1993): 143-148.

Schkade, David A., and John W. Payne. "How People Respond to Contingent Valuation Questions: A Verbal Protocol Analysis of Willingness to Pay for an Environmental Regulation." *Journal of Environmental Economics and Management* 26, (1994): 88-109.

------. "Where Do the Numbers Come From? How People Respond to Contingent Valuation Questions." In *Contingent Valuation: A Critical Assessment*, edited by Jerry A. Hausman. Amsterdam: North Holland Publishers, 1993.

Schuman, Howard, and J. Scott. "Problems in the Use of Survey Questions to Measure Public Opinion." *Science* 236 (1987): 957-959.

Schuman, Howard, and Stanley Presser. *Questions and Answers in Attitude Surveys*. New York: Academic Press, Inc., 1981.

Smith, Tom W. "That Which We Call Welfare By Any Other Name Would Smell Sweeter." *Public Opinion Quarterly* 51 (1987): 75-83.

Smith, V. Kerry. "Comment: Arbitrary Values, Good Causes, and Premature Verdicts." *Journal of Environmental Economics and Management* 22, no. 1 (1992): 71-89.

Smith, V. Kerry, and Laura Osborne. "Are Contingent Valuation Estimates Economically Consistent? Visibility Changes at National Parks." Unpublished paper. Resource and Environmental Economics Program, North Carolina State University, January, 1993.

Smith, V. Kerry and Xiaolong Zhang. "Can Contingent Valuation Pass a Challenging Scope Test?: Visual Displays of Marine Debris," unpublished paper, Center for Environmental and Resource Economics, Duke University, January 1995.

Stevens, Thomas H., Jaime Echeverria, Ronald J. Glass, Tim Hager, and Thomas A. More. "Measuring the Existence Value of Wildlife: What Do CVM Estimates Really Show?" *Land Economics* 67 (1991): 390-400.

Schwarz, Norbert and Fritz Strack. "Context Effects in Attitude Surveys: Applying Cognitive Theory to Social Research." *European Review of Social Psychology* 2 (1991): 31-50.

Sudman, S., and N.M. Bradburn. *Asking Questions*. San Francisco: Jossey-Bass, 1983.

Sutherland, Ronald J., and Richard G. Walsh. "Effect of Distance on the Preservation of Water Quality." *Land Economics* 61, no. 3 (1985): 281-291.

Thayer, Mark "Contingent Valuation Techniques for Assessing Environmental Impacts: Further Evidence." *Journal of Environmental Economics and Management* 8 (1981): 27-44.

Thompson, Mark S. "Willingness to Pay and Accept Risks to Cure Chronic Disease." *American Journal of Public Health* 76, no. 4 (1986): 392-396.

Tobin, J., and H.S. Houthakker. "The Effects of Rationing on Demand Elasticities." *Review of Economic Studies* 18 (1951): 140-53.

Tolley, G.S., L. Babcock, M. Berger, A. Bilotti, G. Blomquist, M. Brien, R. Fabian, G. Fishelson, C. Kahn, and *et al. Valuation of Reductions in Human Health Symptoms and Risks: Volume II: Comparative Analysis of Approaches to Valuing Health Risks*. Final report to the U.S. Environmental Protection Agency, January, 1986.

Veisten, Knut, Hans Fredrik Hoen, Ståle Navrud, and Jon Strand. "Valuing Biodiversity in Norwegian Forests." Presented at Meeting of the European Association of Environmental and Resource Economists. Paris, June, 1993.

Walsh, Richard G., Donn M. Johnson, and John R. McKean. "Benefit Transfer of Outdoor Recreation Demand Studies: 1968-1988." *Water Resources Research* 28,(1992): 707-713.

Walsh, Richard G., Nicole P. Miller, and Lynde O. Gilliam. "Congestion and Willingness to Pay for Expansion of Skiing Capacity." *Land Economics* 59, no. 2 (1983): 195-210.

Whitehead, John C. "Ex Ante Willingness to Pay with Supply and Demand Uncertainty: Implications for Valuing a Sea Turtle Protection Programme." *Applied Economics* 24 (1992): 981-988.

Whitehead, John C., and Glenn C. Blomquist. "Measuring Contingent Values for Wetlands: Effects of Information About Related Environmental Goods." *Water Resources Research* 27, no. 10 (1991): 2523-2531.

Wu, Pei-Ing. "Benefit Evaluation of Multidimensional Environmental Policy: An Application to Ohio's Big Darby Creek." Dissertation. *DAI* 52 (1991): 2228. Ohio State University.

7

COGNITION, COMMUNICATION, AND SURVEY MEASUREMENT: SOME IMPLICATIONS FOR CONTINGENT VALUATION SURVEYS

Norbert Schwarz

INTRODUCTION

Contingent valuation (CV) surveys provide a methodological approach for determining the value of non-marketed goods or services (see Mitchell & Carson, 1989, for a discussion of their theoretical and methodological rationale). In a nutshell, respondents are provided with a detailed description of the to-be-valued good or service and are asked to report what they would be willing to pay for it. The value inferred from their responses is contingent upon the nature of the constructed hypothetical market and the good or service described in the scenario, hence the term "contingent valuation". CV surveys are primarily used to assess the passive use values of natural resources and their results are used in cost-benefit analysis and natural resource damage assessment. The first CV study has been published in 1963 and more than 1,400 studies have been documented since.

Despite the frequent use of CV in natural resource valuation, there are no generally agreed upon guidelines for the design of CV studies. Moreover, the use of CV methodology in assessing the damage inflicted by the Exxon Valdez oil spill in Alaska (see Carson et al., 1992) spurred a considerable amount of research, mainly sponsored by Exxon, that questioned the validity of CV findings (see the contributions in Hausmann, 1993). As a result, the U.S. National Oceanic and Atmospheric Administration (NOAA) and the U.S. Department of the Interior are currently developing regulations to guide the future use of CV surveys for purposes of cost-benefit analysis and damage assessment. The crucial role of cost-benefit analysis in U.S. environmental policy (see Kopp & Pease, 1994), on the one hand, and the monetary implications of estimated passive use values in natural resource damage litigation on the other hand, contributed to a heated debate that far exceeds any other controversy about the methodology of social science research. In the present chapter, I address the key issues raised in this debate by drawing on recent psychological research into the cognitive and communicative processes underlying survey measurement.

CHALLENGES TO CV RESEARCH

Recent theoretical and methodological discussions of CV surveys have focused on the observation that "CV responses are *sensitive* to methodological factors that, from the standpoint of economic theory, are irrelevant, as well as *insensitive* to some theoretically relevant factors" (Schkade & Payne, 1993, p. 273). Underlying much of this discussion are the implicit assumptions of what Fischhoff (1991) called a "philosophy of articulated values." According to this meta-theoretical orientation -- which is usually attributed to economists, but is shared by many survey researchers as well (see Strack & Schwarz, 1992, for a discussion of meta-theories in survey research) -- people have well-formed preferences about (nearly) any topic, which they can retrieve from memory and report when asked. Although some economists have rejected this assumption as a caricature of economic theorizing (see the discussion contributions in Hausman, 1993), it has, more or less explicitly, provided the standard for measuring the performance of CV studies.

An alternative approach is based on what Fischhoff (1991) called the "philosophy of basic values". This orientation, which is dominant in psychology and decision making, assumes that people have well-defined values only for very few, and very familiar, topics of high importance. In most cases, they have to construct their preferences when asked. Importantly, these constructions depend on the information considered at that point in time, rendering them highly context dependent. From a psychological point of view, this context dependency is a normal feature of human judgment that is observed in daily behavior and real economic decision making (see Payne, Bettman, & Johnson, 1992; Thaler, 1992) as well CV responses.

Given their different meta-theoretical assumptions, both approaches differ in their evaluation of the context dependency of reported preferences. From an "articulated values" point of view, the context dependency of reported preferences indicates that the measurement methods used are inappropriate for assessing peoples' "true" preferences and need revision until context-independency is reached (if ever). In contrast, the "basic values" point of view suggests that it is the researcher's task to structure the instrument in a way that helps people in constructing meaningful preferences, e.g., by drawing their attention to pertinent information, providing a relevant frame of reference, and so on. Fischhoff and Furby's (1988) extensive discussion of things to do and not do in CV studies illustrates this approach.

In the specific case of CV research, however, the issues seem more complex than in the assessment of other preferences, lets say political preferences in an opinion survey. Survey researchers, for example, want to assess whatever the opinion of people out there is, but are rarely concerned with the rationality of that opinion relative to some normative model. For them, the key criterion to validate reported preferences for a political candidate, for example, is actual voting behavior in an election. If people vote for the candidate for the "right" or "wrong" reasons is of no concern. Not so in the recent debate about CV responses. In this case, observing that a CV survey correctly predicts the outcome of an actual referendum would not satisfy many of the critics. Rather, the compatibility of CV responses with normative economic models assumes crucial importance, shifting the criteria from how people vote on a referendum to whether they vote the way they do for the "right" reason (see the discussions in Hausman, 1993).

Although noneconomists may find it surprising that models that are known to be wrong as descriptions of real economic behavior can serve as the gold standard for contingent economic behavior, addressing the intricacies of this issue is beyond the scope of my expertise. Two issues, however, are crucial to the current debate and I shall address them by drawing on what we know about how people answer survey questions. These issues are, that CV responses are (a) insensitive to factors that are deemed theoretically relevant, but (b) sensitive to factors that are deemed irrelevant. Taking a mental construal perspective, I argue that proponents as well as opponents of current CV methods need to pay more attention to respondents' construal of the to-be-valued good. Based on related research in survey methodology and attitude measurement, I suggest that many apparently irrelevant features of the questionnaire implicitly provide information that is relevant to the valuation task, whereas much of the explicitly provided information may never find its way into respondents' representations of the good. Based on these considerations, I outline relevant research and discuss methodological implications. Before I turn to these issues, however, it is necessary to review the question answering process in surveys.

COGNITION, COMMUNICATION, AND SURVEY MEASUREMENT

That survey data are only as meaningful as the answers that respondents provide has long been recognized by survey researchers. Nevertheless, the cognitive and communicative processes that underlie question answering in the survey context have only recently received theoretical and empirical attention. Drawing on psychological theories of language comprehension, memory, and judgment, psychologists and survey methodologists have begun to formulate explicit models of the question answering process and have tested these models in laboratory experiments and split-ballot surveys. This work links survey methodologists' expertise in the "art of asking questions" to recent developments in cognitive and social psychology, thus providing a useful theoretical and empirical basis for understanding the processes by which survey respondents arrive at an answer (see the contributions in Hippler, Schwarz, & Sudman, 1987; Schwarz & Sudman, 1992, 1994, 1996; Tanur, 1992, for research examples; and Sudman, Bradburn, & Schwarz, 1996, for a comprehensive review).

Much of the work on cognitive aspects of survey responding has focused on attitude measurement and it is informative to highlight some of the differences between traditional attitude surveys and CV surveys. From a cognitive perspective, answering an attitude question requires that respondents solve several tasks, on which researchers have reached wide agreement (see, for example, Schwarz & Strack,

1991; Strack & Martin, 1987; Tourangeau & Rasinski, 1988). Although these tasks are plausibly presented in a sequential order, the actual order in which respondents complete the tasks may occasionally differ from the assumed typical sequence.

Question comprehension

As a first step, respondents have to interpret the question to understand what is meant. If the question is ambiguous, respondents draw on the context of the question to disambiguate its meaning. Relevant contextual information includes the content of preceding questions (see Schuman & Presser, 1981; Schwarz & Strack, 1991; Sudman et al., 1996, for reviews) as well as apparently formal features of the questionnaire (see Schwarz & Hippler, 1991; Schwarz, 1994, 1995, for reviews). Not surprisingly, different substantive interpretations of a question result in different answers. What is more surprising to many researchers is that different substantive interpretations can be triggered by formal features of the questionnaire that are usually not supposed to influence question meaning.

As an example, suppose that respondents are asked to rate how successful they have been in life along a scale from "not at all successful" to "extremely successful." To answer this question, respondents must determine what the researcher means by "not at all successful". Does this term refer to the absence of outstanding achievements or to the presence of explicit failures? Without additional explanation, respondents may turn to relevant features of question context, making use of what the researcher may consider an irrelevant technical feature of the questionnaire. One such feature are the specific numeric values presented as part of a rating scale. According to textbook knowledge, ratings are affected by the extremity of the verbal endpoint labels and the number of scale points provided, but an 11-point scale is an 11-point scale, no matter whether it presents 11 unnumbered boxes or numeric values that run from 1 to 11, from 0 to 10, or from -5 to +5. Trying to make sense of the specific meaning of the verbal label, however, respondents may turn to such apparently irrelevant factors in interpreting the meaning of the question. Thus, we observed in several studies that "not at all successful" was interpreted as reflecting the absence of outstanding achievements when the rating scale ran from 0 ("not at all successful") to 10 ("very successful"), but was interpreted as reflecting the presence of explicit failure when the rating scale ran from -5 ("not at all successful") to +5 ("very successful"), presenting 0 as the neutral midpoint. As a result of this differential interpretation of the verbal anchor, 34 percent of the respondents endorsed a value below the midpoint of the 0 to 10 scale, whereas only 13 percent endorsed one of the formally equivalent values of the -5 to +5 scale (Schwarz, Knäuper, Hippler, Noelle-Neumann, & Clark, 1991). As this example illustrates, design features that are often considered "nonsubstantive" may profoundly change the meaning of a question. As a result, many influences of apparently "irrelevant" features of questionnaire design can be traced to their impact on respondents understanding of the substantive meaning of the question.

The use of contextual information that is reflected in such findings (see Schwarz, 1994, for a review) is licensed by the tacit rules that govern the conduct of conversation in daily life, as described in Grice's (1975) cooperativeness principle (see Clark & Schober, 1992; Schwarz, 1994, 1995; Strack & Schwarz, 1992, for applications to survey research). According to these tacit rules, "communicated information comes with a guarantee of relevance" as Sperber and Wilson (1986, p. vi) noted, and listeners interpret speakers' utterances on the assumption that the speaker is trying to be informative, relevant and clear. If the speaker does not live up to these ideals, listeners may ask for clarification (which they are unlikely to get from the interviewer) or may use related contributions of the speaker to determine the intended meaning. In the survey interview, the contributions of the researcher to the ongoing "conversation" include the content of preceding questions as well as formal features of the questionnaire, rendering them highly relevant as contextual information.

As in other domains of discourse, however, question comprehension requires more than an understanding of the literal meaning of the utterance. Rather, respondents have to identify the pragmatic meaning of the question to determine which information the questioner asks them to provide (Clark & Schober, 1992; Schwarz, 1994). A simple example may again illustrate this point. When asked, "What have you done today?", respondents are likely to understand the literal meaning of the question -- but which information are they supposed to provide? What are the behaviors that the researcher is interested in? Should they report, for example, that they took a shower or not? When the question is asked in an open response format, chances are that hardly any respondent would report taking a shower. But when "taking a shower" is presented as one of the response alternatives in a closed question format, most respondents are likely to endorse it (see Schuman & Presser, 1981; Schwarz & Hippler, 1991).

Findings of this type again reflect that survey respondents rely on the tacit rules that govern the conduct of conversation in daily life (Grice, 1975). These rules ask speakers to provide information that is "informative" for the recipient, rather than information that the recipient may take for granted anyway. Accordingly, information that seems self-evident, that may be assumed to "go without saying", or that has already been provided in response to a previous question is unlikely to be reported unless the researcher explicitly indicates that it is of interest (e.g., by presenting appropriate response alternatives). This hesitancy to report things that "go without saying" has potentially important implications for questions designed to check respondents' understanding of CV scenarios, as we shall see below.

Recall and judgment

Once respondents made sense of an attitude question, they presumably recall the relevant opinion from memory. Or at least this is what attitude researchers usually hope for (in line with an articulated values philosophy), reflecting their disdain for what has often been called "door step opinions" in public opinion research. In most cases, however, respondents are unlikely to have a previously formed judgment accessible in memory, in particular a judgment that matches the specific aspects of the issue addressed in the question. Accordingly, respondents need to "compute" a judgment on the spot (as assumed by a basic values philosophy). To do so, they draw on relevant information that is accessible at this point in time to form a mental representation of the target (see Schwarz & Bless, 1992; Schwarz & Strack, 1991; Tourangeau, 1992; Tourangeau & Rasinski, 1987; for a review see Sudman et al., 1996, chapters 4 to 6).

Which information is accessible depends on respondents' knowledge and the context of the questionnaire. Some information may always come to mind when a given respondent thinks of a given target, and is hence called *chronically accessible*. Other information, however, may only come to mind because it has been used just recently, usually to answer a preceding question. Such *temporarily accessible* information is the source of most context effects in attitude measurement. The larger the amount of temporarily accessible information relative to chronically accessible information, the larger the size of context effects (see Schwarz & Bless, 1992, for a more detailed discussion). Accordingly, attitude researchers would like respondents to draw solely on chronically accessible information in forming a representation of the target. This follows from their desire to generalize from the opinions reported by their sample to the opinions of a population that has not been exposed to the context of the questionnaire. Accordingly, any influence of the information rendered accessible by the questionnaire is deemed undesirable because such influences would lead to context dependent reports that deviate from the opinions presumably held in the population.

What most researchers hope for in conducting a CV survey, on the other hand, seems quite different. In fully developed CV surveys (see Mitchell & Carson, 1989; Fischhoff & Furby, 1988) respondents are supposed to value a specific good that is described to them in considerable detail in the survey. In most cases, they have no experience with the good. In fact, they are usually asked to value some imagined environmental change for which any previously computed value cannot be available. Accordingly, CV respondents are supposed to rely on the information provided in the questionnaire to arrive at a mental representation of the to-be-valued good. To the extent that they draw on information that is not contained in the scenario, they may construct a good that differs from the good the researcher wants them to value, rendering their reported WTP irrelevant to the goals of the study. Below, I return to these issues in more detail. For the time being, however, I note that the procedures underlying fully developed CV surveys clearly follow a basic values philosophy (despite occasional disclaimers, see Mitchell & Carson, 1989).

Many studies reported by CV critics, on the other hand, follow a methodology that is more in line with the assumption of an articulated values philosophy. Consistent with what attitude researchers would do, respondents in these studies are provided with descriptions of the good of less than 10 words in length, aptly described as following "the headline method" (Kahneman & Ritov, 1994). The better of these descriptions meet the criteria for good attitude questions and are sufficient to identify the issue, which should allow respondents to retrieve a previously formed preference, assuming such a preference is accessible. From a construal point of view, however, these descriptions provide insufficient specifications of the good, rendering it impossible to tell what exactly respondents are valuing.

Forming an evaluative judgment, however, does not only require a mental representation of the target of the question (the attitude object or good), but also a mental representation of some standard against which the target is evaluated. Much as the representation formed of the target, the representation formed of a standard is context dependent (Schwarz & Bless, 1992) and may include temporarily as well as chronically accessible information. In general, attitude researchers again hope that respondents draw primarily on chronically accessible information in constructing a relevant standard, for the reasons discussed above. In contrast, CV researchers frequently remind respondents of other public goods to provide a framework for the valuation task, again reflecting a basic values approach.

As these comparisons indicate, it is the use of *context dependent* information, rendered accessible by the questionnaire, that is considered problematic in attitude measurement. In contrast, it is the use of *context independent* information that is considered problematic in CV surveys, although this issue is rarely addressed in these terms. Given that judgments are likely to be based on *both* sources of information in either case, attitude researchers and CV researcher are interested in minimizing the impact of different sources of information.

Formatting

Once respondents have formed a "private" judgment in their mind, they need to communicate it to the researcher. Unless the question uses an open-response format, respondents have to format their judgment to fit the response alternatives provided as part of the question. Attitude researchers as well as CV researchers usually think of response alternatives as simple "measurement devices." As long as the response alternatives allow respondents to express their judgment, they are not considered to influence the obtained results. This assumption, however, is mistaken as the examples reviewed in the context of question comprehension illustrated. The response alternatives constitute an important source of information that respondents draw on in making sense of the question and in constructing mental representations of the target or standard (see Schwarz & Hippler, 1991; Schwarz, 1994, 1995). Below, I address the implications of this perspective for different forms of WTP questions.

Reporting the answer

Finally, respondents may wish to edit their response before they report it, due to influences of social desirability and situational adequacy (see DeMaio, 1984). In this regard, attitudes as well as CV researchers attempt to safeguard against influences of social desirability and survey methodologists developed various procedures that reduce these influences (see Sudman & Bradburn, 1983).

Modes of data collection

In summary, interpreting the question, generating an opinion, formatting the response, and editing the answer are the main psychological components of a process that starts with respondents' exposure to a survey question and ends with their overt report. Several aspects of this process are influenced by the mode of data collection used, resulting in differences between face-to-face or telephone interviews and self-administered questionnaires (see Schwarz, Strack, Hippler, & Bishop, 1991). In the final section of this paper, I address some of the relevant mode differences and their implications for the use of mail surveys in contingent valuation research.

MENTAL REPRESENTATIONS AND SCOPE EFFECTS: WHAT ARE RESPONDENTS VALUING?

"According to consumer theory, for any good, more of that good is preferred to less. Therefore, a scenario offering a higher level of services should yield a higher value" (Desvouges, Hudson, & Ruby, 1994, p. 8), at least if the good has positive marginal utility. Much of the recent debate has focused on the extent to which the responses obtained in CV surveys meet this assumption of economic theorizing. Several studies demonstrated that reported WTP can be insensitive to variations in the scope of the described good, whereas others observed satisfactory sensitivity (see Carson & Mitchell, 1993, in press, for reviews). The crucial question is what demonstrations of insensitivity to scope actually demonstrate: that a given specific survey instrument is insensitive or that CV methodology in general is insensitive to scope? Whereas the former conclusion suggests that the specific instrument needs improvement, the latter conclusion suggests that respondents' valuations may be based on processes that are incompatible with the economic framework that provides the theoretical justification for CV methods (see Carson & Mitchell, 1993 and Kahneman & Knetsch, 1992, for opposing perspectives).

In addressing this question, we face the usual problems involved in interpreting null results, in particular in the presence of other studies that obtained the predicted differences. Psychologists' usual response to null results is to demonstrate (a) that the appropriate experimental conditions have been realized, based on proper manipulation checks, and/or (b) that some other dependent variable shows a pattern that plausibly supports that the experimental manipulation was successful. In the absence of such evidence, psychologists usually refrain from drawing substantive conclusions from null results. Note, however, that making a case for the interpretability of null results does not require *more* than demonstrating the successful realization of the experimental conditions and appropriate statistical power. As Fischhoff (this volume) noted, some CV researchers advocate standards that raise the cost of methodological studies to a level that renders basic research unfeasible. Whereas these criteria may be appropriate for damage assessments, where the absolute value of WTP is of key interest, many of them (including representativeness, sample size, and related variables) are overly restrictive for methodological studies interested in relative differences between experimental conditions.

What, however, does it take to demonstrate that differences in scope have been successfully realized in a scenario? At the minimum, it requires a manipulation check that indicates that respondents do indeed expect that (a) *different quantities* of (b) the *same quality* of the described good will (c) be delivered with *equal likelihood*, if proper payment is provided. This requires that respondents understand the differences in quantity conveyed in the scenario; that their mental construal of the good is not more or less inclusive than intended in the scenario; that the scope does not affect the perceived likelihood of delivery or the perceived quality of what is delivered; and so on (see Fischhoff & Furby, 1988, for an extensive discussion of relevant criteria). Unfortunately, it is unclear to what extent such prerequisites were met in many of the better known demonstrations of embedding effects -- as well as in the studies that demonstrated sensitivity to differences in scope.

Do respondents understand the description of scope?

Obviously, differences in scope described in the scenario will only affect the obtained responses if they find their way into respondents' own mental representations of the good. This requires that respondents notice the scope described in the scenario and that this description makes sense to them. In general, respondents assume that the space and time allocated to an issue in the questionnaire reflects its relative importance (Fischhoff & Furby, 1988; Schwarz, 1994). Accordingly, scope information needs to be elaborated on, rather than mentioned in passing, and respondents' attention needs to be drawn to it.

To illustrate this rather trivial point, consider two studies reported by Desvouges et al. (1993) and Schkade and Payne (1993), based on the same scenarios. Using a self-administered questionnaire in a mall intercept survey, Desvouges et al. asked respondents to value a program that would prevent the deaths of either 2,000, 20,000, or 200,000 migratory waterfowl from oil ponds in the Rocky Mountain flyway. Respondents were further informed that 2,000 birds represent "much less" than 1% of the population, 20,000 birds "less" than 1%, and 200,000 birds "about 2%". The results showed that the described scope had no impact on reported WTP, which seems surprising if one draws on differences in the absolute number of birds involved, but not if one draws on the minor differences in the percentage of birds involved -- which indicate that either 98% or 99% of the birds would not be affected anyway. However, when Schkade and Payne used exactly the same scenario, but asked respondents to think aloud while answering the questions, the difference between 2,000 and 200,000 birds resulted in differential median WTP values of $25 and $50, respectively (or $25 and $60, p = .11, when zero answers were excluded from analysis). Although these differences failed to reach significance with the small sample size used, the pattern of WTP suggests that the think-aloud task fostered attention to detail, resulting in the elaboration of the scope information provided.

As this example illustrates, scope information requires appropriate encoding, which needs to be ensured by procedures that draw respondents' attention to scope information and encourage its active elaboration. This may be accomplished by questions that stimulate respondents to draw on the scope information during the information acquisition phase and to incorporate scope information in their mental representations of the good. That this can be accomplished even for information that is notoriously difficult to convey, such as information about low-level risks, has been successfully demonstrated in several studies (e.g., Mitchell & Carson, 1986). Simply observing that scope information does not affect reported WTP, however, is insufficient to challenge CV methodology at a basic level as the observed insensitivity may always reflect an unsuccessful manipulation that should be addressed in a revision of the instrument.

Inclusive representations

A different problem arises when differences in scope are introduced by respondents' implicit assumptions about the intervention that is supposed to provide the relevant good. This problem increases with respondents' knowledge about the content domain and decreases, at least to some extent, with the explicitness of the scenario. As an illustration, consider the construals of highly sophisticated respondents in a study reported by Schulze, McClelland, and Lazo (1994). According to economic models, the jointly assessed value of preserving a species of blue winged <u>and</u> a species of green winged butterflies in the Amazon rain forest should be equivalent to the sum of the values assigned to preserving only the blue winged butterflies or only the green winged butterflies, when each species is valued by itself (assuming that the two are not substitutable). This prediction presupposes, however, that respondents do indeed treat the preservation of both species as unrelated. Yet, sophisticated respondents may be unlikely to do so, as focus group results reported by Schulze et al. (1994) illustrate. Drawing on their knowledge about the interdependence of environmental processes, sophisticated respondents may reason,

"Butterfly species in the Amazon are becoming extinct because of a loss of habitat. The only way to save one species is to save all of them by saving the forest as well" (Schulze et al. 1994, p. 16). As a result, respondents' representation of the to-be-valued good includes much more than the butterfly species that is to be saved, resulting, in the present case, in a valuation of the complete forest along with an unknown number of other species. Not surprisingly, asking these respondents to value the preservation of several species in the same habitat does not result in higher WTP, reflecting that the valuation of any species includes the value of all other species given the respondents' mental model of the content domain.

To which extent such joint valuations underlie non-additive valuations is an empirical issue. The embedding effect that results from joint valuations, however, does not violate normative assumptions. Rather, it reflects that respondents in the narrow scope condition are valuing a more inclusive good than the researcher intended them to begin with, thus rendering explicit extensions in scope uninfluential. Accordingly, it is crucial to understand what knowledge respondents draw on in forming a mental representation of the good. Because this knowledge is domain dependent, its exploration presents a formidable task.

Of course, better CV surveys usually try to assess what respondents have been valuing after WTP is assessed. Based on what we learned from cognitive research into question comprehension in surveys, however, such questions are not guaranteed to uncover diverging construals of the to-be-valued good. In line with conversational norms, respondents may not elaborate on information they consider self-evident, assuming that some things go without saying (Clark, 1985). To return to Schulze et al.'s (1994) example, a respondent who assumes that butterflies can only be saved by saving their habitat, may also assume that the researcher, who is presumably an expert on the issue, shares this obvious insight. When asked, she may hence respond that she valued the butterfly species, taking it for granted that this implies whatever it obviously takes to reach the goal. One way to address this issue is to explore respondents' reasoning processes in think-aloud studies during the pretesting phase and to develop specific queries for inclusion in the main survey. Much as in the case of the "What-have-you-done-today?" example discussed above, such specific probes would be likely to uncover assumptions that respondents take for granted, although these assumptions would not be reported in response to a more general question.

Scope and certainty of provision

Similar concerns apply to assessments of the scenario's plausibility and the perceived likelihood that the promised good is actually provided. As Fischhoff and Furby (1988, p. 162) noted, "Agreeing to a proposed transaction involves an exchange of promises: to deliver a good and to make a payment. As a result, two defining aspects of any agreement are the probabilities of each promise being kept. The less likely a good is to be received, the less an offer to provide it should be valued."

In general, CV researchers want respondents to assume that provision of the good is certain. To the extent that respondents' perceived likelihood of provision is lower, they undervalue the good relative to the researcher's intended interpretation of the scenario. Although the perceived certainty of provision is affected by many aspects of the scenario (see Mitchell & Carson, 1989), a particularly crucial one is the described scope: The larger the scope, the less likely it may seem that the promised good is actually delivered. Tempting as an investment plan that promises an annual return of 200% may be, we are likely to put more money into a more conservative plan, reflecting that exaggerated promises raise doubts -- in particular if the relevant mechanism of provision does not strike one as plausible. Similar concerns may apply to a plan that promises, for example, to "Rehabilitate all recently released criminals," as opposed to "Rehabilitate recently released young offenders" (see Kahneman & Knetsch, 1992, p. 65, for relevant examples). To the extent that the certainty of provision seems lower in the former case than in the latter, we shouldn't expect that people pay more for the former plan.

In considering respondents' perception of the certainty of provision it is helpful to distinguish between the provision of the promised intervention and the provision of the good that the intervention is supposed to produce or protect. As the rehabilitation example illustrates, both are likely to be affected by scope. On the one hand, the implementation of a rehabilitation program directed at all released criminals may seem less realistic than a program directed at the smaller subset of young offenders. On the other hand, respondents may assume that "young offenders" are more likely to be successfully rehabilitated than seasoned "criminals", as may already be indicated by the respective terms. If so, they may assume that the smaller program delivers more for the money than the larger program. Moreover, one may wonder if respondents spontaneously include young offenders in their mental representation of criminals, reiterating the concerns about the mental representation of scope addressed above.

Again, respondents' general acceptance of the scenario and their perception of provision is assessed in the better studies, usually after respondents reported their WTP. In many cases, these acceptance checks ask respondents to report what they thought the plan would deliver. This question, however, may be difficult to answer as doubts about the plan may suggest it won't deliver what it promises, without specifying what the scope of the actual delivery might be. Hence, the easiest answer is to reiterate the promises detailed in the scenario, possibly resulting in an overestimate of scenario acceptance. To assess the impact of scope on the perceived likelihood and quality of delivery, simple ratings may provide a better way to gauge the plan's perceived effectiveness.

Conclusions

As the above examples illustrate, there is a need for basic research into the mental representations that respondents form of the to-be-valued good. This research needs to take respondents' real world knowledge into account, exploring how the application of this knowledge transforms the information provided in typical scenarios. The bottom line is simple: Respondents do not value the good as described, but the good as represented in their own mental construal of the scenario.

Such construal processes have been explored in attitude measurement (e.g., Schwarz & Bless, 1992), person perception (e.g., Griffin & Ross, 1991), and behavioral decision research (e.g., Payne, Bettman, & Johnson, 1992), but they have found insufficient attention in recent CV discussions. Understanding these construal processes may raise as well as solve problems that are crucial to CV research. On the one hand, such research may uncover that the apparent insensitivity of CV responses to factors that should matter may reflect that these factors are not well represented in respondents' mental construal of the to-be-valued good. On the other hand, a mental construal approach to valuation emphasizes that the exact nature of the valued good cannot be inferred from the scenario alone, rendering it difficult to determine what people value.

HOW MUCH DOES IT TAKE? WTP AND IMPLICIT COST INFORMATION

Given that respondents have no experience with the good, they need to determine their WTP under conditions of considerable uncertainty. According to CV theorizing, respondents are supposed to imagine the described good and to determine what this good would be worth to them. A key variable that people are likely to consider in determining what they are willing to pay for a good is the cost involved in producing the good. Suppose, for example, that your car breaks down and you are asked what you'd be willing to pay to get it restored to its previous condition. Chances are that you'd like to know if all it takes is to fix a loose wire, as opposed to, lets say, replacing the complete engine. And although the outcome is the same -- your car is running again -- your reaction to a $800 bill is likely to be very different in these two cases. As this example illustrates, our willingness to pay is not only determined by the outcome, but also by our assessment of the fair cost of producing that outcome.

Nevertheless, information about the amount of money it takes to produce a good is usually not explicitly provided in CV scenarios, for theoretical as well as practical reasons. In the case of natural resource damage assessments, the scenario is only supposed to serve as a vehicle that provides a plausible framework for eliciting the valuation of a good (e.g., a clean beach) that the plan is supposed to protect. In terms of the above car example, it is the running car that is to be valued, not the repair effort. Much as in the car example, however, respondents are likely to consider "how much it takes" to produce the outcome, in addition to the outcome itself.

As Schkade and Payne (1993, p. 283) observed on the basis of think-aloud protocols, "Perhaps the most common strategy in our sample involved first acknowledging that something should be done and then trying to figure out how much an appropriate amount would be." To determine the "appropriate amount", respondents are likely to consider cost information, resulting in increasing WTP with increasing cost estimates. To arrive at a cost estimate, respondents have two relevant sources of information, namely the complexity of the scenario and the $-value of the WTP question. Thus, scenarios that describe more extended plans, involving, for example, ten rather than one escort ships in oil spill protection scenarios, are likely to convey higher cost and may hence be likely to produce higher WTP -- even under conditions where the same alleged outcome is described.

A more directly relevant source of information is provided by the $-value presented in a referendum question. In general, respondents assume that the numeric values provided as part of a question reflect the researcher's expert knowledge about the issue under study (see Schwarz & Hippler, 1991; Schwarz, 1994, for reviews of relevant research). From this perspective, the $-value of the WTP question conveys the experts' cost estimate for the described plan. To illustrate this point, I recently asked 20 students at the University of Michigan if they would vote YES or NO on a plan to spend either $5 or $50 of their tuition to cover the start-up cost of an extensive recycling program on campus. Subsequently, the students were asked to estimate what the actual start-up cost would be. Not surprisingly, they estimated the start-up cost to be about eight times higher when the plan involved a contribution of $50 rather than $5.

That the $-value offered as part of a WTP question provides implicit cost information has methodological as well as theoretical implications. Whereas the methodological implications are likely to be appreciated by CV researchers, the theoretical implications are more problematic for CV research. On the methodological side, the present perspective suggests that any discrepancies between open-ended WTP questions and referendum questions are a function of the specific $-value presented in the referendum question. If the suggested $-value is higher than the modal value offered in an open-ended format, referendum questions will result in higher WTP estimates; if it is lower, referendum questions will result in lower WTP estimates. Hence, general discussions of whether referendum questions over- or underestimate WTP (e.g., Desvouges, Hudson, & Ruby, 1994; Green, 1992) are likely to be futile because the specific outcome depends on the specific value presented as the experts' estimate of "what it takes."

On the theoretical side, this perspective implies that the $-value offered in a referendum question is best conceptualized as part of the scenario, informing respondents about the cost of the plan. Whereas this cost information is not explicitly provided in the scenario, it is offered by the elicitation question and most likely used by respondents in their mental construal. From this perspective, respondents who are provided with different $-values as part of the WTP question provide valuations of somewhat different goods rather than different valuations of the same good. As a methodological implication, it follows that discrepancies between WTP questions that use an open-ended versus closed response format (e.g., Holmes & Kramer, 1993; Cameron & Huppert, 1991) do not indicate a faulty measurement process that reflects a lack of convergent validity in assessing the value of the same good (in contrast to the conclusion reached by Desvouges et al., 1994).

Rather, it indicates that valuing somewhat different goods results in different valuations -- further emphasizing the need to understand what it is that respondents actually value.

Note, however, that the perspective offered here has a troublesome implication: To the extent that respondents draw on cost information in determining their WTP, the cost information provided by the researcher predetermines respondents' valuation of the good, essentially anticipating what the study is supposed to reveal. As suggested by Schkade and Payne's (1993) protocols, respondents may first determine if something needs to be done and may then try "to figure out how much an appropriate amount would be" (p. 283). If they interpret the referendum question as reflecting the experts' estimate of the contribution that it takes to meet the cost, this latter task is relatively easy, reducing the decision to whether one is willing, and able, to contribute one's share towards the provision of a collective good.

That respondents take such a cost sharing perspective is suggested by Schkade and Payne's (1993) protocols as well as by data reported by Green, Kahneman, and Kunreuther (1994). Schkade and Payne (1993, p. 283), for example, observed that "41% of the sample mentioned the idea that, if everyone did their part, each household would not have to give all that much. In fact, respondents who used this reasoning did give substantially lower WTPs." This theme is reiterated in Green et al.'s (1994) findings. Respondents in their study were asked to report their WTP for a program to teach English to immigrants to the United States. Some respondents were informed that 20 million other households would be asked the same question, whereas other respondents did not receive this information. Those whose attention was drawn to the large number of other households asked, were more likely to offer some payment, but the payment they did offer was lower than the payment offered by those who did not receive this information. Apparently, respondents who were aware that 20 million households would be asked to make a contribution inferred that each household's contribution could be relatively small. This finding suggests that respondents were willing to pay "what it takes", at least within limits, but certainly not more than it takes.

Although these findings are nicely compatible with a contribution model of CV measurement, as Green et al. (1994) suggest, they are not necessarily incompatible with a purchase model. To return to the car example, suppose that your repair bill includes $100 to cover the mechanic's trip to your car. Would your response to this charge differ if the mechanic also repaired three additional cars that broke down within a few yards, charging each one $100 for the trip? It seems that considerations of cost sharing may be as important in a purchase frame as in a contribution frame.

Conclusions

In summary, the conjectures offered here bear on the concern that "CV responses are sensitive to methodological factors that, from the standpoint of economic theory, are irrelevant" (Schkade & Payne, 1993, p. 273), such as the specific format of the elicitation question used. From a psychological point of view, the key assumption of this argument is mistaken: Far from reflecting formal, methodological features without substantive relevance, different forms of the elicitation question provide different information that respondents actively use in solving a complex task. Much as many formal aspects of attitude questions, such as the numeric values of a rating scale (Schwarz, Knäuper, et al., 1991) have been found to change the substantive meaning of the question, so do different elicitation formats provide more than exchangeable "measurement devices." Whereas future systematic evidence bearing on these conjectures may put the concern to rest that CV responses are sensitive to "irrelevant" factors, these conjectures raise a potentially more troublesome concern by suggesting that the referendum questions recommended by the NOAA panel predetermine respondents' valuations by providing implicit cost information.

MODE OF DATA COLLECTION

Survey responses are to some extent affected by the mode of data collection used. This reflects, in part, that face-to-face interviews, telephone interviews and self-administered questionnaires pose somewhat different cognitive tasks (see Schwarz, Strack, Hippler, & Bishop, 1991, for a detailed discussion). Moreover, the different modes of data collection provide differential opportunities for respondent self-selection. Below I address two key differences between (face-to-face or telephone) interviews and mail questionnaires that seem particularly relevant to CV surveys, namely respondent self-selection and the degree to which the researcher can control respondents' exposure to relevant information. In combination, these two factors argue against the use of mail surveys in CV research.

Exposure to information

One of the key differences between self-administered questionnaires and face-to-face or telephone interviews is that self-administered questionnaires provide no control over the extent to which respondents understand the material presented to them and the order in which questions are read (see Schwarz, Strack, et al., 1991). As several studies indicated, an unknown proportion of respondents is likely to read parts or all of the questionnaire before filling in an answer, resulting in influences of subsequent questions on answers given to preceding questions (e.g., Schwarz & Hippler, 1995). In addition, relevant issues may be discussed within the household, introducing other influences that are difficult to identify. For CV surveys, this lack of control has several potentially problematic implications.

First, it remains unclear to what extent respondents have carefully read the often lengthy and cumbersome scenarios. Hence, an unknown proportion of respondents may answer the questions on the basis of a rather superficial understanding of the scenario. The previously discussed observation that Schkade and Payne (1993) obtained differences in WTP as a function of scope when they requested respondents to think aloud while answering the questionnaire, whereas Desvouges et al. (1993) did not when they administered the questionnaire without a think-aloud requirement illustrates this point. On the other hand, respondents who are sufficiently interested in the topic have more time to think about the scenario under self-administered conditions than they would under interview conditions. At the extreme, they may return to the questionnaire at a later time, discuss it with others, gather additional information, and so on. Such an increased elaboration of the scenario is only likely for highly motivated respondents and its specific impact on WTP is likely to depend on how plausible the scenario seems, once one scrutinizes its details.

Second, to the extent that respondents read ahead, their interpretation of the scenario may be affected by their knowledge of the questions that follow it, including the $-value mentioned in the WTP question or the manipulation checks that ask them if they believed the information that was presented in the scenario. At present, it is unclear what the exact implications of knowing these questions are, but it seems likely that knowing the $-value affects the encoding of the scenario and that reading the manipulation checks may raise doubts about the reliability of the information offered.

Third, the possibility to discuss the issue with other household members or to gather more information may introduce information that is not contained in the scenario, further affecting respondents' construal of the to-be-valued good.

As these possibilities illustrate, mail survey conditions render it even more difficult to determine what respondents are actually valuing than interview surveys, reflecting that the researcher has less control over respondents' exposure to relevant information. Note, however, that some of these potential problems are of less concern when self-administered questionnaires are used under controlled laboratory conditions, where respondents may be discouraged from reading ahead and have to complete the questionnaire without interruption. Accordingly, self-administered questionnaires are a feasible instrument for basic research under controlled administration conditions, although their use under the uncontrollable conditions of mail surveys cannot be recommended.

Respondent self-selection

Adding to the above problems, mail surveys are particularly prone to respondent self-selection, as Schuman (1994) noted. This follows from the simple fact that mail survey respondents can screen the questionnaire before they decide to participate, whereas face-to-face and telephone surveys do not provide this opportunity. As a result, nonresponse in interview surveys reflects the impact of variables that are unrelated to the specific content of the survey, whereas nonresponse in mail surveys is, to an unknown degree, affected by content. Hence, mail surveys are likely to over represent individuals who find the topic interesting and important.

Although this issue becomes less problematic as the response rate of mail surveys increases, self-selection problems remain even at high response rates. As an illustration, suppose that a mail and a telephone survey both obtain an 80% response rate. In the telephone survey, the 20% nonresponse includes participants who refuse because they are called at a bad time, are on vacation, or whatever. However, it does not include respondents who thought about the issue and decided it is not worth their time. In contrast, mail respondents can work on the questionnaire at a time of their choice, thus potentially reducing nonresponse due to timing problems. On the other hand, however, they have the possibility to screen the questionnaire and are more likely to participate in the survey if they find the issue of interest. As a result, an identical nonresponse rate of 20% under both modes is likely to be unrelated to the topic under interview conditions, but not under mail conditions. Hence, similar response rates under different modes do not necessarily indicate comparable samples.

Moreover, the variable that drives self-selection under mail conditions is respondents' interest in the topic, which may be only weakly related to sociodemographic variables. Accordingly, topic driven self-selection may be present even if the completed sample seems representative with regard to sociodemographic variables like age, sex, income, and so on. To assess problems of topic related self-selection, one needs to assess respondents' interest in the topic. The current considerations predict that mail surveys include a higher percentage of respondents who report high interest than face-to-face or telephone surveys, even if the samples are comparable on sociodemographic grounds. If this differential self-selection results in an over- or underestimation of WTP, however, is difficult to determine because interest in the topic may reflect favorable as well as unfavorable attitudes towards the issue.

In combination with the lack of control over respondents' understanding of the provided information, the problem of topic related self-selection renders mail surveys unfeasible for CV research.

SUMMARY

In summary, the above discussion suggests that CV research may benefit from a more detailed consideration of the cognitive and communicative processes involved in answering CV questions, for which recent advances at the interface of cognitive psychology and survey methodology provide a highly relevant background. In drawing on this interdisciplinary work, which has mostly been conducted in the domain of attitude research, it is important to keep in mind that attitude researchers and CV researchers are pursuing different methodological goals. Attitude researchers typically want to minimize the impact of contextual information, hoping that respondents report an opinion that is independent of the information brought to mind by the questionnaire. In contrast, CV researchers want respondents to draw solely on the scenario information provided in the questionnaire and want to minimize the impact of other knowledge on respondents' construal of the to-be-valued good. Hence, CV surveys follow what Fischhoff (1991) has called a basic values philosophy of survey measurement (although this straightforward implication of the empirical approach used is not always reflected in the field's theoretical discussions). Recent research into the cognitive and communicative processes underlying survey responding bears on two aspects that are central to the current controversy about CV surveys, namely (a) the influence of apparently irrelevant factors and (b) the apparent lack of an influence of relevant ones.

With regard to the first issue, I reviewed recent applications of psychological theorizing to survey methodology which demonstrated that many apparently "formal" and "irrelevant" features of questionnaire design provide information that respondents actively use in determining the meaning of the question asked and in constructing a mental representation of the target of judgment. This research suggests that apparently irrelevant features of the questionnaire may influence respondents' representation of the to-be-valued good, resulting in valuations of somewhat different goods as a function of different features of questionnaire design. On one hand, this implies that demonstrating an influence of apparently "irrelevant" features on WTP does not necessarily cast doubt on the validity of the obtained responses. On the other hand, it also implies that apparently formal features of questionnaire design, such as the $-value presented in the elicitation question, should be considered substantive parts of the scenario. Preliminary results supported this perspective, which needs to be explored in more systematic experimental studies.

With regard to the second issue, it is important to emphasize that the sheer fact that some piece of information was presented in a scenario does not guarantee that it found its way into respondents' mental representation of the good. Hence, special attention needs to be given to the presentation of the scenario and to respondents' encodings of its key features. Moreover, respondents' representation of the good may be more or less inclusive than intended by the researcher, and may include assumptions about the likelihood and quality of provision, as the reviewed examples illustrate. Hence, appropriate measures to assess respondents' representations of the good need to be developed -- and the currently used questions (reviewed above) are unlikely to be appropriate. Last but not least, the most dramatic demonstrations of insufficient sensitivity to the described provision of the good are based on rather rudimentary scenarios that require respondents to fill in the gaps, thus rendering it impossible to tell what respondents were valuing. Clearly, future research will need to develop appropriate manipulation checks to probe respondents' mental representation of the good before strong conclusions can be drawn.

Finally, mail surveys provide insufficient control over respondents' encoding of the scenario and are open to self-selection bias based on topic interest, thus rendering them unfeasible for well-controlled CV surveys.

REFERENCES

Cameron, T., & Huppert, D. (1991). Referendum contingent valuation estimates: Sensitivity to the assignment of offered values. *Journal of the American Statistical Association, 86*, 910-918.

Carson, R. T., & Mitchell, R.C. (in press). Sequencing and nesting in contingent valuation surveys. *Journal of Environmental Economics and Management.*

Carson, R. T., & Mitchell, R. C. (1993). The issue of scope in contingent valuation studies. *American Journal of Agricultural Economics*, 75, 1263-1267.

Carson, R. T., Mitchell, R. C., Hanemann, W. M., Kopp, R. J., Presser, S., & Ruud, P. A. (1992). *A contingent valuation study of lost passive use values resulting from the Exxon Valdez oil spill.* San Diego: NRDA.

Clark, H.H. (1985). Language use and language users. In G. Lindzey, & E. Aronson (Eds.), *Handbook of social psychology* (Vol. 2, pp. 179 - 232). New York: Random House.

Clark, H. H., & Clark, E. V. (1977). *Psychology and language.* New York: Harcourt, Brace, Jovanovich.

Clark, H. H., & Schober, M. F. (1992). Asking questions and influencing answers. In J. M. Tanur (Ed.), *Questions about questions* (pp. 15-48). New York: Russell Sage.

DeMaio, T. J. (1984). Social desirability and survey measurement: A review. In C. F. Turner & E. Martin (Eds.), *Surveying subjective phenomena* (Vol. 2, pp. 257-281). New York: Russell Sage.

Desvouges, W. H., Hudson, S. P., & Ruby, M. C. (1994, May). *Evaluating CV performance: Separating the light from the heat.* EPA/DOE Workshop, Herndon, VA.

Desvouges, W. H., Johnson, R., Dunford, R. W., Boyle, K. J., Hudson, S. P., & Wilson, K. N. (1993). Measuring natural resource damages with contingent valuation. In J. A. Hausman (Ed.), *Contingent valuation: A critical assessment.* Amsterdam: Elsevier.

Diamond, P. A., Hausman, J. A., Leonard, G.K., & Denning, M. A. (1993). Does contingent valuation measure preferences? Experimental evidence. In J. A. Hausman (Ed.), *Contingent valuation: A critical assessment.* Amsterdam: Elsevier.

Fischhoff, B. (1991). Value elicitation: Is there anything there? *American Psychologist, 46*, 835-847.

Fischhoff, B. & Furby, L. (1988). Measuring values: A conceptual framework for interpreting transactions with special reference to contingent valuation of visibility. *Journal of Risk and Uncertainty*, 1, 147-184.

Green, D. P. (1992). The price elasticity of mass preferences. *American Political Science Review, 86*, 128-148.

Green, D. P., Kahneman, D., & Kunreuther, H. (1994). How the scope and method of public funding affect willingness to pay for public goods. *Public Opinion Quarterly, 58*, 49-67.

Grice, H. P. (1975). Logic and conversation. In P. Cole, & J.L. Morgan (Eds.), *Syntax and semantics, 3: Speech acts.* pp. 41 -58. New York: Academic Press.

Griffin, D. W., & Ross, L. (1991). Subjective construal, social inference, and human misunderstanding. In M. Zanna (Ed.), *Advances in experimental social psychology* (vol. 24, pp. 319-360).

Hausman, J.A. (Ed.) (1993). *Contingent valuation. A critical assessment.* Amsterdam: Elsevier.

Hippler, H.J., Schwarz, N., & Sudman, S. (Eds.). (1987). *Social information processing and survey methodology.* New York, NY: Springer Verlag.

Holmes, T. P., & Kramer, R. A. (1993). *An independent sample test of yea-saying in dichotomous choice contingent valuation.* Unpublished manuscript. Research Triangle Park: Forestry Sciences Lab.

Kahneman, D., & Knetsch, J. A. (1992). Valuing public goods: The purchase of moral satisfaction. *Journal of Environmental Economics and Management*, 22, 57-70.

Kahneman, D., & Ritov, I. (1994). Determinants and stated willingness to pay for public goods: A study in the headline method. *Journal of Risk and Uncertainty*, in press.

Kopp, R. J., & Pease, K. A. (1994). *Contingent valuation: Economics, law and politics.* Manuscript. Washington, DC: Resources for the Future.

Mitchell, R. C., & Carson, R. T. (1986). *Valuing drinking water risk reduction using the contingent valuation method.* Report to the U. S. Environmental Protection Agency, Washington, D.C.

Mitchell, R. C., & Carson, R. T. (1989). *Using surveys to value public goods: The contingent valuation method.* Washington, D.C.: Resources for the Future.

Payne, J. W., Bettman, J. R., & Johnson, E.J. (1992). Behavioral decision research: A constructive processing perspective. *Annual Review of Psychology, 43*, 87-131.

Schkade, D. A., & Payne, J. W. (1993). Where do the numbers come from? How people respond to contingent valuation questions. In J. A. Hausman (Ed.), *Contingent valuation. A critical assessment* (pp. 271-303). Amsterdam: Elsevier.

Schulze, W., McClelland, G., & Lazo, J. (1994, May). *Methodological issues in using contingent valuation to measure non-use values.* EPA/DOE Workshop, Herndon, VA.

Schwarz, N. (1994). Judgment in a social context: Biases, shortcomings, and the logic of conversation. In M. Zanna (Ed.), *Advances in experimental social psychology* (Vol. 26, pp. 123-162). San Diego, CA: Academic Press.

Schwarz, N. (1995). What respondents learn from questionnaires: The survey interview and the logic of conversation. *International Statistical Review,* 63, 153-177.

Schwarz, N., & Bless, H. (1992). Constructing reality and its alternatives: Assimilation and contrast effects in social judgment. In L.L. Martin & A. Tesser (Eds.), *The construction of social judgment* (pp. 217-245). Hillsdale, NJ: Erlbaum.

Schwarz, N., & Hippler, H.J. (1987). What response scales may tell your respondents: Informative functions of response alternatives. In H.J. Hippler, N. Schwarz, & S. Sudman (Eds.), *Social information processing and survey methodology* (pp. 163-178). New York, NY: Springer Verlag.

Schwarz, N., & Hippler, H.J. (1991). Response alternatives: The impact of their choice and ordering. In P. Biemer, R. Groves, N. Mathiowetz, & S. Sudman (Eds.), *Measurement error in surveys* (pp. 41-56). Chichester, UK: Wiley.

Schwarz, N., & Hippler, H. J. (1995). Subsequent questions may influence answers to preceding questions in mail surveys. *Public Opinion Quarterly, 59*, 93-97.

Schwarz, N., Knäuper, B., Hippler, H. J., Noelle-Neumann, E., & Clark, F. (1991). Rating scales: Numeric values may change the meaning of scale labels. *Public Opinion Quarterly, 55,* 570-582.

Schwarz, N., & Strack, F. (1991). Context effects in attitude surveys: Applying cognitive theory to social research. In W. Stroebe & M. Hewstone (Eds.), *European Review of Social Psychology* (Vol. 2, pp. 31-50). Chichester: Wiley.

Schwarz, N., Strack, F., Hippler, H.J., & Bishop, G. (1991). The impact of administration mode on response effects in survey measurement. *Applied Cognitive Psychology, 5,* 193-212.

Schwarz, N. & Sudman, S. (Eds.) (1992). *Context effects in social and psychological research.* New York, NY: Springer Verlag.

Schwarz, N., & Sudman, S. (Eds.) (1994). *Autobiographical memory and the validity of retrospective reports.* New York, NY: Springer Verlag.

Schwarz, N., & Sudman, S. (Eds.) (1996). *Answering questions: Methodology for determining cognitive and communicative processes in survey research.* San Francisco: Jossey-Bass.

Sperber, D., & Wilson, D. (1986). *Relevance: Communication and cognition.* Cambridge, MA: Harvard University Press.

Strack, F., & Martin, L. (1987). Thinking, judging, and communicating: A process account of context effects in attitude surveys. In H.J. Hippler, N. Schwarz, & S. Sudman (Eds.), *Social information processing and survey methodology* (pp. 123 - 148). New York: Springer Verlag.

Strack, F., & Schwarz, N. (1992). Communicative influences in standardized question situations: The case of implicit collaboration. In K. Fiedler & G. Semin (Eds.), *Language, interaction and social cognition* (pp. 173-193). Beverly Hills: Sage.

Strack, F., Schwarz, N., & Wänke, M. (1991). Semantic and pragmatic aspects of context effects in social and psychological research. *Social Cognition,* 9, 111-125.

Sudman, S., & Bradburn, N. M. (1983). *Asking questions.* San Francisco: Jossey-Bass.

Sudman, S., Bradburn, N., & Schwarz, N. (1996). *Thinking about answers: The application of cognitive processes to survey methodology.* San Francisco, CA: Jossey-Bass.

Tanur, J. M. (Ed.) (1992). *Questions about questions.* New York: Russel Sage.

Thaler, R. H. (1992). *The winner's curse: Paradoxes and anomalies in economic life.* New York: Free Press.

Tourangeau, R. (1992). Attitudes as memory structures: Belief sampling and context effects. In N. Schwarz & S. Sudman (Eds.), *Context effects in social and psychological research*. New York: Springer Verlag.

Tourangeau, R., & Rasinski, K.A. (1988). Cognitive processes underlying context effects in attitude measurement. *Psychological Bulletin, 103*, 299 - 314.

8

WHAT DO PSYCHOLOGISTS WANT? CONTINGENT VALUATION AS A SPECIAL CASE OF ASKING QUESTIONS

Baruch Fischhoff

INTRODUCTION

For a hundred years or so, psychologists have been asking people evaluative questions. In order to gain approval for their work, they have had to satisfy peer reviewers in disciplinary journals run primarily by other psychologists. In this world, technical reports carry little credibility. Psychologists' training typically includes graduate and undergraduate courses in research design, culminating in an experimental dissertation. Unless they are high rollers, they stick to methods that are incremental improvements on existing ones, with (what are believed to be) well-understood strengths and weaknesses. Somewhat more innovation is tolerated in creating theoretical accounts. Top journals seldom accept studies motivated primarily by practical, rather than theoretical issues. Great emphasis is placed on anticipating criticisms -- by raising alternative explanations, explicitly citing sources of residual uncertainty, and identifying research needs.

For twenty years or more, economists have been asking people questions in the specific context of contingent valuation studies. The audience for this work has included juries, lawyers, regulators, and fellow economists. Their work is as likely to appear in technical reports as scientific journals. Reviewers tend to be restricted to CV practitioners and professional critics. They may even try to advance private interests rather than public understanding. Combatants' formal training usually is in the standard fare of economics: sophisticated theory and statistical analysis of archival data. Rather than being considered the elite of their profession (a fancy entertained by experimental psychologists), CV researchers are often hounded by traditional economists for daring to trust expressed preferences. Their clients often impose a siege mentality, discouraging the active pursuit and admission of problems.

If this characterization is even roughly correct, then most experimental psychologists and CV investigators have quite different backgrounds and perspectives. The fact that they are ostensibly in the same business, that of asking questions, has encouraged the naive assumption that they can speak directly to one another. However, their interactions have rarely been in settings suited to cultivating mutual understanding: working collaboratively on common problems, with equal status and commitment. (Viscusi [in press] and Schulze et al. [in press] cite some productive exceptions.) A few conferences have offered the limited opportunities for understanding afforded by formal papers and responses (e.g., Cambridge Economics, 1992; Peterson, Driver & Gregory, 1988). Occasionally, psychologists have been on advisory panels, able to offer comments, but too far from the action to shape the basic design of studies. As a result, they find themselves constantly carping, without the hands-on role needed to "sign off" on results. Sometimes, psychologists are hired to savage CV studies by clients more interested in damaging adversaries than in evaluating natural resources. Radical skepticism makes one few friends, however competently it is executed. These unsatisfactory public interactions are augmented by countless hours of private fuming.

These are not a pleasant or productive circumstances. As a possible step toward bridging this gap, I will describe what I, as a psychologist, see -- and miss -- in conventional CV studies. These observations lead to several recommendations for removing barriers to mutually acceptable research. The second half of the paper confronts psychology's own inherent limits when addressing the challenges facing CV. These limits are revealed in the course of offering an alternative methodology, violating the norms of both professions. Given the social, environmental, and economic stakes riding on the pricing of nonmarket goods, it would be a shame not to pool our respective training and talents. Cooperation might reduce the risk of our becoming pawns in the machinations of those hoping to distort natural resource policy by manipulating science. The spirit of this essay is that of a member of the loyal opposition. I would dearly like CV to work. It is, indeed, too important to fail. However, those stakes make it critical to face problems coming from all quarters. Being an uncritical friend would be a disservice.

From my (limited) viewpoint, CV seems to be at a turning point. Investigators increasingly conduct studies that are conceptualized as experiments. In so doing, they can look for better methods, rather than having to claim to have definitive ones. In this shift, CV goes from an exercise in applied basic social science (adapting existing techniques to applied problems) to an arena for basic applied social science (addressing fundamental issues arising in applied problems). Although this promises to be an exciting period, it may create tensions between those who view CV as a playground, where fascinating topics are pursued, and those who view it as a workshop, where authoritative estimates are produced. Balancing these conflicting objectives requires both good will and a strategic plan. The first half of this paper hopes to clarify some sources of misunderstanding, while the second half offers a possible bridge.

What follows are personal opinions, derived from following CV with some intensity for a decade and more passively for somewhat longer (e.g., Fischhoff, Slovic, & Lichtenstein, 1980).[1] I won't claim to speak for all psychologists, although I suspect that many of these tastes are shared (Ajzen & Peterson, 1988;

Baron, 1994). I won't attempt to document my claims systematically, beyond reference to what I have written already (Fischhoff, 1988, 1990, 1991; Fischhoff & Furby, 1986, 1988; Furby & Fischhoff, 1989).

THE PSYCHOLOGICAL STUDY

The American Psychological Association's *Publication Manual* (1984) sets our standard for reporting research results. Although much of it involves arbitrary rules (e.g., how to format tables, where to place acknowledgments), it also reflects psychology's evolving philosophy of science, regarding the essential elements of a study.[2] I will organize my comments according to the sections that the *Manual* prescribes for the standard psychological paper, in part because of its comprehensiveness, in part to emphasize the deep-seated conventions shaping our perceptions. The plea for full, consistent reporting by NOAA's Contingent Valuation Panel (Department of Commerce, 1993, at p. 4608) is one indication of how slowly such norms evolve.

Components of Psychological Reports

Introduction

When reading a scientific paper, psychologists expect to see a new hypothesis that attempts to accommodate all existing studies and resolve some uncertainty in them. Ideally, that hypothesis is rooted in existing theory. For example, prospect theory (Kahneman & Tversky, 1979) builds on results in psychophysics and adaptation-level theory in order to explain some choice anomalies. Once a study has passed peer review, the burden of proof shifts to those who would ignore its results.

In CV studies, I see less interest in theory testing, in deference to the practical goal of evaluating particular amenities. I see little awareness of the relevant psychological literature. I see dismissal of studies satisfying our methodological norms, for failing to satisfy the norms of CV investigators. Moreover, those norms seem inconsistent and unstable. At any one time, different CV investigators uphold different inviolate standards. Over time, norms seem to change for unsatisfying reasons (e.g., shifting tastes, producing unduly high estimates). The NOAA panel's attempt to legislate methodology feels like the sort of action that might be undertaken by clinical psychologists, a professional guild that we hold at arm's length (Dawes, 1994). As a result, CV studies seem to be introduced in ways that exclude much of what is dear to us.

Design

For psychologists, valid measures are sensitive to relevant changes in the measured object and insensitive to irrelevant changes (Campbell & Fiske, 1959).

This test is easy to apply when relevance is defined independently (e.g., with length or weight); it is much harder with subjective phenomena like values or beliefs. Psychometrics is psychology's philosophy of measurement for coping with subjectivity (Dawes, 1972). It requires the active pursuit of problems, systematically varying factors that should or should not affect measurement. For cognitive psychologists, interested in *how* people think, even measurement failures can be useful if they reveal new behavioral phenomena. Indeed, experimental psychology has been described as a process of converting methodological artifacts into theoretical main effects, worth studying in their own right (McGuire, 1969).

In CV studies, I see a conscientious effort to design the single best evaluation question. All resources are then invested in securing a large sample of responses to it. CV investigators typically rely on impressionistic summaries of pretest interviews with individuals or focus groups. Although they can uncover problems, these techniques create conditions quite different than those of the actual interviews (Merton & Kendall, 1946; Merton, 1987). As a result, there is uncertainty about how actual respondents have interpreted their task.

Stimuli

Psychologists place great importance on mapping the elements of their experimental set-ups onto the concepts in their theories. This means making the theory as explicit as possible, describing its boundary conditions, and excluding irrelevant factors from the task (e.g., giving no hint at the investigator's intent). There is a strong bias toward simplicity, focusing subjects on the investigators' issues and reducing cognitive load. We are, nonetheless, probably too optimistic regarding how well our stimuli are understood and accepted. Even when the words are simple, the underlying concepts and context may be quite foreign to respondents (Fischhoff, 1993).

CV studies necessarily use much richer stimuli, in order to describe complex environmental goods. However, I often cannot see how the specific details were selected. As a result, CV stimuli look quite arbitrary. Seeing the great variation in the features that different CV investigators chose to specify, Lita Furby and I created a framework (Fischhoff & Furby, 1988) for the features that should be addressed in a fully specified evaluation task. The typical CV study omits many of these details, forcing (or allowing) respondents to guess at what was meant. Nonetheless, most CV studies still present more detail than subjects could reasonably absorb in a typical interview. In the absence of comprehensive manipulation checks with actual subjects, I remain skeptical that subjects are answering the intended question. In a study using simplified stimuli, we found that the embedding effect (Kahneman & Knetsch, 1992) decreased when we interpreted responses in terms of the task that subjects reported answering rather than the one we had actually posed (Fischhoff et al., 1993). Without this manipulation check, we would have been unduly optimistic about our ability to communicate and unduly pessimistic about subjects' ability to respond.

Response mode

Psychologists hope is to get as much information as possible out of subjects without creating (and not just revealing) preferences. The late Clyde Coombs articulated this philosophy in his *A theory of data* (1964). There, he showed techniques for eliciting the most precise preferences that subjects can give (e.g., pick the single best and worst options, pick the three best options). We seldom elicit anything stronger than interval scale responses.

CV investigators share our aversion to reactive methods. However, their tasks seem extraordinarily demanding: monetary evaluation of goods whose precise formulation must be very unfamiliar. That formulation must be understood even if evaluations are expressed in a referendum format. Although ostensibly simple, referenda may obscure the difficulty of a task, by making it easy to respond casually in ways that look sensible. I suspect that subjects often translate CV tasks into something more manageable under the time constraints (e.g., "does this merit a large, medium or small standard contribution -- given that I'm supposed to pay something for it."). Or, they may just flee with "protest responses." Strack and Schwarz (1992) use "implicit collaboration" to describe subjects' attempts to make sense out of unreasonable tasks.

Subjects

Cognitive psychologists tend to be casual about sampling. Because we believe that basic thought processes are widely shared, we are content with convenience samples. Because effects must be fairly large in order to have theoretical interest, relatively small samples will have adequate statistical power (although, left to our own intuitions, we tend to overestimate that power [Cohen, 1962; Tversky & Kahneman, 1971]). When individual differences matter, we assume that correlations are invariant across samples. Our primary worry is truncating the range on a variable, so that there is too little heterogeneity for correlations to emerge.

In CV studies, I see a diligent commitment to recruiting representative samples. This befits determining *what* the population as a whole thinks. Less understandable is concentrating all those resources on the single best question. The resulting precision is misplaced without a trustworthy elicitation methodology. It seems more efficient to develop such a methodology with experiments using small, diverse samples. Insisting on large samples for any CV-related study represents a restraint of inquiry, by disenfranchising investigators who cannot command the needed resources.

Results

Our training typically includes a graduate year of "Statistics for Psychologists" and several supervised experimental projects. One taste that this training inculcates is having a large tool kit of statistical of procedures. A second taste is letting the responses speak for themselves, reporting them in something like their original form and avoiding heavily interpretative statistical models. A third is discarding subjects with great reluctance.

In CV studies, I see a problem that we rarely face: many subjects spontaneously rejecting their task or providing unreasonable answers. Deleting such responses makes the effective sample in many CV studies less representative than is intended (and sometimes claimed). It raises doubts about the responses that are retained, some of which may seem reasonable just by chance. CV's reporting norms are improving. However, it is still often unclear what responses mean to those who provide them, nor how respondents' residual confusion should be reflected in data analyses (Hamm et al., 1992). In order to exploit the power of econometric procedures, CV investigators often require stronger assumptions, regarding the orderliness of subjects' decision-making, than most psychologists would be comfortable making.

Discussion

In this section, psychologists pick up the themes laid out in the Introduction, consider alternative explanations for their data, and identify needed future research.

In CV studies, I often see an aggressively defensive attitude, making stronge claims, with little self-criticism. Concern is often focused on issues that we tend to ignore, like strategic responses (Orne, 1962; Schwarz, 1994). It is hard for me to distinguish what CV researchers really believe from what their clients need to hear.

Some recommendations

This is, of course, a caricature. CV studies vary widely in their quality, just as we deviate from psychology's standards more than we would like to think or claim. Nonetheless, there seems to be a clash of paradigms here. The fact that some psychologists and economists have found ways to co-author papers suggests reason for hope. Reason for despair can be found in the incentives for unqualified claims and critiques in a litigious and politicized society. Too many people involved with CV cannot take "yes" or "no" for an answer, but must be ruthless proponents or opponents. Perversely, this unreasonable environment has gotten a hearing for psychology (Department of Commerce, 1993), although in a context that kept psychologists at arms length. Here are some institutional and intellectual suggestions that might help tilt the odds toward the optimists:

Institutional suggestions

Make resources available for basic research on elicitation, without having to evaluate environmental resources that are currently "in play" or conform to current CV norms.

Make psychologists and economists equal partners in allocating resources, directing projects, and reviewing papers -- forcing them to work together.

Encourage cross-disciplinary postdoctoral work, producing scholars who have undergone both apprenticeships.

Include independent peer review in CV projects; publish some reviews, along with responses, as a way of airing differences.

Intellectual suggestions

Accept the legitimacy of studies meeting the standards of each research tradition, if they recognize the standards of the other (e.g., "we sampled haphazardly," "we performed no manipulation checks," "these procedures are not widely accepted within psychology").

Perform studies that systematically vary potentially relevant and irrelevant features of CV scenarios, within an independent framework for determining their relevance.

Provide complete descriptions of responses, including reliability estimates, manipulation checks, no-response rates, and protest-response rates.

Accept the possibility that respondents do not know what to think about the specific questions we pose; grapple with helping them to articulate their values and with using incomplete values in decision making.

Interim conclusion

Most of these suggestions are controversial. For example, a National Research Council (1982) report recommended independent peer review of "survey measures of subjective phenomena," only to provoke a passionate dissent from a leading figure in the survey research industry. Some would be hard to implement. Nonetheless, CV seems ripe for wrestling with core issues, rather than dealing with symptomatic conflicts. CV could become an exciting arena for interdisciplinary contact, or remain a frustrating one.

The next section describes a constructive approach to addressing these issues. It is intended as a zero-based approach, unconstrained by existing ones, but drawing on their hard-earned experience. It is unlikely to satisfy any discipline entirely. Economists may be particularly offended by its claim of taking the contingent market metaphor more seriously than they have (i.e., improving on the economics of CV). Psychologists (and survey researchers) might be particularly aghast at its abandoning the conventional commitment to nonreactive measurement.

The exposition begins with the criteria that a method for eliciting environmental valuations should satisfy. The next section outlines the proposed method, in terms of its organizing metaphor and basic methods. The following section elaborates on how it addresses the criteria and how one should validate an implementation. Finally, the proposal is critiqued, in terms of related approaches and the work to be done. Some differences among approaches are empirical questions, which could be resolved by studying the data that each produces. Other differences are matters of principle, regarding what kind of environmental values should be used in policy decisions.

A CONSTRUCTIVE APPROACH TO ELICITING ENVIRONMENTAL EVALUATIONS

Criteria for value elicitation procedures

In order to fill the niche that CV claims, a procedure should meet these seven criteria:

General applicability

A method for eliciting public values should be accessible to any citizen willing to invest the effort. Thus, it cannot require extensive prior knowledge, nor discourage individuals without it.

Well-formulated policy issue

Participants must receive information on all issues that they deem essential. Vague questions may encourage vague responses (e.g., general expressions of sympathy), while leaving too much freedom to interpret what those responses mean. Participants should not have to read between the lines of the questions; readers should not have that option with the answers.

Standardized response mode

In order to be summarized efficiently and objectively, respondents' beliefs must be expressed in a common format. That summary should capture the critical features of subjects' values, including how deeply they are held.

Understanding of science

In order to provide informed consent of the governed for the actions based on their evaluations, respondents must understand the size and predictability of the environmental changes at stake.

Articulated preferences

Once they have understood the issues, participants must identify the responses that reflect their values. If that process normally requires rumination, conversation, and consultation, then the elicitation procedure must provide the functional equivalent.

Validation

Any scientific study must assess the quality of its measures. That includes determining how sensitive responses are to relevant and irrelevant changes in procedure.

Impact clarity

The consumers of research need a bottom line, summarizing what the results mean for their concerns. They must be able to decide whether the estimates are good enough to justify action, and whether alternative procedures might have fared very differently.

None of these criteria seems controversial.[3] The proposed approach tries to takes each seriously. In some cases, there is much to build on; in other cases, it is largely guesswork. It is called constructivist because it assumes that meaningful responses to novel tasks must be created at the investigators' demand (Burgess, Harrison & Limb, 1988; Fischhoff, 1991; Gregory et al., 1993; Lazo et al., 1992; Schulze et al., in press; Whittington & Davis, 1993).

Some organizing metaphors

Contingent valuation might be seen as having two organizing metaphors. One is the *contingent market*, within which respondents imagine their behavior. The second is the *opinion poll*, within which respondents report their current thinking on some issue. Table 1 shows some examples of people's willingness to respond.

TABLE 1: SOME POLL RESULTS
65% of Americans believe that frozen pizza will never be any good, and there is nothing that science can do about it.
10% of Americans would pay $5 to see Sen. Orrin Hatch battle a big mean dog on television. 80% would root for the dog.
45% of Americans think that rain doesn't feel as good in real life as it seems to in the movies

(margin of error = 9%)

Source: TV Nation, NBC, July 20, 1994

Our approach accepts the former metaphor, perhaps even more seriously than is usual. However, it rejects the latter, as incompatible with the seven criteria. People cannot have existing opinions on the specific CV scenario that they receive. Even if respondents have thought about the good (e.g., a watershed), the terms of a well-specified proposal are inevitably novel. People cannot instantly absorb its details and convert them into valuations. It may take a while even to conceptualize environmental effects as "goods," with a price tag no less. As a result, a process of learning and value construction is inevitable, making measurement inherently reactive. Participants must change if they are to respond meaningfully. A measurement procedure must face and manage those changes.

Reactive measurement seems compatible with the contingent-market metaphor. Participants in actual markets can provide flash estimates for the worth of novel commercial or financial products. However, they might not want to be held to those answers in any consequential setting. Markets work when people can identify specific actions that serve their general interests (Viscusi & Magat, 1987). A properly functioning market should capture *stable* expressions of participants' preferences, in the sense that nothing changes upon further reflection or additional information. Ill-informed responses represent (contingent or conventional) market failure.

Citizens may vote on a complex ballot measure with similarly little prior thought. These casual votes might be predicted by flash responses to an opinion poll. However, that would mean predicting a failed electoral process. A successful referendum is preceded by extensive doses of such democratic processes as partisan proclamations, academic analyses, conversations with peers, question-and-answer sessions, and time to think about the specific proposal. Indeed, one might argue that the referendum metaphor should be used only by investigators who deliver these accouterments (Barber, 1991; Verba & Nie, 1972).

"Referendum" has typically been appropriated for much more casual presentations in CV studies.

For serious elicitation, a more appropriate metaphor is the citizens commission: A representative sample of citizens is selected to learn about an issue, on behalf of the electorate. Their opinions are interpreted as resembling those that other citizens might adopt, if offered the same opportunity. An elicitation procedure instantiating this metaphor would have to capture the salient features of such a commission, including balanced briefings, partisan testimony, group discussions, and the chance to explain complex opinions (Crosby, Kelly & Schaefer, 1986; Fiorino, 1990; Reich, 1985). This metaphor is adopted here, with one important exception: Evaluations are collected privately, in order to reduce the effects of group processes and provide estimates of individual preferences.

Metaphors matter, not only because of the claims they make, but also because of the guidance they provide. Opinion polls on real issues attempt to simulate the conditions of the ballot box (secret responses, no proximal campaigning, etc.). Although they might ask how respondents they expect their opinions to change by election day, polls would not attempt to simulate that change process. With artificial issues, like those necessarily posed by CV, opinions must evolve (on the specific CV proposal, if not on the underlying issues). The commission metaphor embraces that change. It aspires to simulate an idealized political process, with all the access that participants would want to information, analysis, discussion, and rumination. It replaces the polling norm of "tell them nothing" with an attempt to "give them everything." It seeks the thoughtful public values needed for environmental policy. It attempts to confront and exploit the reactivity that is anathema to most psychology and survey research.

Procedural overview

Table 2 outlines the method. It begins with a recruitment procedure that explains the study, introduces the issue, and solicits initial responses on a questionnaire designed to get participants thinking. A confirming phone call allows for clarifying questions. Group sessions provide the opportunity to present and discuss the issues in detail. (The number of sessions depends on the complexity of the issues.) Only private responses are analyzed.

TABLE 2: STANDARD TASK SEQUENCE	
Recruitment	Letter of Invitation (introducing issue and procedure) Letter of Acceptance (including brief questionnaire) Phone Confirmation (and clarification)
Initial Group Session	Introductions (clarifying questions, no discussion) Procedure CV Transaction Underlying Science (natural, social) Preliminary Evaluations (assisted interview) Group Presentation and Mediated Discussion Summary Evaluations (proposal, procedure)
Additional Group Session(s)	Procedural Discussion Clarifying Questions Opening Evaluation Group Presentation and Mediated Discussion Summary Evaluations (proposal, procedure)
Follow-up (sub-samples, with/without intervening events)	

The initial meeting introduces each element of the procedure, including the CV scenario, the relevant science, the response modes, and the organizing metaphor -- so that participants will know what is wanted of them. After this introduction, respondents complete each evaluation form (in private), in order to clarify the task and elicit initial impressions. In keeping with the metaphor, these are treated as tentative preliminary views, subject to change as subjects have time to learn, talk, and think. The remainder of the session is devoted to introducing and discussing the issues. It concludes with the first "serious" evaluations. The following sessions involve more of the same: presenting information, clarifying uncertainties, discussing implications, and eliciting evaluations in private.

Participants evaluate the procedure as well as the issues. They perform manipulation checks, rate fairness, comment on the interactions, and request changes. These evaluations guide the process, in addition to characterizing its quality. Because moderators respond to requests and problems, different groups may receive nominally different material, in order to achieve functionally equivalent experiences. This adaptive strategy takes seriously the "conversational" approach to survey design, which assumes that respondents apply the norms of everyday conversation to interpreting survey questions (Dietz, 1987; Strack & Schwarz, 1992). With unfamiliar topics and heterogeneous audiences, no one wording may be interpreted similarly (and appropriately) by all respondents (Quadrel, Fischhoff & Palmgren, 1994). As a result, geting the message across requires actual conversation.

For most respondents, the elicitation process ends with the final session. Some are interviewed later in order to assess the stability of responses. Additional interviews might be conducted later, if events occur that should change evaluations (e.g., the release of significant scientific findings).

A Work plan

Table 3 lists the tasks involved in implementing this approach and, arguably, any approach to value elicitation that addresses the seven criteria. Each task raises basic research issues, some of which are discussed below, organized by the criterion that each is most closely attached to achieving.

TABLE 3: INSTRUMENTS AND MATERIALS (by primary criterion)

General Applicability	Sampling Frame and Size
Well-Formulated Policy Issue	Specification of CV Scenario
Standardized Response Mode	Proposal Evaluation Protocol Procedure Evaluation Protocol
Understanding of Science	Explanation of CV Scenario Explanation of Underlying Science
Articulated Preferences	Supporting Materials Moderator Guidelines

Validation	Manipulation Checks Validity Tests Reliability Tests
Impact Clarity	Summaries for Policy Makers

General applicability

Sampling frame and size. A procedure that assesses public values should include a representative sample of the citizenry. That could mean random population sampling with aggressive call backs. However, those recruitment efforts would reduce the resources available for interacting with respondents. The value of random sampling is further limited by frame omissions, refusals to participate, and protest responses. The method proposed here should cost more per subject because of its intensity, but less per subject because of its group administration. It also makes a larger capital investment in stimulus development. Having fewer subjects would be justified by having better responses. Response rates might also improve if a more involving procedure increased cooperation. The tradeoff between sample size and response precision deserves some basic research attention.

At this developmental stage, we are selecting participants at random from the membership rolls of diverse organizations (churches, clubs, etc.). This allows assembling people in groups with similar backgrounds, a setting where opinions are often shaped. Responses could be summarized as representing known groups (and not just atomized citizens), or extrapolated to populations of people with similar characteristics. At present, our main concern is establishing a method that is widely applicable. Alternative approaches to representativeness are another topic for future research.

Well-formulated policy issue

Some years ago, Lita Furby and I reviewed thirty-odd studies eliciting evaluations of atmospheric visibility. We were struck by the great variability in the features that different investigators chose to specify. Concluding that there was little consensus on what constituted a "market," we created a framework for specifying "transactions," within which a *payment* is exchanged for a *good*, within some *social context* (Fischhoff & Furby, 1988). It attempts to identify all issues that respondents might wish to consider.

Because respondents may guess at missing features, our framework also identifies the opportunities to read between the lines of a CV scenario. It does not, however, show how to plug the gaps. In some cases, knowledge of the substantive issues will tell us what to say. In others, we may lack answers to participants' questions (e.g., who else will pay? what else am I going to be asked to pay for? who will implement the promised change? what if I want to contribute time, rather than money? how will my responses be used? what are others saying? how would I pay?). Where we cannot answer authoritatively, it may be tempting to remain silent. We may even have normative reasons why a feature should not matter. However, saying nothing about a feature need not prevent respondents from making assumptions on their own. Indeed, they may feel compelled to do so, in order to render the task meaningful. Deciding how to fill in the blanks is another research challenge.[4]

Standardized response mode

Proposal evaluation protocol. Complex, novel proposals may evoke complex, novel opinions. People might be pressured to summarize those feelings in a simple way. However, that summary captures but a portion of their opinions, leaving observers to guess at their full meaning -- just as election results leave room to speculate about the meaning of voters' choices, not to mention their abstentions.[5]

The ambiguity of election results appeals to politicians, leaving them freedom to interpret the mandate that they have gained or lost. It is not, however, very helpful for determining future actions. That requires supplementary research, like detailed exit polls. Whatever format is used, responsible use of CV results requires understanding what respondents meant. Given the latitude that CV investigators have in specifying their scenarios, one needs to know how alternative tasks would have affected responses. To this end, our subjects evaluate the proposals from a variety of perspectives, including how strong their preferences are, how various changes in the proposal would affect them, how fair the proposal seems, and how their responses would change if the science changed.

Procedure evaluation protocol. Interviews are a special kind of social interaction. As a result, the procedure itself may color participants' responses. For example, "protest responses" may represent objections to the proposals or to the opportunities to understand them (Hamm et al., 1992; Schkade & Payne, 1994). In order to clarify sources of random error, our respondents evaluate statements like "I think that I know enough about the issue to make an informed decision about it," "I found the explanation confusing," "I think that my views will be taken seriously by policy makers," and "I think that my position is well represented by my responses." In order to clarify sources of bias, respondents evaluate statements such as "I felt pressure to answer the question in a particular way," "The proposal was not stated honestly," and "The environmental effects were exaggerated." Such questions might both explain puzzling results and reveal problems with seemingly orderly ones (e.g., cases where respondents adopt a mechanical response strategy, in order to get through a frustrating task).

Understanding of science

CV investigators have often worked hard to convey their scenarios. For example, simulating different levels of atmospheric visibility was once a major methodological pursuit. Concern over embedding has increased the attention paid to conveying quantitative features. In this volume, Navrud (in press), Schulze et al. (in press), and Schwarz (1994) all discuss presentation issues. Our approach builds on this work, and on basic research in scientific communication:

Explanation of CV scenario. An obvious challenge is the complexity of CV scenarios, which would only get worse if they were specified completely. Lazo et al. (1992) propose simplifying scenarios by asking subjects how relevant particular facts are, then confirming these judgments by deleting irrelevant facts in scenarios presented to additional subjects. They report promising results (i.e., similar evaluations with and without those facts). A residual risk is artificial convergence, should subjects give roughly the same value to all scenarios, regardless of their details.

Quadrel, Fischhoff and Palmgren (1994) offer a related procedure, differing in two ways: (a) Subjects think aloud as they read proposed experimental materials, in order to avoid the potential problems with retrospective introspections (Ericsson & Simon, 1984; Nisbett & Wilson, 1977). (b) Confirmatory studies test whether people show the same sensitivity (and insensitivity) in structured tasks as emerged in the think-aloud tasks (Fischhoff, 1992; Stokol & Altman, 1986). A minimal test of efficacy is manipulation checks, asking subjects (in actual studies and not just pretests) to report how they interpreted their task.

Explanation of underlying science. One recurrent result in communication research is that people have difficulty processing information that does not correspond to their "mental model" of the situation. They may even reject factual assertions that do not make sense. Thus, successful communication requires knowing the preconceptions that people bring to a task and presenting new information in that context. In effect, respondents need to be taught some science and not just given quantitative end states (diSessa, 1993; Gentner & Stevens, 1983). That education might involve economics, as well as natural science (Furnham, 1989; Green, in press; Voss, Tyler & Yengo, 1983).

For topics that occur in many studies, it might pay for CV to create a science of lay understanding (e.g., How do people estimate the personal effects of "higher prices for goods and services?" or How do they assess the feasibility of referenda on designated taxes for environmental goods? What loopholes do they imagine in the contract offered by a CV transaction?). Specific goods (e.g., groundwater pollution, ozone-related health effects) may require dedicated studies. The methods are quite inexpensive, considering the stakes (e.g., Bostrom et al., 1992;

Fischhoff et al., 1993; Jungermann, Schutz, & Thuring, 1988; Leventhal & Cameron, 1987; Schulze et al., in press).

Articulated preferences

Supporting Materials. Articulated preferences are ones that remain stable in the face of additional time to think, additional information from neutral sources, and additional perspectives from partisan ones. They are immune to framing effects, often observed in confrontations with unfamiliar tasks (Hogarth, 1982; Tversky & Kahneman, 1981). The order in which issues arise might affect the path by which preferences evolve, but not their final state. As a result, it is critical to present a balanced set of evaluative perspectives as well as scientific facts (saying, in effect, here's a way that you could think about this problem). One test of balance is asking partisans whether we have captured their views.[6] Finally, we apply a simple test suggested by the late Cathie Marsh, asking subjects who they think produced the materials.

Moderator Guidelines. The interactive character of our method reflects a belief that the norms of conversation (Schwarz, 1994) require actual conversation. That is, however diligent the pretests, no single wording can address the diverse perspectives that respondents bring to a CV study. They need individual help to understand the issues and develop positions. We have chosen to provide this help in group sessions, both for efficiency and because complex information is often processed socially. Following the underlying metaphor, our moderators are expected to suppress their own opinions, and encourage the expression of diverse views. Their success is monitored by reviewing session tapes and asking participants.

Validation

Types of validity. A measurement procedure's success is often seen as having three components: (a) *face validity*, does it include the critical features of the concepts that it represents?; (b) *predictive validity*, does it predict behavior in some designated situation (e.g., an election)?; and (c) *construct validity*, do responses fit a theoretically derived pattern?

Ordinarily, face validity is a minimal condition. The need to define a complex transaction makes it a particularly demanding test for CV tasks. Previous sections describe our procedures for ensuring that the right things get said (well-formulated policy issue) and heard (understanding of science). Process evaluations and manipulation checks measure our success at conveying the intended context and content. They involve (a) asking respondents to interpret the task in front of them, (b) eliciting their memories for tasks that they have just completed, and (c) posing inferential questions regarding the implications of the literally stated task (Kintsch, 1986; Reder, 1985).

Predictive validity is relevant for CV tasks that have clear real-world analogues. CV tasks have often done fairly well in such tests -- when they involve familiar goods and settings. There is nothing in the world to predict, however, for the typical CV scenario (Mitchell & Carson, 1989; Smith & Osborne, in press; Viscusi, in press). Our procedure should predict the result of a comparable public debate.

Construct validity means showing sensitivity to meaningful changes in conditions and insensitivity to non-meaningful ones. Our framework (Fischhoff & Furby, 1988) distinguishes between *substantive* features, which subjects can choose to value or neglect (e.g., visibility, species preservation), and *formal* features, determining the amount of the substantive features (e.g., the probability that the promised environmental change will be as described or that the promised payment will be collected). CV researchers need independent indicators of relevance, followed by empirical tests of sensitivity. The most extensive tests of sensitivity to a formal property involve scope, with mixed results (Baron, 1994; Carson & Mitchell, 1993; Green, Kahneman & Kunreuther, 1994; Schulze et al., in press). Sensitivity tests should also be conducted for other formal properties, and for substantive features of demonstrated relevance or irrelevance. A systematic research plan is need for identifying and prioritizing such tests.

Reliability. The limiting case for testing insensitivity to irrelevant changes is test-retest reliability. The obvious obstacle to such tests is that subjects will remember their previous responses (but be interpreted as having generated them consistently). Increasing the time period between tests decreases the role of memory, while increasing the risk that intervening events will change beliefs. We use an intermediate time period as a compromise, and also test secondary judgments (e.g., confidence, evaluation of alternative proposals), which should be less memorable. Reliability is necessary, but not sufficient for validity; people might routinely pay the same flat fee for poorly understood goods that investigators force upon them.

Impact clarity

Summaries for Policy Makers. The proposed method creates "thick" descriptions of respondents' beliefs, showing what they thought at several junctures about many issues. Some readers will want to know it all, in order to get an encompassing view of public perceptions. Other readers will focus on particular responses (e.g., final best-guess estimates, first-cut confidence, robust protests). Data need to be summarized coherently for each such audience. Readers who are unfamiliar with a methodology need epistemological guidance as well, telling them how solid the method is. The NOAA review panel provided a narrative summary for some aspects of conventional CV studies. Funtowicz & Ravetz (1990) review and propose some more formal summaries.

Our method will eventually include guidelines for creating summaries. Its implementation would have to be evaluated empirically, using directed readings -- in which individuals from each target audience read materials aloud, commenting on the conclusions that they derive and the confusion that they experience (Schriver, 1989).

CONCLUSION

In some senses, this proposal is quite consistent with conventional CV practice. It could, for example, be viewed as a way to achieve Carson and Mitchell's criteria for "a valid CV response," namely, that respondents "(i) clearly understand the characteristics of the good they are being asked to value; (ii) find the CV scenario elements related to the good's provision plausible; and (iii) answer the CV questions in a deliberate and meaningful manner." (1993, p. 1267)

However, the analysis opening this chapter suggests a clash of paradigms, in which people using the same words are still speaking different languages.[7] Inappropriately assuming common meaning can exacerbate conflicts, by obscuring the existence and source of differences. The acrimony of the debates over CV, the personal recriminations, the differing evidentiary standards -- all suggest disciplines that are solving different problems.

Comparison with alternatives

In that spirit, I will conclude by accentuating some differences between this approach to measuring environmental values and others. These differences are partly empirical questions and partly matters of principle.

Public debate

An obvious source of insight into the public's values is listening to what they say. In principle, all citizens can take part in public debates, formulating issues in their own terms and saying what they want. In practice, though, citizens may know too little to participate effectively, may posture for rhetorical purposes, may fear airing unpopular views, may speak off the (CV) topic, and may express themselves imprecisely. Our proposed approach attempts to create and capture the best of such discourse, while overcoming its weaknesses.

Public hearings

Properly conducted hearings allow participants to study in advance, to organize their thoughts, and to set them down in a formal record. Cross-examination and discussion can clarify ambiguities. Thinking may even evolve, as participants hear other opinions and dwell on the issues. However, comments may address different issues and use different modes of expression, making them hard to summarize. Here, too, strategic responses and heated exchanges can obscure underlying beliefs. Those who speak may represent the population poorly, being skewed toward those who can pay (or get paid) to appear, develop testimony, etc. The present approach attempts to capture the focused and evolutionary character of hearings, with better specified tasks and broader participation.

Focus groups

Every city has firms that pay citizens to join group discussions on specific topics, under the direction of moderators trained to encourage contributions and manage conflict. Such groups can uncover unexpected views on an issue, as can open-ended individual interviews (Chi, in press; Merton & Kendall, 1946; Schriver, 1989). They are less suited to systematically presenting information, airing views, and eliciting individuals' values. Focus groups are usually analyzed impressionistically, as befits their heuristic value (Merton, 1987). The present approach attempts to capture the learning potential of well-moderated groups, but with more systematic sampling, presentation, and elicitation. It elicits values privately.

Opinion polls

Surveys are the obvious method for systematic research into public opinion, and have often shown the public's willingness to sacrifice for the environment. They elicit views in relative privacy. However, they share many limits of public debates. Respondents may be ill-informed about the issues in general and about the specific proposal. If so, they must choose between certain disenfranchisement (by refusing to answer) and some risk of misinterpretation (by answering without understanding). Moreover, what they can say is restricted to a few structured response options, with little chance for elaboration. Survey researchers' commitment to using a single formulation for the entire population means keeping questions simple -- and still leaving some respondents behind. The present approach aspires to elicit any citizen's private views, but abandons the constraints that require simple, uniform, and uninformative questions.

Contingent valuation

Over time, CV research has increasingly freed itself from the constraints it inherited from survey research. CV studies present much more elaborate information and ask much more complicated questions than almost any surveys. In order to do so, CV researchers have developed increasingly involved procedures for preparing, testing, and presenting material. However, these changes seem incremental, without an overall approach to the paradigm shift that they involve. By consciously adopting an alternative philosophy, our approach is forced to face some issues that do not seem to have emerged spontaneously. One such issue is how to create a fully specified scenario, not just with a lot of detail, but with all the detail that respondents need. A second issue is how to convey these details and help subjects articulate their responses. A third is how to assess the success that we, and subjects, have had. The fourth is how to extract the policy implications of the inevitable imperfections. A fifth issue is how to conceptualize and manage the actual elicitation process.

Multi-attribute utility theory (MAUT)

Looking at some of the same issues, Gregory et al. (1993) proposed using multiattribute utility theory to elicit environmental values. They draw on a well-developed technical literature, with techniques for decomposing diverse situations, in order to reduce decision-makers' cognitive load (Keeney, 1993; Keeney & Raiffa, 1976). MAUT accepts the need to help people understand issues and articulate responses. However, its implementation here would face questions for which MAUT lacks complete answers (e.g., framing effects, information selection, failures of introspection, strategic responses). It is unclear if the benefits of decomposition in familiar domains extend to such unfamiliar ones (Fischhoff, 1980; Dawes, 1988).

As a CV substitute, MAUT eliminates the market metaphor, addressing just the environmental good. It assumes that respondents will view that good in isolation, while ignoring the other issues raised in our transaction framework. Although Gregory et al. (1993) call MAUT a "constructive" approach, that seems to be in the sense of assembling overall evaluations from component judgments rather than allowing the evolution of emergent values. As a result, its attitude to reactivity is unclear. Psychology as a whole is still grappling with how to handle situations in which people might not know what they want (Fischhoff, 1991; Fischhoff et al., 1980; Hogarth, 1982; Tversky & Kahneman, 1981).

A Two-fold strategy

The elicitation side of CV has been an exercise in applied basic social science, using existing techniques in unfamiliar settings. The limits to those techniques have prompted CV investigators to innovate continuously. However, there may be limits to ad hoc changes. Our procedure offers a comprehensive alternative view. It is one version of what psychologists might have created had they been given a chunk of the CV budget. Its elaboration shows the need for basic applied research, examining new fundamental issues highlighted by this application. Some studies of "embedding" have this character. Failure to distinguish between basic applied and applied basic research (Baddeley, 1979) has contributed to the acrimony of this debate (Cambridge Economics, 1992; Harrison, 1993; Nickerson, 1993; Smith, 1992), as has neglecting the clash of paradigms.

The economic side of CV has attracted much more basic applied research, looking at such issues as how to identify strategic responses and how to extract continuous estimates from discrete choices (Kristrom, in press; McConnell, 1990; Mitchell & Carson, 1989; Viscusi, in press). From my perspective, these challenges seem to be addressed with greater equanimity than those coming from psychologists. Perhaps the threats are less serious; perhaps economists present their critiques less caustically; perhaps a member of a profession will not rock the boat too vigorously. Our framework (Fischhoff & Furby, 1988) is, in a sense, an unconventional exercise in economic research, asking how to create a well-specified contingent market. We are, in effect, asking what a market is, perhaps not a question that an economist would raise or a psychologist should answer -- alone. Raising these questions might prompt the sort of mutually respectful relations that their solution requires.

ENDNOTES

1 My initial interest was in the choice anomalies (e.g., starting point bias) that CV investigators had documented, with more systematic samples (and larger budgets) than psychologists had ever mustered. My naive plan was to let the economists collect the data, from which we would then make science. The same data could serve quite different roles for economists trying to get the bugs out of a method and psychologists trying to account for response patterns (Fischhoff, 1991).

2 Other sections deal with matters of principle, such as how to avoid sexism in writing (gracefully), how to attribute credit fairly to research collaborators, and how to reassure readers regarding the protection of human subjects and the archiving of research materials.

3 Gregory, Lichtenstein & Slovic (1993) offer another set of criteria for this general niche. Generally speaking, I believe that the present set subsumes four of their criteria (accommodate the multi-dimensionality of value, exclude irrelevancies, separate facts from values, ask the right question). However, I reject Gregory et al.'s fifth criterion, minimize response refusals, believing that subjects may have principled objections to a task; capturing those concerns is part of a full description of results. Accepting the legitimacy of such expressions of discomfort should reduce any implicit pressure to suppress them.

4 Fischhoff (1993) discusses the analogous problems in experimental psychology. In a sense, these problems are much more severe than with CV, because so much more is typically left unsaid and there is so much less real-world context to provide guidance.

5 The failure of California's "Big Green" initiative provides an example of the ambiguous message of a clear electoral majority. The vote told little about which of its many provisions were critical, much less how well they were understood. Equally inscrutable is the June 1994 failure of a California initiative combining environmental protection and crime control, but appearing on the ballot along with three initiatives for earthquake-related spending.

6 We have used this procedure in creating risk communications for controversial fields (e.g., the health effects of electromagnetic fields) (Morgan, 1991).

7 Witness Carson and Mitchell's distinction between "a WTP question" and a "CV response" (1993, p. 1267), sacrificing one important term to the opposition in order to preserve a distinct meaning for a more critical one.

REFERENCES

Ajzen, I. & Peterson, G.L. (1988). Contingent value measurement: The price of everything and the value of nothing? In B. Driver, G. Peterson, & R. Gregory (Eds.), *Evaluating amenity resources*. New York: Venture.

American Psychological Association (1984). *Publication manual* (second edition). Washington, D.C.: American Psychological Association.

Baddeley, A. (1979). Applied cognitive and cognitive applied research. In. L.G. Nilsson (Ed.), *Perspectives on memory research*. Hillsdale, NJ: Lawrence Erlbaum.

Barber, B. (1991). *Strong democracy*. Berkeley, CA: University of California Press.

Baron, J. (1994). Rationality and invariance: Response to Schuman. Unpublished manuscript. Presented at DOE/EPA Workshop on Using Contingent Valuation to Measure Non-Market Values.

Bostrom, A., Fischhoff, B. & Morgan, G. (1992). Characterizing mental models of hazardous processes: A methodology and an application to radon. Journal of Social Issues, 48(4), 85-100.

Burgess, J., Harrison, C.M. & Limb, M. (1988). People, parks and the urban green. *Urban Studies*, 25, 455-473.

Cambridge Economics. (1992). *Contingent valuation: A critical assessment*. Cambridge, MA: Author.

Campbell, D.T. & Fiske, R.W. (1959). Convergent and discriminant validity by the multitrait-multimethod matrix. *Psychological Bulletin*, 56, 81-105.

Carson, R.T., & Mitchell, R.C. (1993). The issue of scope in contingent valuation studies. *American Journal of Agricultural Economics*, 75, 1263-1267.

Chi, M. (in press). Analyzing the content of verbal data to represent knowledge: A practical guide. *Journal of the Learning Sciences.*

Cohen, J. (1962). The statistical power of abnormal social psychological research. *Journal of Abnormal and Social Psychology, 65*, 145-153.

Coombs, C. (1964). *A theory of data.* New York: Wiley.

Crosby, N., Kelly, J.M. & Schaefer, P. (1986). Citizen review panels. *Public Administration Review, 46*, 170-178.

Dawes, R.M. (1972). *Fundamentals of attitude measurement.* New York: Wiley.

Dawes, R.M. (1988). *Rational choice in an uncertain world.* San Diego, CA: Harcourt Brace Jovanovich.

Dawes, R.M. (1994). *House of cards.* New York: Random House.

Department of Commerce (1993). Report of the NOAA Panel on Contingent Valuation. *Federal Register*, 58(10), 4602-4614.

Dietz, T. (1987). Theory and method in social impact assessment. *Sociological Inquiry, 57,* 54-69.

diSessa, A. (1993). Toward an epistemology of physics. *Cognition and Instruction, 10,* 105-225.

Ericsson, A. & Simon, H.A. (1984). *Verbal reports as data.* Cambridge, MA: MIT Press.

Fiorino, D.J. (1990). Citizen participation and environmental risk: A survey of institutional mechanisms. *Science, Technology & Human Values, 15,* 226-243.

Fischhoff, B. (1980). Clinical decision analysis. *Operations Research* 28, 28-43.

Fischhoff, B. (1988). Specifying value measurements. In B. Driver, G. Peterson, and R. Gregory (Eds.), *Evaluating amenity resources* (pp. 107-116). New York: Venture.

Fischhoff, B. (1990). What's it worth to you? A review of *Using surveys to value public goods: The contingent valuation method* by R.C. Mitchell & R.T. Carson. *Public Opinion Quarterly, 54,* 286-294.

Fischhoff, B. (1991). Value elicitation: Is there anything in there? *American Psychologist, 46,* 835-847.

Fischhoff, B. (1992). Giving advice: Decision theory perspectives on sexual assault. *American Psychologist, 47,* 577-588.

Fischhoff, B. (1993). Transaction analysis: A framework and an application to insurance decisions. *Journal of Risk and Uncertainty, 7,* 53-69.

Fischhoff, B. & Furby, L. (1986). *A review and critique of Tolley, Randall et al. "Establishing and valuing the effects of improved visibility in the Eastern United States".* ERI Technical Report 86-8. Eugene, OR: Eugene Research Institute.

Fischhoff, B. & Furby, L. (1988). Measuring values: A conceptual framework for interpreting transactions. *Journal of Risk and Uncertainty, 1* 147-184.

Fischhoff, B., Quadrel, M.J., Kamlet, M., Loewenstein, G., Dawes, R., Fischbeck, P., Klepper, S., Leland, J., & Stroh, P. (1993). Embedding effects: Stimulus representation and response modes. *Journal of Risk and Uncertainty, 6,* 211-234.

Fischhoff, B., Slovic, P. & Lichtenstein, S. (1980). Knowing what you want: Measuring labile values. In T. Wallsten (Ed.), *Cognitive processes in choice and decision behavior* (pp. 117-141). Hillsdale, NJ: Erlbaum.

Funtowicz, S. & Ravetz, J. (1990). *Uncertainty and quality in science for policy.* London: Kluwer.

Furby, L. & Fischhoff, B. (1989). *Specifying subjective evaluations. A critique of Dickie et al.'s interpretation of their contingent valuation results for reduced minor health symptoms.* USEPA Cooperative Agreement #CR814655-01-0. Eugene, OR: Eugene Research Institute.

Furnham, A. (1989). *Intuitive theories.* London: Plenum.

Gentner, D. & Stevens, A.L. (Eds.) (1983). *Mental models.* Hillsdale, NJ: Erlbaum.

Green, D.P., Kahneman, D. & Kunreuther, H. (1994). How scope and method of public funding affects willingness to pay for public goods. *Public Opinion Quarterly, 58,* 49-67.

Gregory, R., Lichtenstein, S., & Slovic, P. (1993) Valuing environmental resources: A constructive approach. *Journal of Risk and Uncertainty,* 7, 177-197.

Hamm, R.M., Bennett, L., Howe, C., & Wunderlich, K. (1992). Contingent valuation: Stability and meaning of "not willing to pay" responses. Unpublished manuscript. Institute of Behavioral Science. University of Colorado, Boulder.

Harrison, G.W. (1993). Valuing public goods with the contingent valuation method: A critique Kahenman & Knetsch. *Journal of Environmental Economics and Management, 23,* 248-257.

Hogarth, R. (Ed.) (1982). *Question framing and response consistency.* San Francisco: Jossey-Bass.

Jungermann, H., Schutz, H. & Thuring, J. (1988). Mental models in risk assessment: Informing people about drugs. *Risk Analysis, 8,* 147-155.

Kahneman, D. & Knetsch, J. (1992). Valuing public goods in the purchase of moral satisfaction. *Journal of Environmental Economics and Management, 22,* 52-70.

Kahneman, D. & Tversky, A. (1979). Prospect theory: An analysis of decision under risk. *Econometrica,* 47, 263-281.

Keeney, R.L. (1993). *Value-focused thinking: A path to creative decision making.* Cambridge, MA: Harvard University Press.

Keeney, R.L. & Raiffa, H. (1976). *Decisions with multiple objectives.* New York: Wiley.

Kintsch, W. (1986). Learning from text. *Cognition and Instruction, 3,* 87-108.

Kristrom, B. (in press). Practical problems in contingent valuation. this volume.

Lazo, J.K., Schulze, W.D.,, McClelland, & Doyle, J.K. (1992). Can contingent valuation measure nonuse values? *American Journal of Agricultural Economics, 75,* 1126-1132.

Leventhal, H. & Cameron, L. (1987). Behavioral theories and the problem of compliance. *Patient Education and Counseling, 10,* 117-138.

McConnell, K.E. (1990). Models for referendum data; The structure of discrete choice models for contingent valuation. *Journal of Environmental Economics and Management, 18,* 19-34.

McGuire, W. (1969). Suspiciousness of experimenter's intent. In R. Rosenthal & R.L. Rosnow (Eds.), *Artifact in behavioral research.* New York: Academic Press.

Merton, R.K. (1987). The focussed interview and focus groups. *Public Opinion Quarterly, 51,* 541-557.

Merton, R.K. & Kendall, P.I. (1946). The focussed interview. *American Journal of Sociology, 51,* 541-557.

Mitchell, R.C. & Carson, R.T. (1989). *Using surveys to value public goods: The contingent valuation method.* Washington, DC: Resources for the Future.

Morgan, G. (1991). *Health risks of electromagnetic fields.* Department of Engineering and Public Policy: Carnegie Mellon University.

National Research Council. (1982). *Survey measure of subjective phenomena.* Washington, DC: The Council.

Navrud, S. (in press). Does the presentation of information matter in contingent valuation studies -- experimenting with video. This volume.

Nickerson, C.A.E. (1993). Valuing public goods: A comment on Harrison's critique of Kahneman and Knetsch. *Journal of Environmental Economics and Management, 25,* 93-102.

Nisbett, R.E. & Wilson, T.D. (1977). Telling more than we know: Verbal reports on metnal processes. *Psychological Review, 84,* 231-259.

Orne, M.T. (1962). On the social psychology of the psychological experiment. *American Psychologist,* 17, 776-783.

Peterson, G.L., Driver, B.L., & Gregory, R. (Eds.), (1988). *Amenity resource valuation: Integrating economics with other disciplines.* State College, PA: Venture.

Quadrel, M.J., Fischhoff, B. & Palmgren, C. (1994). Adolescents' definitions of risky events. manuscript under editorial review.

Reder, L. (1985). Techniques available to author, teacher, and reader to improve retention of the main ideas of a chapter. In S.F. Chipman, J.W. Segal & R. Glaser (Eds.), *Thinking and learning skills* (vol. 2) (pp. 37-64). Hillsdale, NJ: Erlbaum

Reich, R.B. (1985). Public administration and public deliberation. *Yale Law Review, 94,* 1617-1641.

Schkade, D. & Payne, J.W. (1994). How people respond to contingent valuation questions: A verbal protocol analysis of willingness to pay for an environmental regulation. *Journal of Environmental Economics and Management, 26,* 88-109.

Schriver, K.A. (1989). Evaluating text quality: The continuum from text-focused to reader-focused methods. *IEEE Transactions on Professional Communication, 32,* 238-255.

Schulze, W., McClelland, G., Waldman, D., & Lazo, J. (in press). Information, context, and bias in contingent valuation. This volume.

Schwarz, N. (1994). Judgment in social context. In L. Berkowitz (Ed.), *Advances in experimental social psychology, vol 26.* San Diego: Academic Press.

Smith, V.K. (1992). Aribtrary values, good causes, and premature verdicts. *Journal of Environmental Economics and Management, 22,* 71-89.

Smith, V.K. & Osborne, L. (in press). Do contingent valuation estimates pass a "scope" test?: A preliminary metaanalysis. This volume.

Stokols, D. & Altman, I. (Eds.) (1986). *Handbook of environmental psychology* (2 vols). New York: Wiley.

Strack, F., & Schwarz, N. (1992). Communicative influences in standardized question situations. In G.R. Semin & K. Fiedler (Eds.), *Language interaction and social cognition.* London: Sage.

Turner, C.F. & Martin, E. (Eds.) (1984). *Surveying subjective phenomena.* New York: Sage.

Tversky, A. & Kahneman, D. (1971). Belief in the "law of small numbers." *Psychological Bulletin, 76,* 105-110.

Tversky, A. & Kahneman, D. (1981). The framing of decisions and the psychology of choice. *Science, 211,* 453-458.

Verba, S. & Nie, N.H. (1972). *Participation in America.* Chicago: University of Chicago Press.

Viscusi, W.K. (in press). Economic and psychological aspects of valuing risk reduction. this volume.

Viscusi, W.K., & Magat, W.A. (1987). *Learning about risk: Consumer and worker responses to hazard information.* Cambridge, MA: Harvard University Press.

Voss, J.F., Tyler, S.W. & Yengo, L.A. (1983). Individual differences in the solving of social science problems. *Individual Differences in Cognition, 1,* 205-232.

Whittington, D. & Davis, D. (1993). *A review and assessment of techniques for Systematic Client Consultation.* Department of Environmental Sciences & Engineering, University of North Carolina at Chapel Hill.

9

THE EFFECT OF GIVING RESPONDENTS "TIME TO THINK" ON TESTS OF SCOPE: AN EXPERIMENT IN CALAMBA, PHILIPPINES

Dale Whittington
KyeongAe Choe
Donald Lauria

INTRODUCTION

The possible inability of respondents in contingent valuation surveys to offer higher willingness-to-pay amounts for a good or service that the survey researcher believes to be unambiguously better than another good or service has been termed the "embedding " or the "part-whole" problem. Draft guidelines issued by the United States National Oceanic and Atmospheric Administration (NOAA) in 1994 for the use of the contingent valuation method to assess natural resource damages require that at least three split sample "tests of scope" be conducted to determine whether this embedding problem exists. If it does, the accuracy of the CV results is called into question. These "tests of scope" are to offer three different groups of respondents three valuation scenarios in order to see whether respondents value them differently. A "successful" experiment will increase one's confidence that respondents are somehow "sensitive" to the specific good or service described, and are not valuing some other commodity or scenario. How one judges whether a test of scope has been successful (and thus the contingent valuation results can be used) is unclear.[1] Nor did NOAA offer guidance on the appropriate procedures to use when carrying out tests of scope. Future research is clearly required on how best to implement tests of scope.

The objective of this paper is to suggest a possible avenue for such research. We examine the question of whether giving respondents "time to think" about their answers to a referendum question in a contingent valuation survey might help or enable them to better distinguish between different service levels offered. To explore this question, we use data from the first "test of scope" experiment carried out in a developing country. In the next, second section of the paper we provide a brief overview of the city where this contingent valuation study was conducted. In the third section the data set and the experimental design are described. In the fourth section we present the results of our analysis. We examine a different issue in the fifth section: the effect of giving respondents time to think on their answers to high prices in a referendum elicitation procedure (i.e., the effect of a "time to think" treatment on so called "fat tails" in the distribution of respondents' answers). The sixth section offers some brief concluding remarks.

THE CALAMBA STUDY

The contingent valuation study described in this paper was conducted as part of a World Bank-executed project for the Philippines with funding from Japan. The project included the following components: (1) preparation of a national urban sanitation strategy plan, (2) formulation of an action plan for implementing the strategy, and (3) formulation of a local strategic sanitation plan for each of five cities that were selected by the government as representative of urban conditions in the Philippines. In this paper we describe part of the research that was conducted for Calamba, one of the five cities selected as part of this World Bank project.

Calamba is located in the province of Luzon, about 60 km south of Manila; it has a population of about 175,000. The city has a 20-km long east-west axis and is partially bounded on the east by Laguna de Bay, a large inland lake used for commercial fishing. The terrain of the city is generally flat, and the climate is tropical.

The principal objective of our research effort in Calamba was to obtain accurate, reliable information on household demand for improved sanitation services. We sought information that would enable us to predict how different groups of households would respond if they were actually offered the opportunity to purchase an improved sanitation service at a specified price. To accomplish this objective, we designed and carried out a large contingent valuation survey. The contingent valuation questionnaire was drafted in the field in collaboration with a team of Filipino professionals and a large group of local enumerators using a variety of participatory approaches. The survey was executed in November and December, 1992.

About 31 percent of the households in Calamba use a private water connection as their primary water source, 48 percent use a private well, 10 percent obtain their water from neighbors, and 10 percent use public handpumps. The households with private connections are concentrated in the high density urban areas.

The majority of households in Calamba (86 percent) have already installed either flush or pour-flush toilets for the exclusive use of their household members and are quite satisfied with the service these facilities provided. These private facilities were installed by private contractors or by the household members themselves, without government assistance. Flush toilets were most common in the high density areas where more households had private water connections.

These private toilet facilities empty into either lined or unlined septic tanks, which commonly overflow into either drains or ditches that run through town, eventually to empty into Laguna de Bay. Very few private toilets are connected to proper septic fields. Thus, while the existing sanitation system of flush and pour-flush toilets solves the immediate needs of households by removing their toilet wastes from their living space, it creates neighborhood health problems and water pollution in Laguna de Bay.

Study design

The contingent valuation study focused on the majority of households in Calamba that owned their houses and already had flush or pour-flush toilets for their exclusive use, because these households were in a position to make a decision on whether or not to connect to a sewer line in their neighborhood if one were installed. This was not a realistic proposition for renters and households without a pour-flush or flush toilet already in their home.[2]

Our experimental design can be most easily conceptualized by considering our overall stratified random sample of 1500 households in Calamba. Our original sample of 1500 households was split between two groups. First, households with a pour-flush or flush toilet for their exclusive use were targeted to receive one of thirty different versions of the "long" questionnaire. Interviews were successfully completed with 1104 households targeted to receive this long questionnaire. These 1104 households fell into two different groups. For the first group (593 households), a complete in-person interview was conducted with a respondent from each household at one sitting. Either heads of households or their spouses were interviewed. For this first group of households, an interview took an average of 45 minutes.

For the second group (511 households), the in-person interview took place over the course of two or three days. On the first day, the enumerator asked the respondent questions about the demographic characteristics of the household, existing water services, existing sanitation services, and environmental attitudes and perceptions. The enumerator then read the respondent a description of one of three different levels of improved sanitation service (described below) and asked him or her to think about how much the household would be willing to pay per month for this level of service. A brochure with this same information was left with the respondent for members of the household to study and reflect upon. On the second or third day, the enumerator returned to the household, located the same respondent, and completed the rest of the questionnaire.

In addition,each respondent who received the long questionnaire (both those given time to think and those that were not) was offered one of three different levels of improved sanitation service (Table 1). One third of the respondents were offered the lowest level of service (Service Level I): the opportunity to connect their pour-flush or flush toilet system to a sewer line that would run through their neighborhood and would then discharge wastewater untreated into Laguna de Bay. Respondents were shown diagrams of a sewer system in a neighborhood. They were told that the wastewater from their toilet, kitchen, and bath could be discharged into this sewer pipe, and that if they decided to connect, their household would have to pay a monthly fee to the water district, just like a water bill. They were also told that there would be no initial connection fee nor any replumbing costs for connecting to the sewer line (these charges would be paid by the water authority). This group of respondents was told that the benefits of connecting to the sewer line would include improved neighborhood health conditions, but that because there would be no wastewater treatment plant, the quality of Laguna de Bay near Calamba would probably get worse.

TABLE 1:LEVELS OF SANITATION OFFERED TO RESPONDENTS

Service Level I:	Sewer system only -- no wastewater treatment plant	*Implication*: Neighborhood environmental and public health conditions in Calamba would improve, but the quality of water in the lake would get worse.
Service Level II:	Sewer system plus wastewater treatment plant	*Implication*: Neighborhood environmental and public health conditions would improve in Calamba, and the quality of water in the lake would not get worse (it would not improve much either).
Service Level III:	Sewer system plus wastewater treatment plant in Calamba and a regional plan that would ensure that other communities around the lake also treated their wastewater discharges.	*Implication*: Neighborhood environmental and public health conditions in Calamba would improve, and the quality of water in the lake would improve.

The second third of the respondents receiving the long questionnaire were also asked about their willingness to pay for a connection to a sewer line in their neighborhood, but in this case the wastewater collected by the sewer system would be treated at a wastewater treatment plant before being discharged into Laguna de Bay. We termed this next higher level of sanitation service "Service Level II" and hypothesized that households would be willing to pay more for Service Level II than for Service Level I. In addition to the diagrams of a sewer line, respondents were shown large color photographs of a type of secondary wastewater treatment plant in operation about thirty kilometers from Calamba. In this case respondents were told that they would receive neighborhood health benefits if they connected to a sewer system, and that the water quality of the lake would stay about the same. The water quality of the lake would not improve significantly, because there was no assurance that other communities and industries around the Laguna de Bay would clean up their wastewater.

The third group of respondents was offered what we hypothesized to be an even higher level of service (Service Level III). Not only were they given the opportunity to connect to a sewer line with an associated wastewater treatment plant, but they were told that there would be a regional water quality management plan that would ensure that other communities around Laguna de Bay would also clean up their wastewater discharges. The respondents would receive benefits from improved neighborhood environmental conditions and also improved water quality in the lake.

After the enumerator read the respondent a description of the sanitation service level that had been randomly assigned to the household, the enumerator asked the respondent to suppose that it was possible to connect his or her house to a sewer line. The respondent was told that if his or her household decided to connect, they would have to pay a monthly fee just like a water bill. The enumerator then asked:

If the monthly fee to be connected to the sewer line was [25, 50, 100, 150, or 200] pesos, would you want to connect to the sewer line, or would you prefer not to connect? [3]

Which of the five monthly fees (i.e., 25, 50 , 100, 150, or 200 pesos) a particular respondent received was randomly assigned. Each referendum value was followed by a short bidding game.

The study design for the long questionnaire thus results in 30 distinct subsamples (2 treatments for time/no time to think x 3 service levels x 5 monthly fees). Table 2 presents the number of interviews completed in Calamba for each of the thirty "cells." As shown, more than 30 questionnaires were completed for every cell in the study design. Thirty five percent of the "long questionnaire" respondents were asked about Service Level I, 34 percent about Service Level II; and 31 percent about Service Level III. The portion of the sample respondents receiving each of the five monthly fees varied between 19-21 percent. Because the implementation of the fieldwork was considerably more complicated for the respondents given time to think than for respondents given no time to think, fewer time-to-think interviews were successfully completed (511 vs. 593).

TABLE 2: NUMBER OF QUESTIONNAIRES COMPLETED IN CALAMBA FOR HOUSEHOLDS WITH FLUSH OR FOUR-FLUSH TOILETS (Different Versions of the Survey Instrument)

	Type of Improved Sanitation Service Offered the Respondent			
Price of Sanitation Service Indicated to Respondent (pesos per month)*	Sewerage only	Sewerage and treatment	Sewerage, treatment, and regional plan	Total
		Respondent Given No "Time to Think"		
25ppm	45	43	37	125
50 ppm	43	43	38	124
100 ppm	40	34	39	113
150 ppm	44	35	34	113
200 ppm	44	38	36	118
		Respondent Given Time to Think (1-2 days)		
25 ppm	34	35	32	101
50 ppm	35	32	33	100
100 ppm	34	36	33	103
150 ppm	35	37	31	103
200 ppm	35	38	33	104
Total No. of Interviews	389	369	346	1104

* US$1 = 25 pesos

Our experiment was intended to test whether giving respondents "time to think" would affect their ability to judge the relative value of these sanitation service levels. We intended for Service Level III to be unambiguously better than Service Level II, and for Service Level II to be better than Service Level I. Of course, we did not know *a priori* how respondents would perceive the magnitude of these differences in the improved service levels.

TABLE 3: POSSIBLE OUTCOMES OF EMBEDDING EFFECTS FROM EXPERIMENT		
	Embedding Effect.....	
	Present	*Not Present*
Respondent given....	(Service Level I vs. II)	(Service Level I vs. II)
	(Service Level II vs. III)	(Service Level II vs. III)
	(Service Level I vs. Service Level III)	(Service Level I vs. Service Level III)
No time to think	cell 1	cell 2
Time to think	cell 3	cell 4

Possible Outcomes of Experiment

(A) Cell 1 and Cell 3: Embedding effect present--"time to think" treatment does not change theproblem.

(B) Cell 1 and Cell 4: Embedding effect present--"time to think" treatment eliminates the problem.

(C) Cell 2 and Cell 4:Embedding effect not present-- No problem for CVM.

(D) Cell 2 and Cell 3: "Time to think" treatment creates embedding effect.

POSSIBLE OUTCOMES

There are four possible situations that could occur for the two split-samples of respondents given "no time to think" and given "time to think." These four situations are shown in Table 3 for Service Level I vs. Service Level II:

(1) The respondent is given "no time to think" and the "embedding problem" is present, i.e., the respondent does not bid more for Service Level II than for Service Level I (Cell 1);

(2) The respondent is given "no time to think" and the "embedding problem" is not present, i.e., the respondent does bid more for Service Level II than for Service Level I (Cell 2);

(3) The respondent is given "time to think" and the "embedding problem" is present, i.e., the respondent does not bid more for Service Level II than for Service Level I (Cell 3);

(4) The respondent is given "time to think" and the "embedding problem" is not present, i.e., the respondent does bid more for Service Level II than for Service Level I (Cell 4).

These four situations are repeated in our experiment for Service Level II vs. Service Level III, as shown in Table 3.

For all three pair-wise comparisons of service levels (Service Level I vs. Service II, Service Level II vs. Service Level III, and Service Level I vs. Service Level III), there are four possible outcomes of the experiment:

1. Outcome A (Cell 1 and Cell 3) : The embedding effect is present when the respondent is given "no time to think," and giving the respondent the "time to think" treatment does not eliminate the "problem" (i.e., embedding still exists).

2. Outcome B (Cell 1 and Cell 4) : The embedding effect is present when the respondent is given "no time to think," and giving the respondent the "time to think" treatment eliminates the embedding problem (i.e., embedding no longer exists).

3. Outcome C (Cell 2 and Cell 4) : The embedding effect is not present when the respondent has "no time to think," nor when the respondent is given "time to think."

4. Outcome D (Cell 2 and Cell 3) : The embedding effect is not present when the respondent has "no time to think," but is present when the respondent is given "time to think." In this perverse case, the "time to think" treatment creates an embedding effect.

Results

To analyze the results of this experiment, we split the total sample into two groups: those given "no time to think," and those given "time to think." We then ran the following six multivariate models of the determinants of the WTP bids:
(1) OLS model with subsample of respondents given "no time to think";
(2) OLS model with subsample of respondents given "time to think";
(3) Tobit model with subsample of respondents given "no time to think";
(4) Tobit model with subsample of respondents given "time to think";
(5) Probit model with subsample of respondents given "no time to think";
(6) Probit model with subsample of respondents given "time to think";

Table 4 presents the definitions of the variables used in the models; Table 5 presents the model results.

Table 4: Description of Selected Variables Used in the Multivariate Analysis

Variable name	Mean (S.D.)	Description	Expected sign
		Dependent variables	
HIGHBID	53.37 (48.15)	maximum monthly amount household would pay for specified services (pesos): the amount was taken from the last yes to the bidding questions (for OLS & TOBIT models)	
RFRDMBID	0.34	yes and no responses taken from the first bidding questions: 0= Respondent is not willing to pay bid mount for specified service 1= Respondent is willing to pay bid amount for specified service (for PROBIT model)	
		Independent variables	
TTT	0.46 (0.50)	1=if respondents were given time to think 0=no time to think	-
START	104.54 (64.40)	starting point of bidding game taken as continuous values; 25, 50, 100, 150 and 200 pesos	+
TYPE3	0.31 (0.46)	1=service level 3 (sewer, treatment plant & regional plan) was offered 0=otherwise	+
TYPE1	0.35 (0.48)	1=service level 1 (sewer only) was offered 0=otherwise	-
FEMLRESP	0.61 (0.49)	1=if gender of respondent is female 0=otherwise	?
PEDGRDRP	9.31 (3.43)	years of education for respondent	+
WCONNECT	0.32 (0.47)	1=if the major source of drinking water is from NAWASA connection 0=otherwise	?

Table 4: Description of Selected Variables Used in the Multivariate Analysis

DISCHTNK	0.16 (0.37)	1=if waste water from kitchen or bath goes to septic tank 0=otherwise	-
NCMPLTNK	0.64 (0.48)	1=if septic tank does not have either concrete wall or floor 0=otherwise	+
SATIS2	0.41 (0.49)	1=if respondent is very satisfied with existing sanitation system 0=otherwise	-
FISHQLTY	0.57 (0.50)	1=if respondent believes water quality of lake over last 20 years has gotten worse (or much worse) and also very concerned about contaminated fish 0=otherwise	+
SEWKNOW	0.10 (0.30)	1=if respondent is somewhat (or very) familiar with sewer system 0=otherwise	+
TPKNOW	0.13 (0.34)	1=if respondent is somewhat (or very) familiar with treatment plant 0=otherwise	+
HHINCOME	6.52 (3.98)	total monthly income for all wage earners of a household (1,000 pesos/month)	+
FLOOD	0.22 (0.41)	1=if house is located in flood zone 0=otherwise	+
LOCSUBD	0.26 (0.44)	1=if house is located in subdivision 0=otherwise	?
DENHI	0.17 (0.37)	1=if respondent lives in high density (*poblacion*) area 0=otherwise	+
DENMD	0.59 (0.49)	1=if respondent lives in an area which has agricultural activity 0=otherwise	-
INTVQLTY	0.32 (0.47)	1=if enumerator assessed the interviewee made effort to answer WTP questions truthfully and also think the interview quality was good 0=otherwise	+

Table 5: Multivariate Analysis, Time to Think Effects Experiment, Calamba

	OLS				TOBIT				PROBIT			
Variables	sub-sample of no time to think only		sub-sample of time to think only		sub-sample of no time to think only		sub-sample of time to think only		sub-sample of no time to think only		sub-sample of time to think only	
Dependent var. Independent var.	HIGHBID		HIGHBID		HIGHBID		HIGHBID		RFRMBID		RFRMBID	
INTERCEPT	15.103 (1.200)		-0.880 (-0.082)		6.807 (0.469)		-7.175 (-0.569)		0.004 (0.014)		-0.118 (-0.326)	
START	0.062 (1.716)	+	0.060 (1.864)	+	0.060 (1.439)		0.037 (0.999)		-0.010 (-10.167)	*	-0.014 (-10.613)	*
TYPE3	0.919 (0.157)		-10.616 (-2.124)	#	0.498 (0.075)		-12.965 (-2.239)	#	-0.064 (-0.421)		-0.037 (-0.215)	
TYPE1	-14.551 (-2.564)	#	-23.866 (-4.744)	*	-20.392 (-3.120)	*	-30.846 (-5.217)	*	-0.228 (-1.563)		-0.442 (-2.540)	#
FEMLRESP	0.699 (0.140)		1.067 (0.246)		-0.137 (-0.024)		2.206 (0.437)		-0.093 (-0.714)		-0.026 (-0.176)	
PEDGRDRP	2.037 (1.412)		1.289 (1.983)	#	1.219 (1.443)		1.628 (2.139)	#	0.013 (0.736)		0.025 (1.154)	
WCONNECT	-19.550 (-3.184)	*	-1.981 (-0.359)		-21.387 (-3.040)	*	-1.061 (-0.166)		-0.168 (-1.055)		-0.015 (-0.083)	
DISCHTNK	-5.135 (-0.810)		-9.021 (-1.515)		-8.964 (-1.222)		-12.078 (-1.718)	+	0.005 (0.033)		-0.126 (-0.603)	
NCMPLTNK	-9.846 (-1.958)	#	7.315 (1.624)		-11.619 (-2.014)	#	5.891 (1.120)		-0.257 (-1.998)	#	0.076 (0.493)	
SATIS2	-4.127 (-0.756)		-6.096 (-1.227)		-6.134 (-0.978)		-9.197 (-1.585)		-0.973 (-0.700)		-0.253 (-1.457)	
FISHQLTY	14.812 (2.924)	*	11.685 (2.658)	*	17.774 (3.061)	*	14.233 (2.774)	*	0.147 (1.137)		0.212 (1.397)	

Table 5: Multivariate Analysis, Time to Think Effects Experiment, Calamba

SEWKNOW	2.725 (0.270)		-14.094 (-1.426)		-1.612 (-0.138)		-18.500 (-1.610)		-0.045 (-0.175)		-0.608 (-1.846)	+
TPKNOW	-3.395 (-0.374)		-1.258 (-0.150)		-2.021 (-0.194)		0.402 (0.042)		0.096 (0.414)		0.125 (0.445)	
HHINCOME	2.570 (4.213)	*	2.108 (3.893)	*	2.612 (3.736)	*	2.262 (3.620)	*	0.768 (4.393)	*	0.073 (3.459)	*
FLOOD	11.785 (1.957)	+	2.736 (0.520)	+	12.569 (1.828)		1.616 (0.263)		0.128 (0.864)		-0.023 (-0.132)	
LOCSUBD	-2.167 (-0.374)		5.278 (0.957)		-2.373 (-0.358)		4.572 (0.714)		-0.008 (-0.056)		0.128 (0.684)	
DENHI	31.471 (3.486)	*	24.303 (2.922)	*	38.984 (3.671)	*	27.420 (2.837)	*	0.353 (1.522)		0.362 (1.285)	
DENMD	8.859 (1.320)		11.355 (1.958)	#	13.145 (1.705)	+	12.844 (1.901)		0.092 (0.533)		0.347 (1.713)	+
INTVQLTY	25.027 (4.430)	*	22.966 (4.672)	*	28.919 (4.463)	*	26.938 (4.710)	*	0.521 (3.590)	*	0.552 (3.167)	*
log (L)	-		-		-2524.3		-1920.2		-286.93		-213.10	
X^2	-		-		-		-		165.52		197.13	
Pseudo R^2	-		-		-		-		0.225		0.315	
R^2	0.161		0.202		-		-		-		-	
Adjusted R^2	0.131		0.167		-		-		-		-	
F value	5.429		5.750		-		-		-		-	
N	528		427		528		427		568		490	
% Correct predicted	-		-		-		-		73.9%		78.2%	

-The numbers in parentheses below the estimated coefficients are the ratio of these coefficients to the estimates of their asymptotic standard errors.
* indicates null hypothesis of b=0 is rejected at 1% of significance level. # indicates null hypothesis of b=0 is rejected at 5% of significance level
\+ indicates null hypothesis of b=0 is rejected at 10% of significance level.

The key findings for this experiment are found by examining the differences in the coefficients and test statistics of the variables TYPE1 (Service Level I) and TYPE3 (Service Level III) for the two subsamples (analyzed separately). Consider first theresults of the probit models (last two columns in Table 5). When respondents were given "no time to think," there was no statistical difference between the answers to the first price offered to those respondents who received Service Level I and the answers to the first price offered to those respondents who received Service Level II. Nor was there any statistical difference between the responses to the first price offered for Service Level II and the first price offered for Service Level III. However, when respondents were given "time to think," there was in fact a statistically significant difference between the responses for Service Level I and Service Level II, and respondents bid *less* for Service Level I as expected. In this case the treatment (giving respondents "time to think") seems to have eliminated the "embedding problem" (Outcome B; Table 3). However, the results for the variable "TYPE3" in the probit model indicate that respondents did not respond differently to the first price offered for Service Level II and III-- either when they had no time to think, or when they were given "time to think" (Outcome A; Table 3).

For the OLS and tobit models, respondents had no trouble distinguishing Service Levels I and II--either when they had "no time to think," or when they were given "time to think" (Outcome C). Respondents in both subsamples clearly bid less for Service Level I than for Service Level II (as indicated by both the OLS and the tobit models). The magnitude of the difference is significantly larger for respondents who were given "time to think" than for those who were not (24 pesos per month vs. 15 pesos per month for the OLS model; 31 pesos per month vs. 21 pesos per month for the tobit model). The difference between these results and the probit results is probably due to the fact that the probit model just used the respondents' answers to the first price offered, while the OLS and tobit models used the respondents' answer to the last price accepted. The data used for the probit model were thus "coarser" and contained less information (although they were perhaps more incentive-compatible) than that used in the OLS and tobit models.

The results with regard to Service Level II vs. Service Level III are interesting. For the subsample of respondents with "no time to think," just as with the probit model, there was no statistically significant difference between the WTP bids of respondents who received Service Level II and those who received Service Level III. This was true for both the OLS and the tobit results. However, for the subsample of respondents who were given "time to think," there was a statistically significant difference between the WTP bids of respondents who received Service Level II and those who received Service Level III--and respondents who received Service Level III bid *less* than those who received Service Level II. This effect is not only statistically significant, it is also relatively large in magnitude (11-13 pesos per month). These results suggest that when respondents had "time to think" about the regional plan for water quality management of Laguna de Bay described in the survey, they liked it less.

There are two plausible (*ex-post*) explanations for this result. First, people given time to think may have realized that water quality in Laguna de Bay was a public good, and they may have attempted to free ride by not participating in the regional water quality plan (and hoping other communities *would* participate). Second, the fact that respondents who were given "time to think" bid *less* for Service Level III than for Service Level II may simply reflect people's concerns about the ineffectiveness of government programs in the Philippines and their desire not to become involved in a large collective action program.

The Effect of time to think on respondents' answers to high referendum prices

Over the last few years there has been discussion in the contingent valuation research community about possible limitations of the referendum elicitation procedure and the problem of many respondents accepting what seem to be unrealistically high referendum prices (i.e., "fat tail" problem). The older literature on the contingent valuation method might attribute this tendency (when it exists) to compliance bias or "yea" saying. More recently, others have attributed it to poorly designed questionnaires.

In this study we did not have an implausibly high proportion of respondents accept our high referendum price of 200 pesos (US$8) per month. The percentage of respondents agreeing to this price varied from 6-11% depending on the service level (Table 6). It is interesting, however, to examine these sample averages in more detail by disaggregating the data for respondents into those given no time to think and those given time to think. Figure 2 shows the number of respondents who received the 200-peso price for each of the three service levels, and the number that accepted it, for both those who were given time to think and those who were not.

Table 6: Percent of Respondents Who Gave Positive Response to Referendum Question (by Referendum Amount)

	Percent of respondents agreeing to referendum amount for...		
Referendum amount (pesos**/month)	Sewerage only	Sewerage and treatment	Sewerage, treatment, and regional plan
25	57	71	71
50	39	57	62
100	35	27	29
150	9	21	14
200	8	11	6

* For households with pour-flush or flush toilets for the exclusive use of their members ** US$1 = 25 pesos

For example, 44 respondents received Service Level I, no time to think, and the 200-peso price. Six of these 44 respondents accepted the 200-peso price. On the other hand, of the 35 respondents who received Service Level I, time to think, and the 200-peso price, none accepted it. The results are essentially identical for Service Level III. Thirty six respondents received Service Level III, no time to think, and the 200-peso price: 4 accepted it. Thirty three respondents received Service Level III, time to think, and the 200-peso: none accepted it.

This apparent effect of time to think on reducing acceptance of high referendum prices does not exist for Service Level II. Here 38 respondents had no time to think and 4 accepted the 200-peso price; of the 36 respondents who had time to think and Service Level II, 4 also accepted the 200-peso price.

These sample sizes are too small to draw statistically significant conclusions. However, if we combine the observations from respondents who received all three service levels and both of the high referendum prices (150 pesos per month and 200 pesos per month), the effect of the time-to-think treatment on the acceptance of the high prices is statistically significant. As shown in Figure 3, over 13 percent of these respondents who were given no time to think accepted the high referendum price compared to 8 percent of those who had time to think.

CONCLUSIONS

The results of this experiment are obviously mixed and cannot be easily generalized. Nevertheless, we believe they suggest that giving respondents "time to think" may help them better distinguish (or discriminate) between different commodity descriptions. If this proves to be true in other applications, it would suggest that respondents should generally be given "time to think" about the commodity offered and their willingness to pay for it before they are asked the valuation questions.

Our results also indicate one of the potential pitfalls in the application of NOAA's 1994 draft guidelines regarding tests of scope. *Ex-ante* we thought we had designed a "test of scope" experiment in which Service Level III was unambiguously superior to Service Level II. We found that actually respondents preferred Service Level II to Service Level III when they were given time to reflect upon this choice. Should we thus conclude that the contingent valuation exercise failed to reveal accurate, reliable information? Surely such a conclusion is premature. *Ex-post* it seems more likely to us that we made a mistake (not the respondents). At the very least, contingent valuation researchers must acknowledge this possibility and consider means of determining which of these outcomes is more plausible.

More generally, these results point toward the need for more careful consideration of and research on possible treatments or approaches to eliminate problems respondents may have answering contingent valuation questions, rather the rigid application of "test of scope" experiments designed simply reject contingent valuation results.

ENDNOTES

1 In fact, there are very few pairs of goods or services for which the survey researcher can predict with assurance that one good in the pair should be clearly *much* preferred to the other (Carson and Mitchell, 1995). In this sense the "embedding effect" as it has been discussed in most of the contingent valuation literature is not a well-defined problem. Rather it is more of a subjective concern or sense on the part of some contingent valuation researchers that respondents are not "properly answering" the contingent valuation questions as they were intended. If respondents do not distinguish or value differently two goods, it may be because they have not understood what the CV researcher was offering in the hypothetical scenario, or it may simply be because they do not prefer one to the other for some reason that the CV researcher has failed to perceive.

2 Renters and households without pour-flush or flush toilets for their exclusive use were also surveyed; they received a shorter, different questionnaire not described in this paper. For further details on the study design, see Lauria et al.,1995.

3 At the time of our survey US$1 = 25 pesos.

REFERENCES

Carson, Richard, and Robert Mitchell. (1995). " Sequencing and Nesting in Contingent Valuation Studies." *Journal of Environmental Economics and Management*. Vol. 28, No. 2, March. pp. 135-154.

Lauria, Donald T., Dale Whittington, KyeongAe Choe, Cynthia Turingan, and Virginia Abiad. (1995). "Household Demand for Improved Sanitation Services: A Case Study of Calamba, Philippines." In *Valuing Environmental Preferences: Theory and Practice of the Contingent Valuation method in the US, EU, and Developing Countries*. Edited by Ian J. Bateman and Ken G. Willis. Oxford University Press.

PRACTICAL PROBLEMS IN CONTINGENT VALUATION[1]

Bengt Kriström

ABSTRACT

This paper discusses some practical problems that arises within contingent valuation experiments. I discuss the data collection process, scenario construction, questioning modes, how to optimally design an experiment and the use of various econometric techniques when closed-ended valuation questions are used.

INTRODUCTION

The contingent valuation method (CVM) is a practical survey technique, designed to shed empirical light on matters of resource allocation. Survey techniques are the main tool for generating data within the social Sciences. Household expenditure surveys, employment surveys, health surveys, opinion polls and surveys used to compile the national accounts are examples of essential data-generating processes in the social Sciences. Indeed, surveys are the life-blood of empirical studies for economists, psychologists, sociologists and for vast number of other researchers.

At first blush the CVM is very straightforward; simply ask a set of people how much they would be willing-to-pay (WTP) for obtaining a particular good. As is now well understood, this is only a bad caricature of a state-of-the-art application, which needs input not only from economic theory, but also from several other disciplines, including sociology, psychology, statistics and survey research.

While some potentially serious theoretical problems are involved, e.g. the possibility of designing an incentive-compatible valuation question, it is fair to say that the problems of a practical nature outnumber the purely theoretical ones. Unfortunately, the number of practical problems that arises within any single application of the CVM, outnumbers those that can be covered in a paper of the current length. There exist many excellent recent papers and books on the practical problems of the CVM. Some recent extensive reviews of the practical problems in contingent valuation include Mitchell & Carson (58), Hanemann

(23), Hoevenagel (29), Jakobson (30) and the review of the NOOA-panel (62). In point of fact, the detailed review of the practical problems carried out by the NOOA-panel (62) led to a number of guidelines and recommendations that were integrated in the subsequent regulations (63).

Given the existence of these papers and books, I shall only devote little space here to problems that have been extensively covered in the literature. For example, I skip the choice between willingness-to-pay (WTP) and willingness-to-accept (WTA) valuation questions. Neither do I discuss the choice of welfare measure (i.e. the choice between the mean or the median),[i] the possibility of calibrating hypothetical responses[ii] nor the choice between different delivery modes (i.e. telephone vs. mail surveys, interviews vs mail surveys etc.). Finally, I will not discuss the so-called embedding problems, see (29) for a recent summary and Carson & Mitchell's paper in this volume.

The outline of this paper is as follows. Section 2 discusses some problems related to what I shall call the data--collection process. I shall consider the response-mechanism (what incentives are there to answer a questionnaire?); the "extent of the market" (whose welfare is actually affected by the project?). and non-response issues. Section 3 discusses the problem of constructing a scenario. While a scenario is easily described in mathematical terms, it is considerably more difficult to portray this scenario in a questionnaire. In particular, how much information should be given to the respondent? A second issue concerns the kind of information supplied in the questionnaire. Current studies typically portrays scenarios without uncertainty. I discuss advantages disadvantages of including realism in terms of uncertainty and provide some empirical illustrations. Section 4 then turns to the straightforward, but difficult, choice of questioning mode. Should we ask the respondent to consider a price for the good or should we ask the respondent to state his willingness-to-pay? The following two section focuses on problems that are unique to the "yes/no" (dichotomous choice, "take-it-or-leave-it" etc.) valuation question, which is currently dominating applied work. Two key problem arise; first, just what prices should the respondents be asked? This problem has received attention in recent literature, not the least because of the paramount importance of a good design of the so-called "bid-vector". Section 5 discusses the theory of optimal design by means of illustrating various designs that have been developed. This review leads to a personal assessment of how to approach the extra-ordinarily important practical design problem in CVM. Section 6 discusses estimation. From information on the proportion of acceptances to each single bid, the problem is to elicit some useful statistics on the unknown variable WTP. I shall discuss parametric and non-parametric approaches. I also present some recent elaborations, including the so-called "spike-model" and the possibility of interpreting answers to a "yes/no" question in terms of a legal contract. Section 7 concludes the paper.

THE DATA-COLLECTION PROCESS

The structure of the paper follows, more or less, the practical problems as they arise within a given application. Consequently, it is natural to begin our analysis at the starting point of all empirical analysis -- the data-collection process.

Responses as games

Contingent valuation is interactive, in the sense that the researcher and the respondent interact to produce an outcome which is mutually beneficial. The researcher's objective is to obtain a set of responses that reflect the individual's "true" sentiments about the issues raised in the questionnaire. The researcher is also concerned with issues that pertains to properties of the sample, such as a "high" response rate and an "unbiased" set of respondents. What, then, can be said about the respondent's incentives to deliver a response which is consistent with the researcher's objective?

First and foremost we must consider whether or not there will be any response at all. Most surveys do not obtain a 100% response rate for a myriad of reasons. The intended respondent might not have received the questionnaire or may have passed away, or did not understand the questionnaire etc.

We might assume that there is some benefit b_i (i=1,2,...N) of responding that respondent i compares to the costs of responding, c_i. Using an indicator function I( ) we can represent the decision to respond in the following manner;

$$I_i^R(b_i - c_i)$$

where $I_i^R(b_i - c_i) = 1$ if $(b_i - c_i) > 0$ and $I_i^R(b_i - c_i) = 0$ otherwise. Hence, we observe "1" if the individual finds it worthwhile responding and "0" otherwise.

A further layer of complexity may be introduced by differentiating between the accuracy of the response. For strategic reasons, the respondent may select to report a set of answers that differs substantially from the "true" values. In the simplest possible case, there are only two sets of answers: "true" or "not true". If the individual responds, it may be assumed that he calculates the benefits and costs of responding truthfully to the questionnaire. It is possible that the investigator has worked out the best responses to each of the possible strategies the respondent may select to use.

What parameters may be involved in the functions describing the benefits and costs of participating in the survey? Let us be deliberately vague as to the exact composition of these functions, so that c_i denotes the monetary costs of responding to the questionnaire and b_i the monetary benefits of responding (gross of the costs).

Following Bowden (6) assume that the benefit function $b_i(p,\theta)$ is a function of the proportion in favor of a particular proposal ρ and the proportion of people answering the questionnaire, denoted θ. If "enough" people are in favor of the proposal, then it will go through. The credibility of the survey is assumed reflected in the response rate; a lower response rate reduces the credibility of the survey and the likelihood that the proposal passes.

While this set-up seems only remotely similar to a CVM-application, we often interpret them as referendums. This is evident when the "yes/no" valuation questions are used and it turns out that one can often frame such questions in terms of a (hypothetical) referendum (see Hanemann & Kriström (25) for an example).

The fact that people respond to questionnaires even though there is a real cost involved implies that individuals, for whatever reason, want to "get involved". It is, typically, very difficult to explain from first principles why people vote in elections, because the individual cannot expect to affect the election outcome.[iii] Still, people vote and also respond to contingent valuation questionnaires.[iv] Because there is invariably some fraction of non-respondents, it is interesting to discuss the effects of non-response. The next section briefly outlines some of the key issues involved.

Non-response Bias in Referendum-type Models

The above model can be utilized to discern the effect of non-response on certain important parameters in a typical (modern) contingent valuation experiment. Let $z \in \Re^1$ denote an environmental index and denote a *project* $z^0 \rightarrow z^1$. For simplicity, a project is assumed to affect *z* only and leave prices and incomes unchanged in the economy. Let $V_i\ (z^j, b_i, c_i, y_i)$, where $j = \{0,1\}$ and y_i is individual i:s income, be individual i:s indirect utility function. Hence, utility depends on environmental quality, the net benefits of participating in the survey and income.

Suppose that the project is subject to a referendum. The project will be carried out if a simple majority accepts to pay a sum A. Ignoring the costs of responding, the net benefit *(NB)* to the individual is then $NB_i\ (z^1, z^0, y) - A$ where CV is the compensating variation. If $NB_i\ < 0$ then the individual is unfavorable towards the proposal, while if $NB_i\ > 0$ he is favorable. Assume that $CV - N\left(\mu\sigma^2\right)$ so that

$$\Pr\left(NB_i\ > 0\right) = 1 - \Phi\left(0; \mu, \sigma^2\right.$$

where $\Phi\ (o)$ denotes the cumulative distribution function for the normal distribution. Following Bowden [6] consider the simplest possible model of how the net benefits of participating in the referendum might affect the final outcome. Assume that there is a fixed threshold-cost *c*, such that the individual responds if and only if:

$$\left|NB_i\right| > c$$

Hence, if the individual finds the absolute value of his net benefits large enough he will respond. The effect of introducing the costs *c* is simply to remove some of the mass of distribution of *NB*, i.e. observations in the interval $NB_i\ \in\left[-c, c\right]$ The probability that a yes-answer is obtained is then;

$$\Pr(\text{"}yes\text{"}) = \Pr\left(NB_i\ > c\right) = 1 - \Phi\left(r; r\sigma, r\sigma^2\right) = \Phi\left(r - \frac{c}{\sigma}\right)$$

where $\Phi(r) = \Pr\left(NB_i\ \right) > 0$. By the symmetry of the Normal distribution one finds that

$$\Pr(\text{"}no\text{"}) = 1 - \Phi\left(r + \frac{c}{\sigma}\right).$$

We can define the "observed vote in favor" as

$$p_c = \frac{\Phi(r - \frac{c}{\sigma})}{\Phi\left(r - \frac{c}{\sigma}\right) + 1 - \Phi\left(r + \frac{c}{\sigma}\right)}$$

Consequently, as $c \rightarrow 0$, $p_c \rightarrow \Phi(r)$, the "true" proportion of people in favor of the proposal. It can be shown that the cost parameter is biasing the observed p_c upwards, if the true proportion is greater than 0.5. Similarly, the bias is downwards if $p<0.5$.

A related investigation can be performed when continuous responses are recorded, i.e. the case when people are asked to state their *WTP* directly (see Bowden [6] (p.57-60)). Assume that log so that $(WTP) \sim N(\mu,\sigma^2)$ so that *WTP* is distributed as a log-normal with median $= e^{\mu}$ and mean $= e^{(\mu+\sigma^2/2}$. Assume further that the
response-mechanism can be represented in the following way;

$$I_i\left(\beta_0 - \beta_1\left(NB_i - \mu\right) + \upsilon_i\right.$$

where, again, $I_i(x) = 1$ ("response"), if $x > 0$, and $\beta_k (k = 0,1)$ are constants and υ_i a random error term. Let $i \in R$ denote the set of respondents to the survey. The joint density of *NB* and R is then

$$\Pr(NB,R) = \int_{-\beta_0+\beta_1(NB-\mu)}^{\infty} \Pr(NB,\upsilon)d\upsilon$$

Normalizing the variance of v to unity (without loss) it can be shown that the conditional density of *NB* is given by;

$$\Pr(NB|R) = \frac{\phi(NB;\mu,\sigma^2)\Phi[\beta_0 + \beta_1(NB-\mu)}{\Phi(\beta_0;0,1+\beta_1^2\sigma^2)}$$

Thus, $Pr\ (NB \mid R)$ differs from $\phi(NB;\mu,\sigma^2$, the density of the normal distribution, by a factor equal to

$$\frac{\Phi[\beta_0 + \beta_1(NB-\mu)}{\Phi(\beta_0;0,1+\beta_1^2\sigma^2)}$$

If we want an estimate of μ we will underestimate it by computing mean *WTP* from those who reply. Bowden [6] shows that if the response rate is less than 50\%, which corresponds to $\beta_0 < 0$, the estimate of μ may be severely biased. His model implies that the results from a questionnaire receiving less than a 50% response rate must be interpreted with care. It should be noted that these results hold for the particular assumption that *WTP* is log-normally distributed. While this assumption seems to be well-supported in the CVM-literature, it is difficult to say how general Bowden's result is.

The above results may differ with respect to elicitation format. It may be argued that the constructions above best describe the case when the survey-instrument is distributed by ordinary mail. The structure of benefits and costs may look rather different when we consider the case of personal interviews. Space precludes a more detailed discussion of this possibility.

The Extent of the Market

Given an idea of the sample size one needs to decide upon the target population. If K is the universal set of potential interviewees, one needs to decide upon a subset $\kappa \subset K$ from which to draw the sample of interviewees. In order to construct such a subset, it is necessary to make a prior judgment on the potential welfare effects of the suggested project. If non-use values -- or passive use values -- are considered important, then one can argue that $\kappa = K$; a sample should be drawn from the population at large. Perhaps one can envision a CVM-survey with respondents from all countries in the world. In practice, no such study -- to the best of my knowledge -- has been undertaken, although 'inter-country' studies are being planned. [v]

The practical problems of choosing κ are often less difficult than they may seem, because the problem under study typically leads to a natural choice of κ. Consequently, when Johansson, Kriström & Nyquist [36]were asked to study the welfare impacts of large ferries in the Stockholm archipelago, they selected to ask only those living along the route. While other people may certainly be affected by the ferries, their main environmental impact is the damages due the created waves. Similarly, when Jakobson [30] studied the value people in Victoria placed on biodiversity, it was natural to ask Victoria residents only. One may certainly argue that other Australians, and even people in other countries, may value biodiversity in Victoria, but given the link to a state-tax that would help finance the project, the choice of κ was natural (to me). In summary, there is not much one can generally say about the 'extent of the market' in my view, except that the guiding principle is to consider those who has a legal or economic standing in the matter.

The damage assessments following the Exxon Valdez oil spill in 1989 led to substantial controversy regarding the choice of p. According to Exxon-economists, such as Milgrom [57], only direct users of the damaged Prince William Sound have an economic or legal standing in the matter. More fundamentally, Milgrom [57] argues that including non-users in the cost-benefit calculation implies a kind of double-counting, if passive use values are based on altruism towards other people. Economists hired by the State of Alaska argued, in contrast, that the relevant "market" is the U.S. proper, see [12].

The difference between these two viewpoints, in terms of the number of people potentially affected, is at least 200-fold[vi] Either viewpoint is not without support from first principles. Johansson [34] has shown under what circumstances Milligram's double-counting argument is valid. Essentially, the argument seems to go through if "my utility function is included in yours" and vice versa. If this is the case ,then a pure altruist cares not only about the increased environmental quality the other person can enjoy, but also the fact that the other person must pay something for the project. In a sense, which is made precise in [34], these two factors cancel in a cost-benefit analysis. Milgrom's argument does not hold water if altruism is modelled differently. Note, finally, that Milgrom's [57] argument does not change the way we should ask the contingent valuation questions; it is always correct to ask for the total value of the resource, as is explained in [34].

Response Rates

A practical problem of much concern to the CVMpractitioner is the response rate[vii]. This is because non response may have substantial impact on the bias of an estimate. The literature suggests that the response rate is in the range of 30 to 60%, with a tendency toward the lower bound for CVM-surveys directed towards the general population [30].

It has long been recognized in the literature on sample survey practice that a satisfactory survey design should include a "special plan for the treatment of the non-response problem" (Dalenius [16], (p.232)). Some examples can be found of this in the CVM-literature. Fredman [19] provides a recent test of non-response bias in a CVM-study. He used two different follow-up surveys, one including both respondents and non-respondents, the other only non-respondents. The results suggest that non-response did not significantly effect the original *WTP*-estimates. His results agree with those found by Mattsson & Li [54] but disagrees with those in [15].

While it is desirable to keep the non-response to a minimum, there is a benefit and a cost of obtaining an additional response. They very act of forcing a response may lead to bias worse than would have resulted from accepting the non-response (e.g. [16], p. 227, footnote 1)). Because we know little about the shape of the benefits and costfunctions, it is difficult to specify an acceptable response rate a priori.[viii]

Cornfeld (1942, cited in [16]) suggests a potentially useful method for mail CVM-surveys. The idea is then to personally interview a sample of the non-respondents. If CV_r is an estimate of mean *WTP* for respondents and CV_{nr} is the corresponding estimate for non-respondents, then the overall mean is, of course;

$$\tilde{CV} = \tau CV_r + (1-\tau)CV_{nr}$$

Hansen et al (1946 (cited in [16], p. 232))\ suggests that if the non-response rate can be determined (i.e. "guesstimated") in advance, one can calculate the number of people to be surveyed in total, such that any given level of precision is obtained at minimum costs.

Non-response makes it much more delicate to expand sample data to population data. Loomis [51] analyzed a number of different approaches to deal with this problem. The simplest approach is to assume that the obtained sample is representative and then aggregate. Results in Dalecki et al[15] suggest that this might be a dangerous approach. They used a standard procedure, using observable characteristics to infer something about the nature of the non-respondents. Non-response was correlated with some of those characteristics, hence suggesting a biased sample of respondents.

Constructing A Scenario

A key ingredient in any CVM-application is the description of the *project*, i.e. the suggested environmental change $z^0 \rightarrow z^1$. While the mathematical description of the project is trivial, it might be much more difficult to describe the intended project in an effective way. It will not be necessary to repeat here the excellent recommendations given e.g. in [59] and [11]. Some of the key problems may be discussed briefly, however.

The Information Issue

The scenario provides, essentially, a description of the good to be valued, the payment vehicle and the condition under which the good is delivered. It might also be helpful to remind the respondent about the budgetconstraint and possible substitutes.[ix] An essential requirement is that the scenario is consistent with underlying economic theory. This being the case, one must carefully evaluate what the restrictions from economics imply in terms of the scenario development. Johansson [33] provides an excellent illustration of this fact. To illustrate his argument, consider the following indirect utility function;

$$V(p, w, y + \Pi(p, w,), z)$$

where p is a price-vector of private goods, w is the wage-rate, y is lump-sum income Π (p,w) is a profit function (and z the environmental quality index.). Consider now a large-scale project, which potentially changes all prices in the economy. The individual's compensation variation *(CV)* for this project can be written;

$$V\left(p^1, w^1, y^1, + \Pi\left(p^1, w^1\right) - CV, z^1\right) = V\left(p^0, w^0, y^0 + \Pi\left(p^0, w^0\right) z^0\right.$$

Hence, the individual must be informed about the projected changes in prices, wages and profits, as well as the change of environmental quality. The extra-ordinary complexity of such a scenario would lead many researchers not to use it[x] For the purpose of a cost-benefit analysis, one can in fact ask a "partial" *WTP*-question, e.g. portraying a scenario where no prices or lump-sum incomes nor profits are supposed to change. If the information is subsequently going to be used in a cost-benefit analysis, it will be necessary to add to the projects net benefits those changes that were not covered in the scenario.

Given a scenario that is consistent with underlying economic theory, the first issue that arises is that of information -- just how detailed should the scenario be? As Hanemann [23] has emphasized, "surveys are an exercise in communication, and this is always sensitive to nuance and context. Moreover, preferences are inherently context-laden. A basic lesson of the cognitive revolution is psychology is that context determines meaning.--. It would be simpler if consumers disregarded context and had preferences for commodities in the abstract, as Platonic ideas. But, they don't."

We should expect that *WTP* varies with the information in the scenario, and this hypothesis has much empirical support [2],[30]. Information about related goods can the affect the value of the good under consideration, as shown by Blomquist & Whitehead [5]. In a subsequent paper, Blomquist & Whitehead have shown that people respond to different quality Kentucky wetlands in a predictable way, again supporting conventional wisdom about information effects, this time with an eye towards the issue of validity.

What principles of economics may explain such results? It can be argued, as Glenn Harrison has done, that respondents are valuing a lottery and that information changes the probability of different states of the world. I find this an interesting way of thinking about how respondents perceive the scenario, but it gives no help when it comes to constructing the scenario itself.

The issue of information has an analogy, in my view, with a non-constructive mathematical proof. The substantial literature on information effects does not tell us how to construct a scenario, it says that information is important. My own preference in this regard, which completely agrees with Hanemann's view cited above, is to try to follow the guidelines for scenario construction that e.g. Carson [11] has developed. By using focus-groups one can then iteratively find a scenario and a questionnaire design that may, in the end, be satisfactory.[xi]

Certainty Versus Uncertainty in the Scenario

The overwhelming majority of CVM-studies are based on welfare measurements under certainty. Thus, scenarios are invariably portraying projects where the outcome is supposed to be certain. In some applications, abstracting from an invariably uncertain future might be a reasonable assumption. In other cases, this is less plausible. Indeed, scientific understanding of the structure of ecological systems is rarely complete.

In Hammack & Brown [20] Sellar et al. [69] respondents are asked about the value of the last year's activity under consideration. Markets, on the other hand, are forward-looking, "asking" about our *WTP* given the utility we expect to enjoy from the commodity over its expected lifetime. Consequently, scientific uncertainty provides one motivation for including uncertainty in the scenario and 'market resemblance' another.

The first study that explicitly invoked uncertainty in the scenario specification was carried out by Johansson [32], see also Johansson [31]. In his first study, which concerned moose-hunter's *WTP* for a hunting permit, the outcome of the next hunting season was presented as uncertain. Essentially, with probability p the hunting conditions are z_0^1 and with probability $1-p$ they are z_1^1. The value of the hunt in the uncertain case depends on the hunter's attitudes to risk. By asking hunter's to choose between an uncertain hunt yielding the same outcome on average as a certain hunt, Johansson [32] was able to infer something about the individual's attitude to risk. The empirical analysis suggests that about 30% of the hunters are "risk-lovers", about 30% are "risk-averse" and 40% of the hunters in the sample are risk-neutral.

Because the suggested "hunting-package" may have been unrealistic in the eyes of some hunters (it portrayed the outcome of an average hunt), Johansson buttressed his findings by asking each hunter to state the probability of him/her killing 1 or 2 moose the next season. This information is used to calculate the hunter's perceived variance of the bag-outcome. Using these variances in a regression of the *WTP* for next years hunting season, along with other variables, shows that a increase in the expected number of bags increases *WTP*, while a mean-increasing spread of the expected number of bags decreases *WTP*, on the average.

The study of the moosehunters clearly revealed that attitudes to risk vary across the sample. The average risk averse hunter is willing to pay less for a hunting permit compared to the average risk-neutral and risk-loving hunter.

Johansson [32] also compares his results with a parallel study of moosehunters, where they were asked their *WTP* for a permit that would replicate the last seasons outcome. The *WTP* in the uncertain scenario is about 77% of the WTP obtained from the conventional, certain, set-up.

In his second study, Johansson [31] asked a sample of Swedes their *WTP* for four different programs which would save some or all of 300 endangered species in Sweden. One program would save all species with probability 0.5 and every second species with probability 0.5. The other three programs would save 50%, 75% and 100% of the species. Again, the results -- albeit based on a relatively small sample -- indicated differences in risk perception between men and women; a finding that is buttressed by various Gallop polls on attitudes to environmental risks.

While introducing risk in the scenario increases the cognitive burden on the respondents, the fact that uncertainty is an undeniable feature of the real world likely increases the credibility of the questionnaire in the eyes of the respondent. It might also provide better foundations for evaluating 'real-world' projects.

Whether or not to include uncertainty in the scenario specification is ultimately related to the objective criterion which underlies the exercise itself. Thus, the welfare analysis upon which the empirical exercise is based should point to the appropriate structure of the scenario.

QUESTIONING MODES

From a welfare-theoretic point of view, it is easy to design the valuation question; simply ask people to state their *WTP* (or willingness-to-accept). This *open-ended* question has many advantages, including the fact that it immediately gives the information the researcher is looking for. One may also select to present certain intervals and ask the respondent to pick the interval which best represent his *WTP* for the good. As will be detailed below, the *closed-ended* valuation question is now, to some extent, dominating the theoretical and applied literature. Here, the respondent is presented with a price for the environmental good under consideration. A recent extension of this approach is to ask the depends on the reaction to the initial price [24].

your frequency diagram. Since the mean is theoretically unlimited, drawing a connecting line to the abscissa would give away at once all the advantages of the non-parametric approach.

If you have a large number of different values and a very large sampling population, the empirical survival curve itself might be a good instrument for recognizing and testing convergence to a "fundamental opposition" level (which might be unobservable by looking at external criteria). That is, if your curve gets almost flat at the highest values, you might derive the tentative conclusion that some share of the population cannot be convinced by cash payments in this case. In any case, it is good having a visual aid which gives you some idea of potentially dramatic structures in the underlying population. This is not a focus if you do parametric analysis.

PARAMETRIC CVM METHODS

Parametric methods, as already mentioned, assume a well-specified functional form both for the underlying probability density function as well as for the individual's evaluation function. As a by-product, you can arrive at different estimates using different parametric methods.[16] Besides that, parametric methods are computationally difficult. Typically, you have to do maximum likelihood estimation, and you cannot obtain closed form solutions from the first order conditions for the parameter values to be estimated. There are a lot of different methods for numerical solutions around, but if the likelihood function is not well behaved, they might easily generate different[17] estimates.[18] Fortunately, this is not the case for single-bounded designs if you employ the "usual" probability density specification (such as, e.g., log-logistic). Yet, in the case of double-bounded designs, the situation might be quite awkward.[19] In this case, however, you can always resort to single-bounded analysis with a double-bounded design.[20] All in all, parametric results might vary from application to application. This ambiguity centers our attention on what comes out of applying this approach in terms of qualitative outcomes.

But, first of all, it should not go unmentioned that as regards representativeness, the specification of compensation offers as well as the size of the subgroups, parametric models are characterized by less restrictive requirements concerning sampling techniques than non-parametric models.[21] This is due to the fact that assumptions here make up for a lot of things, and, additionally, the approach permits the inclusion of population characteristics as explanatory variables. The latter fact implies that -- besides a widespread inclusion of those potential determinants of individual decisions[22] -- only a minimum variability in these independent variables is called for. Owing to these circumstances, it is possible to do case-sensitive aggregation, because aggregates in general are conditional here, so that the results can suitably be tailored to specific target populations (Cameron 1988, McFadden and Leonard 1993).[23] Hence, questionnaires for parametric applications, above all, ought to be rather "lengthy," since one has to register as many personal characteristics as possible, whereas a representative draw is not necessarily called for, and the overall size of the sample is not that crucial. With regard to how to specify and allocate compensation offers, a lot of controversial statements have been made recently.[24]

However, what is crucial is the fact that the coefficient on the compensation offer has to be strictly positive as a determinant of stating "yes,"[25] and this for every person in the sample. Otherwise, graphing the probability of saying "no" against a monetary compensation axis would not yield a nice survival curve in responses to a treatment. Thus, the coefficient on the (function of the) compensation offer has to be larger than zero if we sketch the probability of acceptance as a function of bid amount. Nevertheless, a zero coefficient on compensation is not a statistical problem, but rather a problem in terms of interpretation of the results. Specifically, if you directly specify a WTA function in advance, as is done by Cameron (1988), you can make it fit into an (indirect) logit or probit approach in the fashion of, say, Bishop and Heberlein (1979) or Hanemann (1984b). The point is that in this case, you have to interpret the coefficient on compensation as the inverse of the variability parameter of the underlying density function. Once one cannot reject the hypothesis that this coefficient is equal to zero, this, however, does not necessarily imply that the variability parameter goes to infinity. It might as well be the case that there does not exist any comprehensive WTA function. Here, it should be mentioned that the approach taken by Hanemann, Bishop and Heberlein and others is to be preferred to Cameron's method, because the latter unduly narrows down the possibilities to interpret 'weird' results, since it takes the existence of a WTA function as given. A test for equality to zero regarding the compensation coefficient is one of the qualitative criteria we have alluded to before. The higher the percentage of people who do not want to accept the project in question for non-monetary reasons, the higher the possibility of not being able to reject the hypothesis of equality to zero. To this end, it is useful to specify high upper compensation offers, when choosing the design points.

The test for a negligible influence of monetary compensation offers is, indeed, a very fundamental one, since it challenges the idea of monetary compensation in a general manner. Whatever the relevant reason, any kind of opposition to the arrangement of a monetary compensation will culminate in the value for that coefficient.[26]

If the compensation coefficient is not significantly different from zero, then it makes no sense calculating median or mean WTA values. Perhaps the significance check might serve as a way to caution against processing some theoretical median which is mathematically possible unless you obtain exactly zero by directly estimating the coefficients. However, the judgment on whether the compensation coefficient is zero has to be based on the information matrix obtained by the maximum likelihood estimation. In the case of single-bounded designs, one can apply the Newton-Raphson procedure, the method of scoring, or Berndt's method, all of which generate an estimate of this information matrix. Here, one only has to bear in mind that the statements hold asymptotically. With double-bounded designs, things are a lot more complicated. Since the likelihood function here is not necessarily well-behaved, all you can do in some instances is estimate the coefficients directly (see, e.g., Goldfeld and Quandt 1972), because indirect methods, which would generate an estimate of the variance-covariance matrix (see Bazaraa and Shetty 1979), might fail to converge, or the extreme value found is a minimum (cf. Hanemann 1984a, 555). In any case, testing for irrelevance of the compensation coefficient makes sense if you limit your analysis to the single-bounded results; but even in this case, the results might not be trusted.

A somewhat more reliable way of tracing qualitative outcomes of parametric CVM analysis is trying to calculate the mean WTA. To this end, you only need the parameter estimates, not the variance-covariance matrix. In the computationally easy Bishop and Heberlein specification, you only have to check whether the coefficient on the log on the monetary compensation offer lies between zero and one. If this is the case, the integral under the fitted survival curve does not converge, and you can be sure that mean WTA for your sample is infinity (Hanemann 1984b, p. 337). This check is, besides its greater reliability compared to the test for equality to zero, also a more sensitive one. While you need to have a considerable share of people for which monetary compensation in the relevant case does not work in order to get insignificance of the compensation coefficient, the presence of a small group is sufficient to obtain an infinite mean, given that the range of the amounts you offer is large enough. This presence produces fat tails, and the mean reacts to this by going to infinity. On the other hand, if you obtain a finite value for your mean WTA, this does not guarantee that there is no protest group, since you might have left out values in the upper range which would have allowed you to trace out fat tails if they had been present. Hence, the greatest merit of parametric analysis is that it makes it possible to check the influence of monetary compensation directly.

Further advantages might derive from the fact that parametric analysis offers a basis for extrapolation and allows for checking subsamples. For example, a question which can be tackled on this basis is the question of a break in structure. Also, spline estimation is feasible. Moreover, parametric techniques allow for multi-stage estimation with a multivariate equation system.

A COMPARISON OF METHODS AND SOME FURTHER SUGGESTIONS FOR RESEARCH METHODOLOGY

Let us now briefly reflect upon what we have derived so far. The least problematic case of all is the one in which the researcher happens to observe 100 percent approval concerning the highest bid specified in the survey. Although this is no guarantee that there are no opponents if your sample is a subset of the population, it is reasonable and statistically feasible to calculate whatever measure you want, by means of the method you prefer. Hence, a first check should consist in looking at the frequency table of your data in order to check whether the highest compensation offer was universally accepted. If yes, one can do any kind of analysis; if not, one might proceed with the methods to follow.

In terms of political economy, the most relevant question is usually if the project in question will catch a majority of votes at some amount of compensation per person. To this end, one should first have a look at the survival curve of the actual sampling data on which non-parametric analysis rests. If one obtains some definite range for an empirical median, that's fine. In a second step, one might then want to proceed to a more detailed analysis centered on observable determinants of the response behavior of individuals. At this level, one has to employ parametric analysis, and one should interpret the results with more caution. The dangers of misspecification are much greater: an ill-suited functional form selection for the underlying distribution function, a poor specification (functional or in terms of arguments) of the argument one plugs into that function, estimation-specific precision problems are common sources of error. In addition, in parametric analysis, one analyzes all of the data before one indirectly derives estimates for the location parameters (i.e., these estimates rely on estimated coefficients as arguments). More fundamental than the potential bias of these estimates[27] is the fact that in using all data points one has to rely on the universal validity of one and only one behavioral function, which at most might depend on criteria one can observe from outside. If one wants to estimate a more case-sensitive median than the one from non-parametric analysis, which is based on only part of the observations, one is facing the danger that there are groups with an ultimately different view, groups that are small enough so as not to affect the empirical, non-parametric median (which therefore can be calculated), with the critical factor determining their opposition being beyond the scope of the researcher and therefore not among the observables in the questionnaire.[28] To find out whether it is worth calculating the parametric median, one might try to calculate the parametric mean first and see whether it has a finite value.

What if non-parametric analysis does not yield a median? In that case, one should be very cautious. It is highly problematic to go on and employ parametric analysis which automatically generates a median. On the other hand, one cannot automatically infer that there is no median. In every closed-ended design, it can always be the case like, e.g., in a study by Kriesel and Randall (cf. Cooper 1993) that one happens to cover only a small part of the relevant distribution with the bids one specifies,[29] although the function itself is quite well-behaved. In that case, it is not meaningless to calculate a median value, although one still has to hope that a break in structure does not arise until the median has been reached.

Therefore, an overall check might be a good idea when one cannot obtain an empirical median (range). The most fundamental test is the one for insignificance of the compensation coefficient, a less fundamental one for an infinite mean value. But even if a finite value can be obtained, it is still possible that there is evidence of a break in structure in the upper area of the actual bid range. Therefore, a test for break in structure is worth applying if the other two tests were passed. If this final test is passed, one could go on and compute the parametric median, under the assumption of stability of the underlying structure at least up to this median value.

AN EMPIRICAL APPLICATION

We conducted a closed-ended CVM study in order to check the acceptance of a nuclear waste repository in some Swiss communities. As already mentioned, we consider the problem of compensation structures. In this case, WTA seems to be the appropriate concept. On theoretical grounds, Mitchell and Carson (1986) make the point for using this concept when it comes to the siting of hazardous waste facilities. Referring to the legal frame, since our study was conducted in Switzerland, the assignment of property rights is present in a form that gives the local community right to veto any proposal which is beneficial to the society.

In our case, we conducted our survey in two of four communities which had been examined for their geographical appropriateness to host a nuclear waste repository. In terms of this and in analogy to the study by Kunreuther, Easterling, Desvousges and Slovic (1990), the content of the questionnaire was not completely hypothetical to the subjects. When questioning the people we made sure that the response pattern in general was not overshadowed by any kind of dissatisfaction with the prior evaluation procedure. Indeed, most people (65 %) stated that the geographers did a decent job.

In order to eliminate any kind of error due to a vague design we consulted psychologists from the ZUMA institute. Later on, many subjects (77 %) admitted that our questions were quite realistic. This assessment may also be due to our hiring of professional interviewers. They interviewed in person the heads of family of one small community in total and a representative draw of them in the second community, a total of 305 people. That sample was randomly split into three subsamples, with 103 of the individuals being confronted with SFr 2500 per inhabitant household member and year, 117 with SFr 5000 and 85 with SFr 7500. All in all, the questionnaire design was mainly set up in line with the remarkable questionnaire by Kunreuther, Easterling, Desvousges and Slovic (1990).[30]

Of those confronted with SFr 2500, 28 (i.e., 27.2 percent) were not against the repository, of those confronted with SFr 5000, it was 33 (i.e., 28.2 percent), and of those confronted with SFr 7500, it was 23 (i.e., 27.1 percent). It is obvious that a non-parametric median value cannot be obtained from these data.

Cautioned by this result, we switched over to parametric analysis. A logit estimation of acceptance conditional upon a constant and the log of the monetary amount, that is a Bishop and Heberlein-like specification,[31] produced an estimate of -1.0303807 for the constant and an estimate of 0.0075073348 (estimated asymptotical standard error 0.29148165) for the coefficient on the log of the monetary compensation offer.[32] A probit estimation produced for the constant the value of -0.63426527 and for the compensation coefficient the value of 0.0044939587 (estimated asymptotical standard error 0.17420463). Thus, the coefficients have the expected negative, respectively positive signs. But it can be seen very easily that the compensation lies between zero and one, so that the mean WTA is infinity, and, moreover, it is not significantly different from zero (assuming the sample is large enough). Therefore, one does not need a more detailed analysis to infer that monetary compensation in this case apparently fails to bring about acceptance. The parametric median exists,[33] but it is not advisable to take it at face value. In the logit case, it would be as high as SFr $1.97*10^{61}$, in the probit case SFr $4.04*10^{59}$ per capita.

It is interesting to have a look at the quality of overall prediction. In both cases, the percentage of correct predictions amounts to 72 percent. At a first glance, this result seems to be quite impressive. But at a closer inspection, it is just the No-answers which amount to 72 percent over the whole sample which are correctly predicted by the model. This suggests the presence of a dichotomous split in the population as regards the question "acceptance of a nuclear waste repository and some (arbitrary?) amount of monetary compensation or non-acceptance of the package in total?" In our case, the data fit into a dichotomous choice story, as in the theoretical model by Hanemann (1984a) which was criticized on theoretical grounds by Cameron (1988). In our case, Cameron's argument of an ordered nature of monetary compensation payments appears to be not valid. People obviously value the alternatives in qualitative terms, at least to a great majority.[34]

Needless to say, the hypothesis of significance of the non-constant factors can be rejected quite easily. The restricted logit estimation, which produces a highly significant value of -0.96734585 (-0.59652566 in the probit case) for the constant,[35] has a restricted log-likelihood value of -179.51252 as compared to a value of -179.51219 of the non-restricted log-likelihood. Therefore, it is not a surprise that the mean WTA goes to infinity since the coefficient of the slope is smaller than 1. Opposition in general implies opposition in the tales, too.

In the questionnaire, people were asked whether they would accept it if the Swiss Parliament decided that their community should serve as the site for the nuclear waste repository. Surprisingly, only 137 out of 305 persons (45 percent) responded that they would not accept this decision. Compare this figure with the rejection of monetary compensation offers by about 72 percent (220 out of 305 persons) of the sampling population. These 220 persons were asked explicitly for reasons why they rejected the offer in a closed-ended form with a yes/no option for each of the offered reasons. Only 11 from all subsamples stated that the compensation amount was not large enough.[36] However, as for a second possible reason, 149 stated that there was *no* compensation for the threat to human life emanating from the repository. An even more impressive number of 184 people declared that they would not allow themselves to be *bribed*. This raises the question as to whether there are alternatives to the general idea of monetary compensation.

Those 137 who refused to accept selection of their community as a host site were asked whether some policy measures could reduce their resistance. These policy items were asked for separately in closed-ended forms. 75 persons still refused to accept the repository if its operation were put under the supervision of Greenpeace, 89 if a second repository were constructed elsewhere;[37] and 95 if the waste were packed into double-coated containers. 114 stated that knowledge of the fact that the same type of facility was operated elsewhere would not affect their resistance to a nuclear waste repository in their own community. All this is, of course, piece-meal evidence. But it suggests that it is worth considering the design of alternatives to monetary compensation.

SOME LESSONS

What basic suggestions result from our study? First, as regards the hotly debated question "mean or median?", our reflections enable us to give a detailed assessment. It is fair to say that the mean as a measure of central tendency is not as reliable as the median. Calculation of the mean requires using all the data one has obtained, and it is, except for very few exceptional cases, only possible to employ parametric techniques with their many specific problems in order to calculate its expected value in a non-arbitrary fashion. An estimate of the median can be derived by non-parametric techniques which use only the less problematic part of the data. However, trying to calculate an expected mean is indirectly a very good exercise. It may serve as a general check in terms of the question whether there exists a finite value for the mean or not, and this perhaps for subsamples, too. The mean is, by its definition, a good indicator of whether the data set for which it is computed is in fact problematic. It may be a good device to caution the researcher. Hence, one should always try to estimate both measures, first the non-parametric median, then the parametric mean as an indicator, then the parametric median. If it can be derived, the non-parametric median should serve as a primary policy guide. Only if a finite value for the parametric mean can be calculated, the parametric median is a meaningful figure. Otherwise, the parametric mean might serve as a device to split up the sample and obtain estimates for subgroups.

All in all, one should not expect some concrete numbers in the first instance. Robust estimation with the whole data set is to be preferred to trimming the data until some numbers result. When parametric estimation is done, the pseudo-R^2 is not an appropriate measure to report. It is more sensible to apply the kind of testing procedure that we have proposed in this paper.

Coming back to the questionnaire design, one should, in light of what we have been saying so far, take into account the following additional rules: Since non-parametric analysis should in any case be applied in a first step, a representative draw is called for. Reliance on the registration of observable individual characteristics as a substitute is dangerous. Furthermore, specification of an amount which seems to be extremely large as the highest compensation offer will be very enlightening (see also Cooper and Loomis 1993, 203). Alternatively, if the figure for the benefits accruing to the project is known, inclusion of a compensation offer which is, in view of these overall benefits, not affordable will be sufficient. In addition, in order to be able to better trace the continuity in the general structure, one might also want to specify some very low offers. Besides that, one should disregard theoretical suggestions which deem sufficient an equal split of the sample over only two different compensation offers, since they rely on strong *a priori* assumptions (see Kanninen 1993b, p. S-2). It is more essential to have a broad range of different values[38] in order to do sensitivity-oriented analysis.

On the other hand, it is also necessary to inquire into a lot of potential determinants of decision-making. Highest priority should be given to factors which influence the way people make their decision. This might enable the researcher to obtain at least some evidence as to the determinants which fundamentally structure the way the problem in question is perceived and processed. Nevertheless, since these produce only vague hints for policy-making due to their interrelatedness and incompleteness, a general check in terms of actual responses is still called for to the effect that ordinary CVM questions remain indispensable.

All in all, a comprehensive survey is called for, which allows for several types of analysis. One cannot get good CVM results cheaply. One has to ensure representativeness, one has to employ interviews with people willing or unwilling to participate, one has to draw a large enough sample with a fairly broad range of compensation offers, and one has to ask intensively about a large number of potential reasons for individual decisions. In terms of analysis, both non-parametric and parametric methods should be applied. As regards the parametric setup, Hanemann's indirect specification rather than Cameron's reduced form WTA should serve as a basis for analysis.

In any case, one should not rely *a priori* on the universal effectiveness of monetary compensation. In order to present suggestions for policy, it is always a good idea to check for the acceptance of alternative policy instruments. Preparedness for a failure of monetary compensation will enable the researcher to design the CVM questionnaire more in line with the range of politico-economic instruments, not only economic ones.

CONCLUSION

This paper has dealt with the CVM approach in a fairly critical manner. However, this is not the kind of impression we would like to advance if one compares the Contingent Valuation Method with other methods of registering preferences for public goods or distastes for public bads, as they are discussed in Pommerehne (1987), for example. From a merely technical point of view, there are situations in which competing approaches do not lend themselves to application. Once you do not have past experience with a problem, many procedures are of no use regarding your purpose. On a more specific level, if you have unobservable determinants of preferences for a specific good, you end up realizing that the hedonic technique, for example, is not at your disposal. This is not a problem once you directly elicit people's positions via questionnaire. And the CVM approach is based on surveys, which are a very powerful tool in many respects.

It is not only that you are enabled to make visible what is invisible by passive observation. Rather, you can be absolutely sure about the important issue of causality. In an interview, at least with regard to your treatment, it is clear what the stimulus and the response are. Moreover, you are not a slave of past events, in that you have the opportunity to systematically choose the levels of your treatment. Indeed, you can even overcome theoretical limitations such as the postulated zero willingness to accept at nonpositive compensation offers. Hanemann (1989, p. 1059) announced that he would make a theoretical inquiry into this question the topic of a forthcoming paper. There is little practical limitation to integrating this problem into CVM questionnaires. The fact that you encounter the zero willingness to accept at the amount of zero as an assumption (cf. Kriström 1990, p. 138, for a remarkably explicit statement) is, in principle, due to the fact that the questionnaire only features positive design points in the specific case.

Furthermore, the sampling method and questionnaire implementation provide ample room for less specific techniques of statistically analyzing people's responses. Of course, one might as well think of a nonparametric analysis in a hedonic framework, but the low degree of control with respect to actual randomness perhaps accounts for the fact that you do not encounter applications of any such methods in this indirect framework. Due to the possibility of randomly selecting your sample in a CVM study, however, this format is no doubt suitable for choosing this method of analysis, and it is quite typical that the main contributions to this area (Kriström 1990 or Duffield and Patterson 1991, e.g.) are presented in the context of the contingent valuation method. It is in fact this very issue which appears to be the crucial one: It is always possible to design and administer a contingent valuation study so that you can analyze the responses with nonparametric techniques, not only with parametric ones, since it rests on a questionnaire technique, where treatments are arbitrarily variable. If this fact were always taken proper account of, that would promote the quality of the results of the ensuing analysis. The reliability of the data themselves aside, it all boils down to the question of *how* CVM is *applied.*

If properly applied, CVM has the potential to overcome, at least to a certain degree, even problems associated with the mismatch (see, e.g., Beed and Kane 1991, p. 590) between simplistic utility theoretic models of human decision on the one hand and the insurmountably complex cognitive mode in which decisions are made in reality. Of course, there remains the gap between statement and actual behavior, but as regards statements, as reliable as they are in the context, they can be taken at face value by looking just at response and treatment. Those two elements are identifiable in a survey, as well as the underlying causality. Anything else is taken good care of, to some extent, if the sampling is done in a randomized manner. The major problems occur if the researcher is lured by his own model into thinking he could substitute randomization by a causal model of determinants of people's decisions, thus giving away all the potential that CVM as a questionnaire method offers to him.

Parametric analysis can be done additionally to nonparametric analysis. It seems problematic to make the former one the exclusive basis for further analysis from the outset. You never know how many determinants really influence people's decisions, a fact that gives rise to biases, not to mention the problem of how to implement a causal model if people's decisions are taken in a multiple layer cognitive framework. As our study indicates, it indeed seems to be the case in some instances that a good many people make macro-decisions without proceeding to the micro-level, where the typical economic calculus is at least one of several candidate frames. It cannot be excluded that people perceive problems as "concepts with multi-dimensional attributes" (Beed and Kane, 1991, p. 592), in which case it seems hopeless trying to single out partial influences as factors smoothly affecting actual behavior.[39] If it is properly described, you can then only test for your subject's assessment of such a conglomerate in general. Fischhoff (1994, p. 7 and p. 19) for instance, who explicitly acknowledges the possibility of a multi-attribute utility framework, advocates practicing multimethod analysis. Indeed, it seems worthwhile to pick up this opportunity which is present in the CVM and try to look for robustness of the results.

Thus, we are left with the conclusion that from the empirical side, CVM has, perhaps, more to offer than other methods of eliciting people's preferences. Due to the possibility of applying nonparametric statistics, it has neither to be assumed that the object in question is perceived as either a good or a bad unilaterally, nor is it indispensable to postulate that the willingness to accept decreases on the aggregate if you raise the compensation offers. The challenge lies in designing and administering the survey, so that parametric analysis can be complemented by nonparametric analysis. It is imperative to look at median WTA, not only mean WTA. The main problem seems to consist in getting policy-makers to adopt the viewpoint of CVM. But this is a problem of any method of elicitation of preferences for public goods, perhaps, however, to a degree which varies according to the method. Thus, it would be interesting for future research to gather more evidence about how policy makers themselves react when confronted with one or the other method. Some intuition from such a political-economic perspective, but from a context only loosely related to CVM, can be found in Opaluch et al. (1993), but we need to know much more about possible interactions, perhaps in order to enhance the performance of the CVM in turn as regards describing realistic policy scenarios, if the method is politically accepted at all in the long run. Evidence on this point (for a quite unique item in this category, see Kopp and Pease 1994) is still rather spotty at the moment.

ENDNOTES

1 We are well aware of the fact that in many situations CVM remains the only method applicable for eliciting preferences for unpriced goods; see Brookshire and Crocker (1981) as well as Pommerehne (1987, p. 241).

2 Another difficulty is posed by the absence of "scope effects" (for evidence see, e.g., Smith and Desvousges 1987). In the present paper, we are not going to touch upon this type of problem, we rather consider the case where the amount of a disamenity is fixed while the "dose" of monetary "treatment" (compensation) may vary.

3 A notable exception is Kanninen and Kriström (1993, p. 199), who speculate that the problem of fat tails might have to do with "anomalies."

4 Kunreuther and Easterling (1990) raise the decisive question of whther tradeoffs are possible at all. Georgescu-Roegen (1954, p.521) hints at the consequence of such a non-existence of tradeoffs, namely that we can "no longer" be "sure that indifference exists."

5 Schkade and Payne (1993, p. 275) are among the few who reflect on this possibility. They write, "if different people use many different strategies, or if the same person uses different strategies in different situations, these facts would be difficult to reconcile with the standard economic model."

6 This group would be "immune" to the monetary treatment.

7 This is indirectly suggested by Mitchell and Carson (1989, p. 37).

8 There are some auxiliary devices like protocol analysis (Schkade and Payne 1993), but their workings are indirect all the same.

9 Bishop and Heberlein (1979, p. 929), e.g., warn against generalizing their results which are based on a specific case study.

10 So that you do not have to do excessive "white noise" smoothing to get a nonincreasing "rejection" function depending on the compensation amounts offered.

11 In open-ended designs you are faced with the problem of zero values in the case of protest-bidders (WTP), unless they did prefer to break off.

12 McFadden and Leonard (1993, p. 168) point out that the possibility to extrapolate is a specific advantage of parametric approaches.

13 It should be mentioned that extrapolation schemes between the data points of the survey are necessarily somewhat inaccurate, since you have to linearize. Nevertheless, a theoretical median range can be calculated. If you take the higher of the two bids in the median range as your compensation amount, you can be pretty sure that nothing will go wrong.

14 Even in this case, there is some arbitariness, since you have to assume that the probability of saying “no” equals one at a compensation offer of zero (cf. Kriström 1990).

15 Perhaps some kind of curve-fitting comes to mind. This, however, would require giving up the non-parametric character of the analysis, since groupwise logit estimation over the actual "logits" would result in a parametric interpretation of the data in terms of slopes and treatment effects.

16 It is, for example, always possible to assume an asymmetric, fat-tailed probability density instead of the usual, symmetric logit or probit specifications (cf. Kanninen and Kriström 1993, p. 199).

17 See the impressive examples with applications of different algorithms to the same problem in Goldfeld and Quandt's (1972) introductory chapters.

18 If you manage to get them at all!

19 Cameron and Huppert (1991, p. 913) report that their (multiple-bounded) models were "fundamentally nonlinear in parameters." They were forced to apply the Davidon-Fletcher-Powell algorithm, an approach which does not yield an estimate of the variance-covariance matrix as a by-product.

20 Hanemann, Loomis and Kanninen (1991) do this in their double-bounded design by analyzing only the first round answers. A minimum requirement for this to be feasible is the prespecification of at least two different first round levels.

21 There are some quotations in Duffield and Patterson (1991, p. 231) to the effect that in logit analysis, specification of only two different bid levels suffices.

22 Economists especially might systematically lack imagination as regards *a priori* specifications of potential influences. They are used to thinking in terms of relative prices, deliberately closing their eyes to the possibility of influential attitudinal factors, for example. This will inevitably result in severe misspecifications (cf. McFadden and Leonard 1993, p. 168). This danger is not present in non-parametric analyses. The openness of parametric design to explanatory factors, hence, does not have only merits.

23 However, the aggregation itself of necessity suffers from inherent aggregation problems the more case-sensitive the estimated conditional WTA functions are (for a good description see, e.g., Bowker and Stoll 1988, p. 377). You have to plug in the more mean or median values of the characteristics, the more explanatory variables you have (for an illustration see Pommerehne and Römer 1992, p. 191). Even the question whether you should substitute mean

or median values has not been settled so far (see Hanemann 1989, p. 1060). Like Hanemann, Mitchell and Carson (1989) advocate the use of medians, since medians are more reliable.

24 See, e.g., Kanninen (1993b, p. S-2).

25 The model we have in mind, is, in a logit-case, the following one: $Pr(yes) = 1/(1 + exp(-dV))$, with $dV = \hat{A} + \beta \ ln(X)$, where X refers to the size of the monetary compensation offered (cf. Hanemann 1984b, p. 334).

26 Even infinite perceived damage expectation with some individuals will only partly be reflected in the constant but rather in the compensation coefficient.

27 As Kanninen (1993a) has shown, the estimates of the location parameters can, in general, only be derived by calculating some function of the ratio of the coefficient *estimates*.

28 Perhaps they might even be unconscious of the causes for their rejecting the proposed compensation deal.

29 In Kriesel and Randall's WTP study, "60% of the respondents were willing to pay the highest posted bid" (Cooper 1993, p. 26).

30 Admittedly, the design is certainly not optimal. The three monetary amounts specified should ensure comparability with Kunreuther's results. Finney (1955, p. 148) states that specification of three different treatments is a minimum requirement when there is no confidence that the underlying relationship is linear.

31 As Johansson, Kriström and Mäler (1989, p. 1055) emphasize, Bishop and Heberlein's model, although theoretically incorrect, may be viewed as a handy first order approximation to Hanemann's rigorous specifications. They also correctly point out there that "if individuals are not identical, such an approximation may be as reasonable as assuming a single well-behaved utility function." This is what we, too, assume in our paper.

32 In order to trace out differences in comparing the various calculations, it makes sense to report results from our analysis as accurately as possible. Thus, we report a great number of digits behind the decimal point.

33 In the logit case, the appropriate formula is exp(-1.0303807/0.0075073348), in the probit case it is exp(-0.63426527/0.0044939587).

34 Georgescu-Roegen (1954, p. 521) points out that "continuity does not apply either to 'rejection' or to 'preference' which are states described in no other way. ...it is not at all necessary that between two states there should always be an intermediary one."

35 The estimated asymptotic standard errors are 0.12816362, and 0.076523652, respectively.

36 This result indicates that we might draw confidence in a fairly appropriate choice of the design points in our survey.

37 This proposal has its analog in the U.S. Nuclear Waste Policy Act which was guided by the idea of implementing a "fair procedure."

38 (1993b, p. S-2) points out that "multi-point designs do have the advantage of being conservative," which is essential if you have no prior Kanninen knowledge, for example about different evaluation strategies in your population.

39 It is plausible to assume that there are a lot of connotations, economic and noneconomic ones, around if people are to judge a real situation. With regard to the second of these two categories, Schkade and Payne (1993, p. 289) state, "our results provide an assessment of the seriousness of those noneconomic considerations: They are frequent and they are significant determinants ..." For an example of the empirical relevance of factors which are difficult to grasp see, e.g., Pommerehne and Hart (1994).

REFERENCES

Axelrod, Robert M. (1984), *The Evolution of Cooperation*, New York: Basic Books.

Bazaraa, Mokhtar S., and C.M. Shetty (1979), *Nonlinear Programming: Theory and Algorithms*, New York: Wiley.

Beed, Clive, and Owen Kane (1991), What is the Critique of the Mathematization of Economics? *Kyklos* 44, 581-612.

Bishop, Richard C., and Thomas A. Heberlein (1979), Measuring Values of Extramarket Goods: Are Indirect Measures Biased?, *American Journal of Agricultural Economics* 61, 926-930.

Bowker, J.M., and John R. Stoll (1988), Use of Dichotomous Choice Nonmarket Methods to Value the Whooping Crane Resource, *American Journal of Agricultural Economics* 70, 372-381.

Brookshire, David S., and Thomas D. Crocker (1981), The Advantages of Contingent Valuation Methods for Benefit-Cost Analysis, *Public Choice* 36, 235-252.

Cameron, Trudy Ann (1988), A New Paradigm for Valuing Non-market Goods Using Referendum Data: Maximum Likelihood Estimation by Censored Logistic Regression, *Journal of Environmental Economics and Management* 15, 355-379.

Cameron, Trudy Ann, and Daniel D. Huppert (1991), Referendum Contingent Valuation Estimates: Sensitivity to the Assignment of Offered Values, *Journal of the American Statistical Association* 86, 910-918.

Carson, Richard T., Jennifer Wright, Anna Alberini, Nancy Carson, and Nicholas Flores (1994), A Bibliography of Contingent Valuation Studies and Papers. Unpublished Paper, National Resource Damage Assessment Inc., La Jolla, CA.

Cooper, Joseph, and John Loomis (1993), Sensitivity of Willingness-To-Pay Estimates to Bid Design in Dichotomous Choice Valuation Models: Reply, *Land Economics* 69, 203-208.

Duffield, John W., and David A. Patterson (1991), Inference and Optimal Design for a Welfare Measure in Dichotomous Choice Contingent Valuation, *Land Economics* 67, 225-239.

Fischhoff, Baruch (1994), What Do Psychologists Want? Contingent Valuation as a Special Case of Asking Questions. Paper presented at the Werner Reimers Stiftung, Bad Hamburg, July 1994.

Finney, D.J. (1955), *Experimental Design and its Statistical Basis*, Chicago: The University of Chicago Press.

Georgescu-Roegen, Nicholas (1954), Choice, Expectations and Measurability, *Quarterly Journal of Economics* 68, 503-534.

Georgescu-Roegen, Nicholas (1971), *The Entropy Law and the Economic Process*, Cambridge, MA: Harvard University Press.

Goldfeld, Stephen S., and Richard E. Quandt (1972), *Nonlinear Methods in Econometrics*, Amsterdam: North Holland.

Hanemann, W. Michael (1984a), Discrete/Continuous Models of Consumer Demand, *Econometrica* 52, 541-561.

Hanemann, W. Michael (1984b), Welfare Evaluations in Contingent Valuation Experiments with Discrete Responses, *American Journal of Agricultural Economics* 66, 332-341.

Hanemann, W. Michael (1989), Welfare Estimation in Contingent Valuation Experiments with Discrete Response Data: Reply, *American Journal of Agricultural Economics* 71, 1057-1061.

Hanemann, W. Michael, John Loomis and Barbara J. Kanninen (1991), Estimation Efficiency of Double Bounded Dichotomous Choice Contingent Valuation, *American Journal of Agricultural Economics* 73, 1255-1263.

Johansson, Per-Olov, Bengt Kriström, and Karl Göran Mäler (1989), Welfare Evaluations in Contingent Valuation Experiments with Discrete Response Data: Comment, *American Journal of Agricultural Economics* 71, 1054-1056.

Kahneman, Daniel, and Amos Tversky (1979), Prospect Theory: An Analysis of Decisions under Risk, *Econometrica* 47, 263-291.

Kanninen, Barbara J. (1993a), Optimal Experimental Design for Double-Bounded Dichotomous Choice Contingent Valuation, *Land Economics* 69, 138-146.

Kanninen, Barbara J. (1993b), Design of Sequential Experiments for Contingent Valuation Studies, *Journal of Environmental Economics and Management* 25, S-1-S-11.

Kanninen, Barbara J., and Bengt Kriström (1993), Sensitivity of Willingness-to-Pay Estimates to Bid Design in Dichotomous Choice Valuation Models: Comment, *Land Economics* 69, 199-202.

Kopp, Raymond A., and Katherine A. Pease (1994), Contingent Valuation: Economics, Law and Politics. Paper presented at the Werner Reimers Stiftung, Bad Hamburg, July 1994.

Kriström, Bengt (1990), A Non-Parametric Approach to the Estimation of Welfare Measures in Discrete Response Valuation Studies, *Land Economics* 66, 135-139.

Kunreuther, Howard, and Douglas Easterling (1990), Are Risk-Benefit Tradeoffs Possible in Siting Hazardous Facilities, *American Economic Review, Papers and Proceedings* 80, 252-256.

Kunreuther, Howard, Douglas Easterling, William Desvousges, and Paul Slovic (1990), Public Attitudes Toward Siting a High-Level Nuclear Waste Repository in Nevada, *Risk Analysis* 10, 469-484.

Mäler, Karl Göran (1985), Welfare Economics and the Environment, in: A.V. Kneese and J.L. Sweeney (eds.), *Handbook of Natural Resource and Energy Economics*, vol. I, North Holland: Elsevier, 3-60.

McFadden, Daniel, and Gregory K. Leonard (1993), Issues in the Contingent Valuation of Environmental Goods: Methodologies for Data Collection and Analysis, in: Jerry A. Hausman (ed.), *Contingent Valuation. A Critical Assessment*, North Holland: Elsevier, 165-208.

Mitchell, Robert C., and Richard T. Carson (1986), Property Rights, Protest, and the Siting of Hazardous Waste Facilities, *American Economic Review, Papers and Proceedings* 76, 285-290.

Mitchell, Robert C., and Richard T. Carson (1989), *Using Surveys to Value Public Goods: The Contingent Valuation Method.* Washington: Resources for the Future.

Opaluch, James J., Stephen K. Swallow, Thomas Weaver, Christopher W. Wessels, and Dennis Wichelns (1993), Evaluating Impacts from Noxious Facilities: Including Public Preferences in Current Siting Mechanisms. *Journal of Environmental Economics and Management* 24, 41-59.

Pommerehne, Werner W. (1982), Empirische Ansätze zur Erfassung der Präferenzen für öffentliche Güter, in: Gottfried Bombach, Bernhard Gahlen, and Alfred E. Ott (eds.), *Möglichkeiten und Grenzen der Staatstätigkeit*, Tübingen: Mohr, 407-492.

Pommerehne, Werner W. (1987), *Präferenzen für öffentliche Güter*, Tübingen: Mohr.

Pommerehne, Werner W., and Albert Hart (1994), Tragic Choices and Collective Decision-Making, Discussion Paper B 9401, University of Saarland, Saarbrücken.

Pommerehne, Werner W., and Anselm U. Römer (1992), Ansätze zur Erfassung der Präferenzen für öffentliche Güter: Ein Überblick, *Jahrbuch für Sozialwissenschaft* 43, 171-210.

Schkade, David A., and John W. Payne (1993), Where Do the Numbers Come from? How People Respond to Contingent Valuation Questions, in: Jerry A. Hausman (ed.), *Contingent Valuation. A Critical Assessment*, North Holland: Elsevier, 271-303.

Smith, V. Kerry, and William H. Desvousges (1987), An Empirical Analysis of the Economic Value of Risk Changes, *Journal of Political Economy* 95, 89-114.

INDEX

Ability to pay, 37, 276
Acceptance, logit estimation of, 309, 310
Accuracy, of survey response, 52n100, 219, 233, 237
Acid rain, 144(table), 145(table), 153n35
Acushnet River/PCB legal case, 30, 52n96
Adding-up test, 36–37, 108–109, 109(table), 110–111, 119n5, 151n18
Advantages/positive impacts, of SHDP development, 279, 284(table), 288–289
Aesthetic impact, 290–291, 294n6
Agricultural impact, 50n81, 279
Agricultural landscape, 143(table), 274, 294n6
Air pollution, 2, 50n81, 105, 144(table), 149n5, 153n34, 204
Air quality, 8–9, 28, 104–105, 153n34
ALCOA, damage assessment process, 55n125
Alternative methodology, 190, 203, 206–208, 247, 310–312
Altruism, 60, 242
American Jewish Federation, 152n29
American Psychological Association, 191
Andreoni's theory of warm glow, 130, 149–150n11
Applied basic social science, 190, 209
Applied welfare economics, 119n6, 250, 263
Arando-Ordaz flexible function form, 258
Articulated preferences, 197, 201(table), 205
Articulated values, philosophy of, 166, 169–170
Asymptotical standard error, 252–253, 309, 318n35
Attitude, 169, 180, 221, 245–246, 276, 289, 290(table)
  measurement, 71, 141, 167, 170–171, 182, 273–275, 278
Automobile accident risk, 95–96, 145(table)
Ayer et al theorem, 261–262
Ayer estimator, 262–263

"Bads," 63, 299–303, 312, 314
Bag-outcome, 245, 246
Basic applied research, 190, 201, 204, 209, 210
Basic values philosophy, 166, 170–171, 183
Bayesian updating process, 85–86, 253
Beach day experience, WTP, 153n32
Behavior, 3, 4, 8, 36, 84–85, 90–91, 96–97, 128, 140, 149n7, 167
  internal consistency condition, 101, 118n1, 119n2
Behavioral model, 71, 130, 299, 308, 314
Beliefs, criteria, 196, 206, 208
Benefit-cost analysis, 52n95, 63, 65, 72, 95–96, 129, 142, 242, 244, 265nX
  ethical motivation and, 50–51n87
  of government policies/regulation, 7, 12, 27
  total value basis for, 25–26, 41–42
  use of CV in, 24–25, 27, 42, 44n9, 165, 300
Benefit function, 238
Benefits, 90, 95, 223, 237–238, 241–243
  estimation, 24–25, 28–29, 50n81, 255–257
Bias, 20, 71, 76, 192, 203, 232, 249–250, 252–255, 308, 314
  CV method subject to, 64–65, 273
  in risk perception, 84, 87–88, 94, 97
  metric, 128, 273
  non-response in referendum-type models, 238–243
  part-whole, 128–129, 273
  probability of provision, 128, 273
  starting point, 210n1, 247, 258
  symbolic, 128, 273
Bids, 153n35, 247, 254, 258, 275, 280, 307, 308, 316n21, 317n29
"Bid-vector," 236, 250, 252, 263
Big Darby Creek program, Ohio, 146(table)
Binary discrete choice elicitation method, 137–138, 142
Binary response models, 263
Biodiversity, 145(table), 241
Biometrics, 249–250
Bird experiment data of Schkade and Payne, 136, 136(table), 137(table), 152n26
Birds/Rocky Mountain oil ponds study, 135–136, 135(table), 141, 145(table), 151n18, 173–174
Bishop-Heberlein regression equation, 255, 257, 307, 309, 317n31
Bob Marshall wilderness area, 134, 151n22
Bottom-up sequences, 132, 150n15, 150n16
Break in structure, test for, 308, 315n11
Bribes, 301–302, 310
Budget constraints, 29, 47n51, 60, 71–72, 95, 151n21, 243
  consumer choice and, 102, 120n8
Burdens, of SHDP, 280–281, 291, 295n12, 295n18
Butterfly species in the Amazon, 174–175

Calamba, Philippines, CV test of scope, 219–234
California's "Big Green" initiative, 211n5
California Water Resources Control Board, 143
Cambridge Economics, Inc. Conference on CV values, 18
Cameron's benefit estimation in closed-ended cases, 256–257

Cameron's reduced form WTA, 312
Cancer, death risk metric, 95–96
Carson & Mitchell's criteria, 144(table), 149n4, 207, 273
Carson *et al*, 37–38, 40, 106, 144(table), 146
Carson-Flores Hypothesis I test, 134, 151n22
Case sensitive aggregation, 305, 316n23
Causal model, 313–314
Central limit theorem, 261
Certainty, 92, 175–176, 183, 245–246
CES utility function, 151n18
Change process, 107, 117, 122n18, 191, 197, 199, 203, 206
Charitable donations, 129, 149n11
Choice, 8–9, 42n2, 47n51, 50n87, 61, 63, 65, 95, 115, 236
  circumstances of, 10–12, 26–28, 43n4
  CV measures and, 2, 5, 105
  economic value, 101–103, 106, 113, 118, 119n2, 121n14, 248
  internal consistency of, 36–38, 101, 107, 119n3
  outcomes of, 4, 118n1
Choice behavior, 4, 35–36, 38, 63, 101
  rational, 34, 36, 84–85, 90–91, 96–97, 107, 118
Choice plans to control marine debris, 112(table), 113, 113(table), 121n16
Chronic bronchitis, risk of, 93, 95–96
Cigarette smoking, risk of, 86, 89
Clean Air and Water Acts, 17, 24, 149n5
Closed-ended design, 299–301, 303, 308–310
Closed-ended question format, 169, 178, 281
  valuation, 235, 246–249, 255–259, 261, 263
Cochran-Mantel-Haenszel statistic, 113
Cognitive mode, multiple layer, 313–314
Cognitive overload, 128, 246, 281, 292
Cognitive process, 4, 165, 167–172, 180, 182
Cognitive psychology, 127, 130, 192–193
Collaboration, psychologists and economists, 189–190, 193–196, 210n1, 210n2
Collective Action programs, 232
Commercial freshwater fishing, 279
Commodity, 62, 74, 95, 116–117, 122n18, 245, 276
Communication devices, 273–292, 293n3, 295n16
  equality hypothesis, 276–278
Communication process, 165, 167–172, 182, 204, 273
Compensable value, 16, 19, 22–23
Compensation, 11, 13, 17, 29, 48n68, 49n75, 308, 309
  alternatives, 302, 310–311
  for risk, 83–84, 93–94
  high upper offers, 306–307, 311
  monetary, 299–306, 310, 312, 315n2, 315n13, 317n25
  resistance to, 301–303, 305–306, 310, 312, 317n28
  valuation, 15n14, 50n95
Compensation coefficient, 306–310, 317n26, 317n27
Compensation offer, 306, 311–314, 315n10
Competitiveness, international, 26, 40–41, 55n125
Complements, 70–71, 103, 122n18, 132
Component sensitivity, test of, 132–133
Composite hypothesis, 37, 101
Comprehensive Environmental Response Compensation and Liability Act (CERCLA), 13–16, 43n5, 45n24, 55n125
Conjoint analysis, 49–50n78
Consistency tests, 101, 108, 119n3, 134
Construal process, 167, 170, 175, 177–178, 181, 183
Construct validity, 37–38, 55n123, 60, 65, 69–77, 141, 205, 206
  equation, 38–39(table)
  two forms of, 55n122, 69
Consumer, theory of, 59–62, 66, 172
Consumer choice, 63, 101–102, 104, 129
Content validity, 60, 65–69, 71–74, 76–77, 205
Contingent valuation (CV), 2, 5n1, 73–74, 103, 134, 165–166
  academic perspective, 3, 34–40, 54n111
  as case of asking questions, 189–210
  controversy, 15, 22, 33–34, 54n117, 59, 69, 76, 190, 235, 236
  cost benefit analysis and, 27–28, 40, 44n9
  direct use survey, 14–15, 46n47
  estimates, 101, 106, 108, 110–111, 120n13, 137, 139–142
  as information source about economic values, 118, 122n18
  OMB and, 26–27, 50n80
  passive use and, 7–13, 18–19, 23–24, 29–40, 42, 46n41, 59, 70
  question response model, 277
  reliability/validity, 20, 22, 24, 27–40, 76
  research, constraints, 166–167, 208–209
  scenario, 195, 198, 200, 201(table), 202–204
  standards/guidelines, 20–25, 48n65, 49n78, 50n83, 50n85
  theoretical basis for, 1, 3, 5, 76, 177
  use in damage assessment, 13, 15, 18, 41–42, 116, 219, 263
  validity assessment, 19, 42, 60, 65, 70, 72, 76
Contingent valuation, surveys/studies, 27, 29, 31–33, 35–37, 41, 47n54, 51n90, 64, 127
  assessing content validity, four steps, 65–68, 76
  Calamba, Philippines, 221–225
  communication devices in, 273–292
  consumer choice and, 101, 105, 107, 122n18
  guidelines, 165–166, 249, 281
  reliability, 108, 134, 219

tests of insensitivity to scope, 127–148
Contingency valuation method (CVM), 1, 2, 4, 165, 219, 247
calculating use/nonuse values, 17, 19, 33
as insensitive to scope, 172, 174, 177
limits to applicability, 299–314
overall validity of, 72–75, 77
practical problems in, 68, 235–265, 273
reliability, internal consistency, 101, 107, 109, 119n2
survey, 241–242
Convergence, 204, 305, 307
Convergent validity, 55n120, 69, 75, 178
C-optimal design, 252–253
Costs, 29, 37, 40, 52n94, 95, 138, 177–180, 247, 250, 256
of survey responding, 202, 237–243
restoration, 14–15, 19–20, 45n35
Criteria, for value elicitation procedures, 196–198, 201
Criterion validity, 60, 65, 73–75, 77
Cultural objects impact, 279–282
Cumulative distribution function, normal distribution, 239

Damage assessment, 12–13, 15, 18–19, 29, 52n95, 72, 242
appropriate measure of, 13–14, 16, 43n7, 43n9
judicial process of, 18, 20, 29–34
passive use values, 40, 42
using CV, 56n125, 59, 65, 68, 75, 165, 173
regulations, 12–23, 24–25, 42, 45n35
Damages, 40–41, 55n125, 260, 261, 300
infinite, 301, 303, 317n26
Data, coherent summarization of, 194, 196, 206
Data collection methods, 172, 180–182, 235–246
Data points, of CVM survey, 301, 308, 315n13
Daubert v. Merrell Dow Pharmaceuticals, 32, 33, 41, 52n100, 53n103, 53n107
Davidon-Fletcher-Powell algorithm, 316n19
Debriefing, respondents, 280–281, 292
Decision making, 63, 67, 78n3, 118n1, 166, 177, 194–195, 209
errors in, 88, 90–91
potential determinants of individual, 305, 312–314
public, CV estimates of passive use, 8–9
Decision to respond indicator function, 237
Demand curve, 153n31, 257, 261
Density function, 306
Density of the normal distribution, 240
Department of Energy, 24–27, 50n85
Department of the Interior (DOI), 13–14, 23, 50n85, 165
natural resource damage assessment regulations and, 13–23, 25, 42, 43–44n9, 44n15, 49n72
rule revisions, 16–17, 21–23, 45n27, 46n43, 46n47, 48n66
Design points, 153n31, 252–254, 304, 306, 313, 318n36
Desvousges *et al.* study, 133, 135–136, 135(table), 141, 146, 151n18, 152n24, 173
Diagrams, use of, 274, 291
Diamond's scope test, 108, 110–111, 120n7, 121n14
Difficulty in answering the WTP question, 278
Diminution in value, 19–20, 52n98
Direct use, 42n1, 141–142, 242, 264nVI
Direct use values, 15, 21, 25, 48n65, 127, 130, 147
CV as a method to survey, 14, 17, 22, 44n15, 45n31, 46n47
Disamenity, 273, 300, 302, 315n2
Discussion, 181, 194, 199–200, 207
SHDP survey and, 283–291
Distributional assumption, 256, 259–261
Distribution function, 262, 308
D-optimal design, 251–252
Double-bounded models, 250, 258, 262–263, 305–306, 316n20
Double-bounded model log-likelihood equation, 258
Drawings, use of, 274, 291
Drinking water quality, 2, 144–145(table), 227(table), 275

Earthquake zone, WTP for, 140, 211n5
Ecosystem impacts, 128, 245, 279–280, 294n11
Econometrics, 68, 76, 235, 255, 258
Economic model, 4, 315n5
Economic rationality assumption, 3–4
Economics/cognitive psychology collaboration, 127, 130, 189–190, 194–196, 210n1, 210n2
Economic theory, 63, 65, 71, 74, 76, 101, 118n1, 129–133, 141–142, 148n2, 235, 243–244, 248, 255
sensitivity and, 142, 166, 172, 180
Economic value, 2–5, 7–12, 29, 42–43n3, 49n68, 50n87, 52n95, 64, 106, 128, 130
constructing measures of, 16, 42n1, 50n81, 101–118
moral value vs., 129, 150n12
WTP/WTA and, 60, 62–63
Egoistic utility maximization, 301, 302
Elicitation, 4–5, 195, 205, 314, 314n1
Elicitation method/format, 147, 193, 196–201, 208–209, 241, 248, 281
Elicitation questions, 178, 180, 183
Elkem Sauda, 279, 283(table)
Embedding effects, 68, 129–130, 134, 148n2, 151n21, 173, 175, 273, 295n16
Calamba experiment, 225, 225(table)
evaluation question and, 192, 204, 209
"perfect," 131, 149,n9

as problem, 219, 225–226, 231, 236
three levels of, 69
Embedding effect tests, 131, 133, 148
Empirical survival function, 261
Encoding, of scenario, 174, 181, 183
Endangered species, 2, 44n11, 128, 140, 246, 275
Environmental amenity, 63, 68–70, 273
Environmental assessment (EA), 275–276
Environmental change, 170, 174, 243, 273–274, 276, 278, 291
evaluation criteria, 196–207
Environmental good, 5, 131, 141, 192, 198, 209, 259, 273
Environmental impact, 241, 273–275, 281–282, 290, 292, 294n9
larger, 284(table), 286(table), 288, 290(table)
Environmental Impact Assessment (EIA), 275–276, 281, 284(table), 296n18
Environmental improvements, 139–140, 143, 249, 254, 260, 289
Environmental insult, 39, 63, 70, 86, 90, 96, 108; *see also* Natural resources, damage to
Environmental protection, 138, 211n5
Environmental Protection Agency (EPA), 24–26, 28, 43n9, 50n83, 148n3, 149n5
Environmental quality, 3, 64, 106, 110, 208, 276
change in the level of, 274, 276–277, 291
index, 238, 242, 244, 248
Environmental regulating, 24–25, 28, 51n92
Environmental resources, 2, 61, 101, 119n2
plan/program, 1–2, 105–107, 109, 112, 115, 120n13, 133, 133(table), 144(table), 145(table), 199
valuation of, 60, 64, 68, 101–103, 111, 209, 276
Equality, hypothesis of, 277–278
Estimated hazard model, 122n17
Estimation-specific precision problems, 308
Ethics, as motivation, 3, 50–51n87
Evaluation, 191–193, 200–201, 203, 302, 309, 318n38
function, 303–305
Evidence, reliability of, 30–33, 53n107
Executive branch, 12–13, 21, 24, 28, 43n6
Executive Order (EO), 21, 24, 50n80, 51n93
Expected utility theory, 119n1, 119n4
Experimental psychology, 189–190, 210n4
Expert opinion, 31–32, 53n102, 68, 175, 178–179, 282
Explicit models, 167, 174, 177–178
External criteria, 20, 35, 303, 305, 308
testing of scope, 132, 142–143
Exxon Valdez oil spill, 1, 17–18, 37–39, 106, 139, 148, 165
damage assessments following, 242, 264nVI, 265nIX
scope experiments, 133–134, 136, 151n20

Existence values, 14, 16, 25–26, 30, 34, 43n9, 45n24, 52n97

"Fat tails" problem, 219, 232, 265nXVI, 299, 307, 310, 315n3, 316n16
Federal Register, 28, 46n42
Federal Rules of Evidence, 30–32, 53n104
Finnish ferry study, 241, 254, 260–261, 279, 293n4
Florida fish management plan, 140
Focus groups, 67–68, 174, 192, 208, 245, 274, 292
Follow-up questions, 68, 200, 258
Forest landscape, 145(table), 274, 276, 279
Fuller's error decomposition model, 248

Geothermal development, New Mexico, 140
Glenn Canyon Dam study, 144(table)
Goods, 66, 127, 130, 134, 170, 175, 177, 179, 183, 301
changing scope of, 137, 153n33
described, 128, 148, 165, 171–173
environmental, 131, 191, 198, 202, 209, 246, 273, 295n16
nested levels, 131–132, 142
Goods and services, value of a, 62–63, 66–67, 69–70, 73, 219
Good-to-be-valued, 137, 170, 173–174, 177, 183, 207, 243–244
construal of, 167, 170, 175, 177, 181, 183
Grand Canyon study, 140, 144(table)
Greenhouse effect, 139, 144(table)
Group processes, and evaluations, 199–200, 202, 205, 208
Groundwater pollution, 28, 50n83, 204

Habitat endangerment, 143, 174–175
Habitat protection, 8–9, 44n11
Hanemann's utility theory regression, 149n6, 255–257, 310, 312, 317n31
Hazardous waste, 12–13, 50n82, 145(table), 309
Hazards, risk valuation of, 86, 88
HBRS, Inc. study, 144(table)
Health outcomes, 93–96, 149n5
Health risk, 83, 90–91, 221–222, 301
"Hearsay" evidence, 30–31, 52n100
Hedonic pricing, 14, 70, 75, 140
Hedonic property value, 103, 104, 105, 107, 109–111, 120n8
Hedonic technique, 312–313
Heteroscedastic survival function, 114(table), 115, 115(table), 122n17
Hicksian compensating/equivalent variations, 61, 131, 265nXIII
Homo economicus, 66, 67, 130
Homo sapiens, 66, 67
Homoscedastic survival function, 114(table), 115, 115(table)

Household's WTP, environmental quality function, 276, 277
Huber-White consistent variance estimates, 117
Hunting package (Moose), 245–246, 249
Hydroelectric development impact, 3, 274, 276–277, 279–281, 284(table), 288–289, 292, 294n9, 294n10, 295n16
Hypothesis of equality of probability of preservation, 278
Hypothesis of equality of respondent's selected change in environmental quality functions, 277

Idaho v. Southern Refrigerated Transport, Inc., 30
Idarado mining case, 41
Ideological values, 128–130
Impact clarity, 197, 202(table), 206
Impact table, 280–281, 291, 294n11
Incentive-compatible valuation question, 235, 248–249, 258
Incentives, 47n51, 64, 67, 147, 231, 237
Inclusive representations, 174–175, 183
Income, individual, 60–63, 70–71, 238, 260, 276, 300–301
  effects on choice, 102–103, 109, 120n7
  WTP and, 70, 131, 141, 151n21
Indirect utility function, 60, 102, 120n8, 238, 244, 276
  choice of trips, equation for, 104, 105
  equation, 103
Individual's compensation variation (CV), 244
Information, 4, 67, 150n16, 176, 182–183, 208–209, 303
  about cost, 177–180
  accessibility, 170–171, 199
  additional, 293n2, 294n11
  amount of, 273, 275, 288, 292, 293n2
  contextual, 168–169, 171, 182
  descriptive survey, 118, 122n18
  individual risk processing, 84–90, 88(table), 93–94, 204
  issue of, 244–247
  matrix, 251, 254, 306
  modes of providing, 89, 167, 174, 177, 180, 274–275, 293n2
  prior, 86, 253
  reliability of, 34–35, 181
  repetition of, 275, 280, 288, 293n2, 295n15
  requirement, 10, 38, 43n4
  scope, 173–174
  self-evident, 169, 175
  supplied in questionnaire, 236, 249, 258
  use of devices to communicate, 276–278, 281
  value elicitation procedure criteria and, 196, 201, 204
In-person interviews, 35, 37, 54n117, 136, 172, 180–182, 221, 223, 241, 243, 280, 296n22, 302, 309
Instruments and materials, 201–202(table)
Interagency working group, 24–28
Internal consistency of choice tests, 101, 107, 110, 119n2
Internal tests of scope, 132, 138, 142–143, 150n15, 150n16
Internal utility evaluation schemes, 302–303
"Intervention" in the economy, 60–61, 63, 66, 75, 78n3
Interviewer instructions, 281–282
Interviews, 67, 181–182, 203, 208, 236, 280, 295n18, 300, 303, 312; *see also* In-person interviews, Telephone interviews
  evaluation questions and, 192, 200
Interview techniques, 31, 35, 53n102
Intrinsic value, lost, 15, 30
Inverse Mills Ratio, 114–115, 114(table), 115(table), 122n17
"Irrelevant" factors, 180, 183, 210n3
Isotonic regression theorem, 261

Joint density of net benefits and set of respondents, 240
Jointly assessed value, 174, 175
Judicial Conference Study Group Handbook of Recommended Procedures for the Trial of Protracted Litigation, 31

Kahneman and Knetsch scope and sequence test, 128, 130, 133–134, 138, 148, 148n3, 149n4
Kakadu Conservation Zone study, Australia, 144(table)
Kaplan-Meier (KM) estimator, 262
Kentucky horse farm preservation, 145(table), 147
Kentucky wetlands programs, 146(table), 244
Knowledge, 10, 28, 32, 174–176, 178, 181, 289, 290(table)
  of risk, 84, 86
  prior, 196, 202–203, 284, 287(table), 318n38
Kruskall-Wallis test, 134

Legal issues, 12, 40, 236, 242, 309
  public good valuation, 7, 12–29
  recovery for passive use values, 29–30, 40, 52n96, 52n97, 52n98, 53n102, 53n103, 53n107
  reliability for passive use value, 30–33
"Lesser of" rule, 14, 15
Levels of the good of interest, 142–143, 145(table)
Lexicographical orderings, 265nXII, 301, 303
Liability, 17, 40
Likelihood function, 135, 305–306
Likelihood of delivery, perceived, 173, 175–176, 183
Linear regression model, 250
Linear valuation function, 257

Litigation, 20, 72, 194, 273, 281, 295n17
Logging of wilderness areas study, 69
Logit model, 252, 286(table), 288–289, 290(table), 306, 309–310, 316n15, 316n16, 316n21, 317n25, 317n33
Log-likelihood equation, 258–261, 310
Log-logistic model, 261, 305
Log-normal data, 136, 152n25
Lung disease, chronic, 50n81, 94

Mail surveys, 172, 180–183, 236, 241, 243, 265, 265nXIV, 302–303
Main contingent valuation anomaly, 134
Manipulation checks, 172–174, 181, 183, 192–193, 195
validation and, 201, 202(table), 204–205
Maps, use of, 274, 280–281, 291, 291(table), 295n12, 295n18
Marginal utility, 172, 254
Marginal valuations, 92–93(table), 104, 106, 109–111, 121n16, 142
Marine debris beach cleanup, 111–115, 145(table), 146, 177
Market-based data, 60–63, 67, 75, 90, 96
Marketplace, 63, 66–69, 73, 198, 202, 209, 241–242, 245, 247
Market price, 14–16, 49n72, 52n98, 63, 73
Marshallian measurement method, 103
Maximum likelihood estimation, 256–259, 261, 263, 305–306
Measurement, 179–180, 196, 198, 205–207
of damages, 14–15, 17, 19–20, 22
of economic value, 7–8, 14, 42n1
of non-use values, 59–77
Measurement methods, 14, 192, 195–196
for economic value derived from choice, 101–107, 118
for economic value, gauging reliability, 107–111
reliability/validity and, 64–74
Memory, psychological theories of, 167
Mental construal, of the good, 170–178, 181, 183, 204
Meta analysis, 115–117, 140, 166
Methodological norms, 191, 193, 196, 198, 204, 206
Methodological studies, cost of, 173, 178, 180, 182–183
Methods, a comparison of, 307–308, 314
Metrics, 83–84, 94–96, 128, 265nXI, 273
Microeconomic theory of nonuse values, 59
Midnight regulations, 19, 46n41
Minimax principle, 254, 301
Minimization problem and function of asymptotic variance of parameter ratio, 251–253
Moderator guidelines, 201(table), 205
Monetary commitment, 63–64
Monetary measures of value, 11, 42–43n3, 74, 83, 95
Monetary compensation, 299–307, 309–312, 315n2, 317n25
Money, 106, 238, 254, 276
Mono Lake water level, WTP study, 143
Monotoxicity assumptions, 132, 136
Montana waterfowl hunting trips study, 144(table)
Moral satisfaction, 129–130, 149–150n11, 150n12
Mortality risk, 83, 84, 88, 94–96, 301, 310
Motives, 129, 136, 150n12, 245
Multi-attribute utility theory (MAUT), 209
Multi-stage estimation, 307, 314, 316n19, 318n30
Multivariate equation system, 229–230(table), 307
Muskoka Lakes cleanup, WTP scope insensitivity, 128–129

National Ambient Air Quality Standards, 50n81
National Health Service, 145(table)
National Oceanic and Atmospheric Administration (NOAA) crafting CV standards, 13, 20–22, 42, 47n52, 165
CV panel, 18–20, 25, 33–34, 107, 120n11, 148n2, 180, 191, 206, 236
natural resource damage assessment regulations and, 13, 15–23, 25, 45n36, 46n38, 46n39, 47n49, 49n72, 49n74, 49n76
panel notes/report, 34–37, 41, 54n111, 54n116, 107–108
proposed/final rule, 23, 50n79, 219, 233
National Opinion Research Center's General Social Survey, 139
National Research Council, 195
Natural resources, 2, 44n11, 101, 106–107, 190
assessment of damage, 12–13, 19–22, 30, 33–35, 40–42, 45n27, 55n125, 165, 177, 219
injuries to, 7, 14–17, 22–23, 29, 37, 47n53, 106, 114(table)
regulations, 21, 23, 45, 51n92
NB conditional density/normal distribution difference, 240
Nerve disease, death risk metric, 95
Nested goods, 131–133, 148
Neutrality hypothesis, 149n11
New Bedford Harbor/PCB legal case, 30, 52n96
Newton-Raphson procedure, 306
Non-consumptive use values, 30, 45n24
Non-health benefits, 140, 149n5
Nonmarketed use valuation methodology, 17, 22, 45n31, 63, 165, 190
Non-negative random variables, 265nXVII
Nonparametric analysis, 261–263, 303–305, 308–314, 316n22

Nonresponse, 35, 181–182, 195, 236, 259, 264nVII, 302–303
bias in referendum-type models, 238–243
Nonuse values, 1, 59–60, 74, 76, 96, 111, 241–242, 273–274, 276, 279; *see also* Passive use value
measuring, 59–77, 281
Normative economic model, 166–167, 175
Norms, 190–191, 195, 203
Northern spotted owls study, 26, 144(table), 146
Norwegian rivers preservation, 279–281, 285–286, 285(table), 286(table), 288–289, 294n9
No-sayer, 302–304, 306, 310
"No time to think," Calamba survey, 223, 224(table), 225–226, 228(table), 231–233
Nuclear waste repository sites, Switzerland, 3, 300, 309–311
Null hypothesis, 74, 114–115, 132, 135, 230(table), 248
interpreting null results, 172–173

Object of choice, 5n2, 8–12, 37, 43n4, 102, 111, 121n14
change in, 102–103, 106–107, 116
set of defining attributes, 9–12, 36, 55n120
Occupation, risk and, 84–86, 88, 90, 96
Office of Information and Regulatory Affairs, 26
Office of Management and Budget (OMB), 21, 24–29, 50n85
Ohio, et al. v. Department of the Interior, 14–19, 21–22, 30, 48n65, 54n111
Oil Pollution Act (OPA) of 1990, 17–18, 20–21, 23, 34, 45n33, 45n35
Oil spills, 12, 17, 38, 41, 60, 106, 135, 145(table), 178
OLS model, 226, 227(table), 228(table), 231, 285, 287(table), 289
Ontario, Canada, lake cleanup, 128–129
Open-ended format, 153n35, 171, 178, 208, 299, 301–302, 315n11, 316n22
Open-ended questions, 35–36, 246–249, 257, 281
Opinion poll, 31, 197–199, 198(table), 208
Optimal design, theory of, 236, 250–255
Option values, 14, 16, 30, 43n9, 45n24
Oral presentations, 274, 279
Organizing metaphors, 197–199, 200
Outdoor recreation trip valuation, 140–141
Overall mean value, WTP for respondent/nonrespondent, 243

Packaged regulations, 28–29, 51n90
Pair-wise coparisons, 226, 234n1
Parameter values, 251, 254, 256, 257, 260, 305, 307
Parametric analysis, 257–258, 262, 304–314, 315n12, 316n15, 316n22, 317n33
Partisan testimony, 198–199
Part-whole bias, 128–129, 219, 273
Passive use value, 1, 14–15, 20–21, 27, 42n1, 44n18, 46n47, 51n87, 127, 147, 241–242; *see also* Nonuse value
CV to calculate, 7–9, 12–13, 16–19, 22–24, 29–40, 42, 46n41, 49–50n78, 130, 165
recovery of, 19, 22, 48n60, 48–49n68
of resource and WTP, 142, 143–146(table), 146
role in regulatory decision making, 24–29
Payment, 67, 173, 175, 202
Payment card, 153n35n 247n 281–282, 293n3
Payment vehicle, 28, 47n51, 66, 74, 102–103, 111, 122n18, 243, 249, 280, 295n17
role of in CV surveys, 137, 142, 150n11, 153n31, 153n35
Peer review, 32–33, 53n107, 68, 189, 191, 195
Perceived probability function, 86–87
Perception, 106, 111–112, 143, 206, 273, 312, 314
of damage, 37, 39, 300, 303
of likelihood of delivery, 173, 175–176
of probabilities, 86, 153n33
of quality of good delivered, 173, 176
of risk formula, 84–87, 89–90, 94, 97, 246
of visibility changes, 115–117, 276
Photography, 274, 277–281, 285(table), 286, 286(table), 287(table), 289, 291–292, 291(table), 293n2, 295n18
Pie charts, 274, 277, 279, 294n9, 295n16
Pilot study, 67, 147, 254–255
Poisonings, 89(table), 91, 92–93(table)
Policy makers, 95, 202(table), 206–209, 312, 314
Policy measures, 90, 95, 196, 303, 310–311
well-formulated, 201(table), 202–203, 205
Political concerns, 7, 12–29, 40–42, 63, 166, 199, 312, 314
Posterior probability that an outcome will occur, 86
Potentially responsible parties (PRP), 49n68
Predictive validity, 73
Preference, 75, 189, 197, 199, 203, 205, 247, 275, 289, 302
assessment, 166, 299, 312
choice decision and, 4–5, 11, 36–37, 101–102, 104–105, 118, 118n1, 119n2, 119n3, 120n7
context dependent, 166, 244, 265nXIII
CV as accurate measurement, 134, 151n20, 300, 312, 318n34
for environmental amenities, 62–63, 69–70
lexicographic orderings, 265nXII, 301, 303
methods of eliciting, 193, 197, 314, 314n1
revealed, 5n2, 17, 43n4, 62, 75, 101, 119n3, 137, 140
Preference of ordering. *See* Utility function
President's Council of Economic Advisors (CEA), 25, 29

Pretesting, 35–36, 67, 93, 108, 111, 127, 175, 192, 204–205
SHDP project, 273, 279–280, 292, 294n10, 294n11
Price for the environmental good, 190, 246, 249
Price of goods and services, 60, 93, 102, 142, 153n31, 204, 244, 246, 249–250, 258, 276, 316n22
Price of marketed goods, function, 104–105, 110
Prince William Sound protection, 38, 106, 242, 265nVI
Prior of the variances of the parameters, 253
Private donations, 4, 149n11
Private goods, 3–4, 8, 244, 261
Probability, 35, 47n52, 86–91, 96, 175, 206, 244, 263
density function, 303, 305
for an acceptance equation, 257
for an acceptance linear valuation function, 257
of favorable/unfavorable net benefits, 239, 245, 246
perceived function, 86–87
of preservation, 278, 286, 288
of provision bias, 128, 147, 151n19, 153n33, 273
of yes or no answer, 256–257, 262, 306, 316n14
Probit model, 114, 226, 227(table), 228(table), 231, 258, 306, 309–310, 316n16, 317n33
Procedure evaluation protocol, 201(table), 203, 205
Profit function, 244
Proportion of yes answers, 238, 240, 255, 261
Proposal evaluation protocol, 198, 200, 201(table), 203
Protest responses, 193, 195, 203, 307, 315n11
Provision of the good, 128, 175–176, 179, 183
Psychological report components, 191–196
Psychology, relevance of, 2, 59, 76, 165, 180, 182
Psychometrics, defined, 192
Publication, evidence reliability and, 32–33, 53n107
Public comment, 22–23, 25, 49n72, 207
Public goods, 3–4, 62, 64, 129–130, 133(table), 140, 232
assessing preferences for, 299, 312, 314, 314n1
multiple, 28, 150n11
as objects of choice, 7–8, 29, 36–37, 51n90, 52n95
Public opinion, 138, 139, 166, 170
Public policy, 3, 59, 72, 75, 119n2, 127, 138–139
Public values, elicitation method, 196, 199, 202, 207
p value, 134–136, 135(table)
Qualitative research procedures, 67–70, 72, 76, 306, 310
Questioning modes, 235–236, 246–249
Questions, 139, 198, 211n7, 258, 277, 299, 302
comprehension, 167–172, 175, 180, 183
CV and asking, 189–210
wording, 138, 147, 152n27, 169, 183
Questionnaires, 31, 53n102, 168–173, 181–183, 199, 236–238, 246, 277, 304, 309, 313
CV survey, Calamba, 220, 223, 224(table), 232, 234n2
design of, 111, 232, 245, 273, 280, 299, 302–303, 311–314
explicit/implicit information, 167, 174, 177–178, 180
response rates, 241, 265nXIV

Random utility model, 120n8, 120n10
Rationality, 4, 34, 36, 101, 107, 118, 166, 263, 301
valuation of risk reduction, 84–85, 90–91, 96–97
Recall and judgment, 169–171
Recreational activities impact, 279–282, 283(table), 286(table), 287(table), 289, 293n5, 294n11
Recreational behavior, 104, 106, 120n10
Recreational services, 63, 273, 276
Recruitment procedure, 199–200, 202
Referendum, 35, 37, 167, 198–199, 232–233, 232(table), 300
approach, 238, 249–255, 264nIV, 265nXIV
elicitation procedure, 219, 223, 232–233
format, 193, 198, 281
question, 178–180
type model, non-response bias in, 238–241
voting in, 63–64, 74
Regional water quality management plan, 223, 224(table), 227(table), 231–232, 232(table)
Regression analysis, 70–71
Regulations, 23, 26, 28–29, 41, 51n90, 51n92, 52n94, 60
Regulatory Decision Making, role of passive use in, 27–30, 42, 50n80
Regulatory impact analysis (RIA), 24–28, 40, 50n83
Regulatory programs, 7, 12–13, 16, 25, 27–29, 40, 44n9
Regulatory review process, 29, 51n93, 51n93
Rehabilitation program, 45n35, 49n75, 176
"Rejection" function, 315n10, 317n27, 318n34
Relevance, 191–192, 195, 197, 204, 206
communicated information and, 169, 171, 177–178, 180–183
Relevant distribution, 308, 318n39
Reliability, 5, 21, 54n111, 94, 96, 106, 181, 195, 206, 262, 300, 307, 313
of CV, 5, 19–20, 29–40

mean/median as measure of central tendency, 311, 317n23
of measures for economic value gauging, 107–111
validity and, 60, 64–74
Research design, 191, 278–282
Resistance/opposition, reduce, 303–304, 307, 310–311
Resource Conservation and Recovery Act, 24, 50n82, 50n83
Response, study/survey, 137–138, 146–148, 171–172, 194–201, 203, 206–208, 210, 210n1, 211n7, 313
Response behavior, 302–303, 308–309, 312–313
Response mechanisms, 236–238, 240
Response mode, 193–194, 196, 200, 201(table), 203, 208–210
Response rate, 21, 49n72, 66, 182, 202, 237–238, 241–243, 247, 249, 264, 265nXIV
Respondents, 167, 169–170, 172, 175, 194, 198, 237, 240
personal charaacteristics of, 174, 304–305
self-selection, 180–183
unresponsive to good being valued, 127, 151n18
Respondents with positive response to referendum question, 232
Restore/replace value, 13–16, 19–23, 45n35, 47n53, 49n76
Risk, 141, 174, 204, 211n6, 245–246, 274, 299
assessment, 86–90, 89(table), 96
Risk-money tradeoffs, 84, 90–96
Risk reduction, valuation of, 83–97, 147, 277
Robbins-Monroe recursion, updating the bid-vector, 252–254
Rogaland/Hordaland counties (RH), 279–281, 283–285(table), 286(table), 287(table), 288–289, 290(table), 291, 291(table), 293n3, 294n9, 295n15, 295n16, 296n19, 296n21
Rudimentary tests, 71–72, 75, 77

Sample/sampling, 66, 76, 111, 127, 140–141, 153n31, 208, 237, 243, 263–264, 300, 302, 304–305
frame, 201–202(table), 202
random, 202, 221, 309, 313
representative, 31, 193–194, 202
split, 47n53, 134, 138, 142, 146–148, 153n32, 219, 225–226, 248, 309, 311–312
Sample size, 65, 67, 76, 173, 201–202(table), 202
larger, 152n17, 261, 304–305
small, 136, 147, 174, 193, 241, 248–249, 264
Sanitation services, 219–221, 222(table), 223, 224(table), 225–226, 225(table), 227(table), 228(table), 231–233, 232(table), 234n2
Sauda, Norway, 279–281, 283–285(table), 286(table), 287(table), 288–289, 290(table), 291, 291(table), 293n3, 294n9, 295n15, 295n16, 296n19, 296n21
Sauda Hydroelectric Development Project (SHDP), 278–289, 293n2, 293n3, 293n4, 294n9, 295n12, 295–296n18, 296n21
Scenarios
construction, 235, 243–246
CV, 148, 169–170, 172–178, 181, 183, 265nIX, 280
psychology procedure recommendation, 195, 198, 200, 201(table), 202–204, 206–207, 209
use of video to communicate, 274, 276, 291–292
Schkade and Payne, 133, 136–137, 136(table), 137(table), 145(table), 152n24, 173–174, 177
Scope, 143–146(table), 148n2, 173–176, 315n2
insensitivity, 127–137, 141, 143–148, 146(table), 149n7, 150n17, 153n33, 172
sensitivity, evidence/arguments, 137–147, 173, 206
Scope tests, 20–21, 23, 36–37, 39, 47n58, 49n72, 55n120, 108, 109(table), 110–118, 119n5, 289
CV studies and, 70–71, 75, 77
time to think, 219–234
Screening/threshold factor, 21, 23, 48n60
Sea turtle extinction, North Carolina, 146(table)
"Secondhand" evidence, 30, 52n101
Selway Bitteroot wilderness, 134–135, 151n22, 151–152n23
Senate Advisory Committee on Rule 703, notes, 31–32
Sequence effect tests, 131–133, 148, 149n10, 150n14, 150n21
Sequencing, 205, 252–253, 293n2, 301
Service-to-service scaling approach, 23, 49n76
Sewer line, 221–223, 224(table), 227(table), 228(table), 232(table)
Shopping mall intercept survey, 135–136, 147, 173
"Simulated market" values, 73–75, 77
Simple logistic model, 260
Single-bounded model, 257–259, 303, 305–307
Site quality, 104–105, 111, 115–117, 120n8, 120n10, 141–142, 278–282
Smith-Osborne scope test, 116, 116(table), 117(table)
Species preservation, 8, 174–175, 206
Spike model estimation function, 236, 259–261, 265nXVIII
Sport fishing toxics study, 145(table), 147
Starting point bias, 210n1, 247, 258
Statistical noise, 71, 76

Substitution effects, 28, 35–36, 70–71, 109–110, 131, 151n21, 174, 243, 293n5, 311
on measures of valuation, 103–106, 109(table), 120n7
Survey administration, 22, 30, 65, 71–72, 76, 181, 313
insensitivity to scope and, 127–128, 146–148, 152n24
problematic situations and, 299, 302–303, 314
standards, 20, 33, 35–36, 49n72, 55n110
Survey design, 59, 165, 190–192, 201, 235, 242, 250–254, 257, 299, 302–303, 309, 313–314
content validity and, 65, 67, 76
flawed, 67–68, 71–73, 87, 90, 96
guidelines, 35–36, 54n116
insensitivity to scope and, 127–129, 146–148
of instrument, 18, 20, 22, 30, 47n54, 50n90, 53n102, 55n120, 107
open-ended, 299, 301–302
single/double-bounded, 303, 305–307
Survey instrument, 47n58, 70, 147, 166, 172, 174, 241
Survey methodology, 84–87, 96, 167, 235
Surveys, 68, 71, 135–136, 147, 169, 191, 238, 242, 244
as admissable evidence, 31–33, 53n102
cognitive and communicative measurement, 165–183
CV, 27, 29, 31–34, 47n54, 313
question formats, 116, 122n18, 167, 172
Survival curve, 262, 301, 305–308
Symmetric diagonal matrix element equation, 251
Symmetric distribution function, 254

Taxation, 4, 63, 66, 113, 150n11, 152n30, 241
preservation tax, 280–282, 295n14, 295n15
surcharge, 28, 38, 51n90
Telephone survey, 69, 111, 133, 147, 149n4, 172, 180–182, 236, 296n22, 302
Theoretical validity, 55n120, 69–71, 73, 77, 132
Think-aloud task, 136, 174–175, 177, 181, 204
Time constraints, 71–72, 193, 206, 277
"Time to think," 198, 219, 223–226, 224(table), 225(table), 228(table), 232–233, 275, 278, 288
Tobit model, 226, 227(table), 228(table), 231, 296n20
Total economic value, 7, 9–12, 24, 42n1, 74–75, 242
basis for cost-benefit studies, 25–26, 28–29, 41–42, 50n83
Tradeoff, 83–84, 86, 90, 94–96, 202, 301, 315n4
decision, 8, 10–11, 20
Tradeoff value of compensation function, 94
Transivity, 62, 70–71
Travel cost model, 14, 63, 70, 75, 103–104, 106–107, 109, 120n8, 140
Trimming the data, 135, 135(table), 140, 311
"True value," 60, 71–74, 76

Unbounded liability, 40, 41
U.S. Congress, rulemaking process, 12, 15, 41–42
Senate Committee on Environment/Public Works, 55n125
U.S. government policy, 3–4, 12, 60, 63, 84, 137–138, 152n28, 165, 232
expenditure, 27, 40, 138–139, 149n11
public goods and obligation of, 129, 149–150n11
regulation, 83, 91, 249, 264nVIII
U.S. Supreme Court, rulemaking process, 12, 32–33
Use value, 13–16, 19, 24, 31, 33, 45n35, 50n83, 60, 74–75, 111, 242, 273–274; *see also* Direct use value
scope sensitivity and, 127, 130, 147
Utility function, 15n18, 62, 94, 119n3, 132, 151n18, 242, 245, 248, 255–257, 265nXII, 265nXIII, 300–301, 303, 317n31
indirect/direct, 102–105, 120n7
multi-attribute, 313–314
Utility maximization framework, 60–61, 276, 281

Validity, 97, 178, 183, 191, 196–197, 205–207, 244, 308
construct, 37, 60, 70, 205–206
of insensitivity tests, 132, 151n22
reliability, 8, 52n100, 54n111, 60, 64–74, 76, 202(table)
Valuation, 16, 18, 22, 43n4, 84, 175, 177–179, 183, 273
concepts, economic models and, 102–107
environmental criteria, 196–207
estimation, 42n2, 50n83, 62, 67–68, 72
functions, 141–142, 248–249, 257
of risk, 90–92, 95
sequence, 131, 131(table), 151n20, 151n21
Value, 1, 23, 60, 62, 65–66, 69–71, 73, 84, 105, 196, 198, 209, 210n3, 237, 242, 253–254, 276
concept of economic, 8–12
finite, 308, 311
implicit, 83, 91, 95
Variables used in multivariate, description, 227–228(table)
Variables, SHDP survey, 283–285(table), 296n19, 296n20
Variance-covariance matrix, 251, 253, 316n19
Variance of the prediction, 251
Variance of the parameter estimate, 251
Victoria, Australia, biodiversity valuation, 241
Video, use in CV surveys, 273–292

Visibility, 115–117, 122n18, 140, 149n5, 202, 204, 206, 274, 280
Visual aids, 291–292
Voting behavior, 10, 35–36, 38, 63–64, 74, 166–167
Voting clout, 64, 264nIV

Wages, risk tradeoffs, 84, 90–94
"Warm glow" theory, 130, 149–150n11
Warning labels, risk and, 88(table)
Washakie wilderness area, 134, 151n22
Waste disposal sites, 274, 294n6, 295n18
Water quality, 8, 30, 50n98, 106, 227(table), 274
  in Laguna de Bay, 221–223, 228(table), 231–232
  national vs. regional study, 140, 144(table), 149n4
Water pollution, 145(table), 221–223, 224(table), 227(table), 228(table), 232(table)
Water diversion project, 274, 279
Weibull Survival Models, 38, 114, 114(table), 115(table)
Welfare economics, 61–62, 65, 70, 78n3
White noise error, 300, 315n10
Wilderness areas, logging studies, 69, 134, 144(table), 151n22, 151–152n23, 279, 294n9
Wilderness set aside program, 9–10, 40
Wildlife preservation, 4, 50n87
Willingness to accept (WTA), 2, 10–11, 29, 46n41, 60, 62, 83, 93, 149n6, 150n14, 236, 246, 250
  estimating the mean/median, 299, 304, 306–307, 310, 314, 316–317n23
  zero, 313
Willingness to pay (WTP), 2–3, 20, 28, 46n41, 47n51, 47n52, 52, 69–70, 116, 127, 142, 146, 149n6, 165, 258, 264nV, 315n11
  alternative sources of evidence regarding, 62–65
  circumstances of choice, 10–11, 51n90
  chosen distribution, 256, 259–261
  communications device, 274, 288
  CVM survey techniques and, 235–236, 242, 249
  defining theoretical, 60–64, 76
  difficulty in answering, 278, 290(table)
  distribution function, 259
  distribution with log-likelihood function, 260
  dollar-value of question, 178, 181, 183
  equation for, 103, 152n25
  estimate, 140, 153n30, 153n32
  for controlling marine debris, 114(table), 115, 115(table)
  for moral satisfaction, 50n87,129, 150n12
  for selected classes of goods, 133(table)
  for Selway wilderness area, 135, 151n22, 151–152n23
  and implicit cost information, 177–180
  marginal/incremental, 92–93, 92(table), 107, 110–111
  maximum, 281–282, 285(table), 293n3
  mean/median, 65, 133(table), 135, 141, 151n23, 243, 248, 252–256, 260–261, 263, 288
  measuring/testing, 59, 64–66
  net, 280, 294n10
  overstated, 178, 182, 248, 277, 288
  questions, 171, 211n7, 245–247, 281, 303
  rational choice assumptions plus, 101, 103, 107
  reported, 170, 172–174, 176
  response mechanism, 39–40, 136, 240–241, 243
  risk reduction and, 83, 91–93, 95
  scope and, 108, 111, 115, 117, 120n13, 128, 139, 181
  SHDP survey, 280, 282, 287(table), 294n9, 295n14
  size of environmental good, 134, 150n17, 151n21
  stated, 20, 291, 295n16
  "time to think" and, 219, 221–222, 226, 227(table), 233
  to preserve environmental sites, 276–279, 281, 284(table), 285, 288–289, 294n9, 295n15
  understatement, 51n90, 54n116, 178–179, 182, 277, 285
  validity/reliability of, 60, 65, 68, 70
  valuation function, 29, 35–38, 47–48n58, 175
  valuation sequence structure, 131–132, 131(table), 150n15
  zero, 259, 261, 278, 285(table), 288, 293n3
Willingness to respond, 197, 198(table)
Within sample test, 140, 150n17
Work plan, 201–207

"Yes" saying, 232, 302, 306
"Yes/no" valuation question, 236, 249, 255, 258, 310

Zero-based approach, 196, 259, 261, 278, 285(table), 288, 293n3, 315n11

GPSR Compliance

The European Union's (EU) General Product Safety Regulation (GPSR) is a set of rules that requires consumer products to be safe and our obligations to ensure this.

If you have any concerns about our products, you can contact us on ProductSafety@springernature.com

In case Publisher is established outside the EU, the EU authorized representative is:

Springer Nature Customer Service Center GmbH
Europaplatz 3
69115 Heidelberg, Germany

Batch number: 10755284

Printed by Printforce, the Netherlands